Biotechnology Law and Practice

Fundamentals of the Biosciences

Legal, Regulatory, Corporate Strategy

Case Law and Best Practices

NEW LONDON CROWN PUBLISHING HOUSE LTD.

10, UPPER BANK STREET TOWER, CANARY WHARF,

LONDON, E14 5EE,

UNITED KINGDOM

Company Number 13137552

Registered in England and Wales

London +44 20 38075002

Tollfree: 1-888-614-1227 US

Fax: 1-888-986-4006

New London Crown Publishing House Ltd Online

https://newlondoncrownpublishing.com

Ordering Information:
Quantity sales. Special discounts are available on quantity purchases by corporations, associations, and others.
For academic sales or text book adoptions, ask for Academic Sales, Contact the publisher at the address above for details.

Please contact New London Crown Publishing House Ltd.

Printed in the United States of America

Publisher's Cataloging-in-Publication data
De Keesee, Wen Biotechnology Law and Practice: *Fundamentals of the Biosciences- Legal, Regulatory, Corporate Strategy- Case Law and Best Practices*
ISBN: 978-1-7362095-0-9

Printing: New London Crown Publishing House
1. The main category of the book —LAW—Other category. SELF-HELP 2. Another subject category —MINI-MBA CERIFICATE 3. More categories —Biotechnology and bioscience business practices

First Edition

Book Design and Formatting Aalishaa

Editor Jeffrey Stein Esq.

Index: Krislit Phd

Web design – Chris Adikaram

Cover Design

Video production – Eduardo Ocampo

Foreword

The Biotech "Gold Rush" is On!

We are entering an explosive new era of medical and scientific discovery and the opportunities are huge for those who grasp the moment.

The Biotechnology Law and Practice, 4-volume book series*, is the most current, important and potentially, most informative series of its kind.*

Heralded by lawyers, scientists and entrepreneurs, these guide books are a precious resource, which you may routinely review on your great new quest!

Simplifying complex issues at the frontiers of the law and biomedicine with over 1500 power packed pages by numerous authorities from biotech and pharma law, intellectual property, and scientists from biomedicine, pharmaceuticals, regulatory affairs and new technologies, you will be introduced into this explosive field, which may inspire new discoveries and dynamic management executives.

Biomedical Business and Legal Management Strategies

Going beyond simple 'science for non-scientists' or 'mini-MBA' offerings, these four (4) volumes describe the convergence of scientific, political, regulatory, and commercial factors that drive the biotechnology industry and define its scope.

Learn the business of biotechnology, how to start and manage biotechnology companies, and how-to turn research into an Agent of Change.

Study, learn, and explore opportunities in biotechnology law, new medicine and advanced technologies!

Assess the potential therapeutic value of discoveries emanating from advanced research in the life sciences and understand ways to accelerate these discoveries into therapeutics, and medical devices.

Lead science-based organizations, including businesses and non-profits, with an understanding of research, business models, intellectual property and regulatory strategies.

Determine the most promising strategy for science-based organizations, including novel ways for expanding access to crucial investment funds and securities offerings.

Understand the financial underpinnings of investment decisions in the life sciences, including real-option approaches to investments, as well as the role of scientific, commercial, and regulatory uncertainties affecting biopharma companies.

Develop approaches to novel therapeutics, including investment in neglected diseases, AI, nano technology, new biologics and medical devices.

The Biotech "Gold Rush" is On! What are you waiting for?
Register Today:

The Masters of Bioscience Law and Technologies MBLAT
– Mini-MBA Certificate Program

International Society of Law and the Biosciences (ISLAB)

ISLAB exists primarily to educate lawyers, physician researchers, students and management professionals regarding the extraordinarily complex set of laws that govern the creation, development, and marketing of new drugs, biologics, medical devices, and other advanced technologies.

Furthermore, ISLAB research fellows produce scholarly white papers, and recommendations for policy on the varied and complex issues posed by a rapidly expanding explosion of new biomedical and emerging technologies, creating a need for awareness and diligence at the crossroads of biotechnology and the law.

The International Society for Law and the Biosciences combines the study of legal theory with practical applications in the biosciences.

International Opportunities

Biotechnology doesn't just happen in the United States or the UK. Legal and regulatory frameworks for successful approvals like the FDA in the US, exist through the world in new, off-shore, multi-billion-dollar markets. In addition, many biotech companies have a presence in multiple countries. If you enjoy travel, speak a foreign language or want the opportunity to influence laws on an international scale, you may enjoy bioscience law.

A Growing Industry

Biotechnology law is an exciting area of practice that can both improve the quality of life for people and benefit society. New disruptive technologies must be discovered, and investigators must pursue alternative and illusive cures on completely new branches of research, which no other scientists have journeyed before! As scientists go forward slowly and cautiously into this dark and unknown frontier, new legal questions and challenges will quickly appear. This reality, is surely coming and must be anticipated if we are to prevail. After all, so many people's lives will be touched by the success of our great work.

Volume one:

Biotechnology and Life Sciences Law

Book series number 1 of 4

Table of Contents:

Chapter 1

Biotechnology Law and Corporate Strategy

With law often playing catch up to ever-changing technology, the study of how law interacts with science and technology is more critical now than ever before.

This guide book provides law students, lawyers, scientists, regulatory professionals, biotech leaders, and visionary entrepreneurs a deep dive into the fundamentals of biotech-biopharma law and business practices.

Entrepreneur is defined as a person who organizes and operates a business or businesses, taking on greater than normal financial risks in order to do so. Many entrepreneurs see a vast potential in this post-pandemic market, predicted to be strong for years to come!

Biotech Stocks are On-Fire!

In a recent interview, Nasdaq's head of healthcare listings Jordan Saxe told Endpoints News the tally was 56 IPOs with a total $11.3 billion raised and year totals may break 70 IPO's with billions more forecasted to finish 020.

By developing a working expertise in this exciting emerging career specialty, you will have a special insider look at this industry with a strong focus on real-world applications and opportunities leading to C-level management, in-house counsel, or launching and leading new technologies and bioscience enterprises.

The concept that lawyers should be integrated with their clients has long been a core precept of law department organization. Despite major differences among our clients in industry, size, geographic location, culture and business objectives, this central organizing principle runs through most, best-in-class law departments.

General Counsel emphasizes the importance of developing a working environment where lawyers are integrated with their clients and are members of the business team - in perception and reality.

When business people perceive their lawyers can provide creative legal solutions with a business perspective, the lawyers are drawn more deeply into business teams as high value-added contributors and trusted advisors.

All larger companies rely on a mix of inside and outside lawyers to meet their legal needs.

Many larger law departments try to handle as much sophisticated, business-critical legal work in-house as possible. In-house lawyers typically perform the majority of their company's legal work, with the most notable exceptions being litigation, investigations, customer-paid transactional work, or international work where the law department lacks local presence and or knowledge.

However, inside lawyers are preferred, especially when they are perceived as being more knowledgeable about the industry, business operations, strategy and new product opportunities than outside counsel.

The International Society of Law and Biosciences (ISLAB) exists primarily to educate lawyers, physician researchers, and management professionals regarding the extraordinarily complex set of laws that govern the creation, development, and marketing of new drugs, biologics, medical devices, and other advanced technologies.

Furthermore, ISLAB research fellows produce scholarly white papers, and recommendations for policy on the varied and complex issues posed by a rapidly expanding explosion of new biomedical and other emerging technologies, creating a need for awareness and diligence at the crossroads of biology and the law.

Is the biotech industry growing?

The global biotechnology market is expected to reach USD 727.1 billion by 2025, according to a new report by Grand View Research, Inc. The emergence of certain key themes in the biotechnology market is expected to drive growth in this industry to a lucrative extent.

These key themes include regenerative medicine and genetics in diagnostics present a plethora of companies focusing on the development of regenerative therapies anticipated to drive sector growth through to 2025.

Technological advancements pertaining to the penetration of artificial intelligence in this industry is expected to fuel progress with potential companies engaged in unleashing machine learning in order to streamline and supercharge drug development and diagnostics.

Developed economies such as UK and the U.S. are also critically monitoring and funding synthetic biology R&D initiatives.

The emergence of certain key themes in the biotechnology market is expected to drive growth in this industry to a lucrative extent.

Further key findings suggest:

- Owing to technological advancements and widespread application of this field in various aspects of healthcare, the health segment is expected to exhibit strong progress in the forecast period.
- Continuous introduction of new biotechnological products to cater to healthcare entities that are involved in diagnosis, prognosis and biopharmaceutical development is estimated to propel the market
- Decreasing costs and rise in number of services in this segment are expected to drive segment with lucrative avenues
- Introduction of technologically advanced products and presence of various biotechnology-based programs such as the UC Davis Biotechnology Program, the University of California Biotechnology Research and Education Program are attributive to drive the growth of sector in the coming years

- Asia Pacific market is anticipated to grow at a lucrative pace due to changing health care infrastructure in this region which drives the demand for these products
- Key players operating include Gilead, Celgene, Abbott, Novo Nordisk A/S, Novartis AG, Sanofi Aventis, and Lonza
- DNA Sequencing
- Nanobiotechnology
- Tissue engineering and Regeneration
- Fermentation
- Cell Based Assay
- PCR Technology
- Chromatography Market
- Others

In today's hyper-aware environment, concerns about food and drug safety are paramount for both companies and consumers. The Food and Drug Administration (FDA) and the US Department of Agriculture (USDA) regulates the areas of biotech, food, and drug law. Additionally, laws including the 21st Century Cures Act, and cGMP (Current Good Manufacturing Processes), regulate industry standards/ norms in food, cosmetics, and other industry-sectors.

Other developments in biotech, surrounding biosimilars, natural fuel production, medical devices, biotechnology, nanotechnology and materials, and the pharmaceuticals industry, have promising futures.

Intellectual Property disputes are a complex area of law, often involving deep dives into complex concepts to understand the issues at play. The United States, the United States Patent and Trademark Office (USPTO/PTO) is the agency involved in registering patents and trademarks. As part of the USPTO, the Patent Trial and Appeal Board settles patent disputes, using a variety of mechanisms to settle issues related to intellectual property. Some of the mechanisms include inter partes review, post-grant procedures and covered business method patent reviews.

Healthcare law is constantly changing, especially in today's data driven online world. Healthcare providers have unprecedented concerns related to privacy and cybersecurity as different technologies and threats intersect in ways never seen before. With the growth of cloud computing and electronic health records, more regulations and greater scrutiny has been given to the industry, as hospitals, medical providers and healthcare agencies are liable in new and different ways.

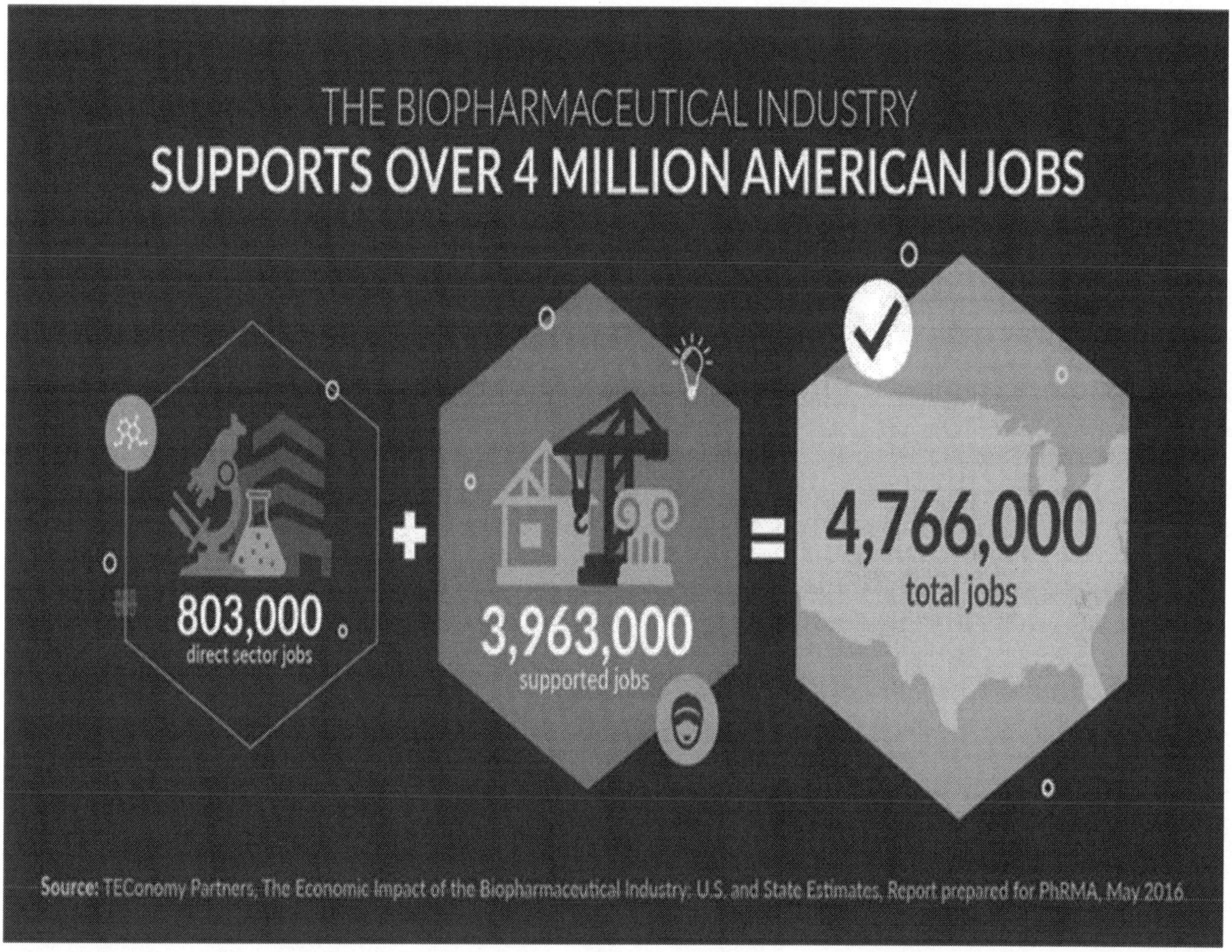

https://innovation.org/about-us/commitment/economic-impact/jobs-supported-by-americas-biopharmaceutical-companies

Biopharmaceutical Sector Jobs in U.S.

811,153 direct sector jobs!

4,738,972 Total Jobs!

Economic Output $1.1 Trillion Dollars!

Biopharmaceutical jobs require diverse skills and educational levels. Employees range from Ph.D. scientists to administrative workers and entry-level technicians. The majority of these jobs are, unsurprisingly, science, technology, engineering and math (STEM) related, ranging from advanced manufacturing positions to those in domestic production. Management and financial occupations account for another 20 percent of jobs. Office and administrative workers spread across the industry account for 13 percent of the workforce.

Production occupations account for 13 percent, and transportation and moving occupations account for 4 percent. Employees are drawn to the high-quality work and the chance to make a difference.

Biotechnology and Life Sciences Law

- Law schools and Universities can increase enrollment when they offer curriculum that meets real-life business and career challenges.
- Look outside of those classroom walls, and make the education process pertinent to real life.

Create Curriculum that Meets Real-World Needs and Provide Unique Choices

As a higher education institution, the keys to success must include the ability to provide real-world learning, listening to graduate student feedback, relevancy to the global population, as well as providing affordable options to the community. These factors better the chances for universities to thrive, while achieving profit at the same time.

Universities can increase enrollment when they offer curriculum that meets real-life business and career challenges.

Adding innovation and entrepreneurship experiences will attract potential new enrollments, and will help your university stay relevant in our fast-paced world.

Law Schools Are Going Online to Reach New Students

Law schools, in the face of marked declines in enrollment, revenue and jobs for graduates, are beginning to adopt innovative new ways of delivering legal education.

Some law schools are moving away from relying solely on classic settings and instead are blending classroom learning with online instruction, that explores disruptive innovation in the biosciences and advanced technologies.

"Law schools are increasingly out of step with shifts in the legal services market.

"Law schools that "are able to pioneer online, competency-based programs that focus outside of the traditional J.D. will have a leg up in the struggle to survive," said Mr. Horn, an author of the newly released report, "Disrupting Law School: How Disruptive Innovation Will Revolutionize the Legal World."

Sticking to the traditional hamper's innovation, warned Deborah J. Merritt, a professor at the Ohio State University Moritz College of Law who tracks such developments.

Educators creating online courses, she said, "tend to replicate conventional courses online, delivering the same content to familiar audiences."

While this may increase options for interested audiences, she said, "it is unlikely to expand the pool of students benefiting from our expertise." The costs of creating, maintaining and updating high-quality online courses are so high, she added, that they could prove more expensive than campus classes.

To attract new and broader audiences, she advised law schools to categorize offerings by subject matter rather than by course or by degree program. One example is a copyright law course developed in conjunction with Harvard Law School. In addition to law students, roughly 500 other people have been attracted to the online course, which is offered in the spring semester and was developed by Harvard using existing technology.

Harvard offers another, moneymaking model with an online certificate course in business basics created by its business school. The course is available to Harvard Law students for roughly $300, but other students must pay $1,800.

This kind of program can be a model for law schools to expand their reach, Ms. Merritt said. But she said that "to justify the costs of online education, law schools need to think big."

She said that means creating courses that "reach out to broader audiences who may also want to learn critical, real world skills and legal principles."

Online subjects and Certificate Programs can help bolster law school's content offerings, filling curriculum gaps, as well as assist with enrollment and budget challenges. ISLAB works to deliver online topics that connect law students with advanced learning and technology.

These subjects diversify programs, attract potential students, and build enrollments to support the core JD mission.

Today's Student

Today, students are educated consumers. They are looking for affordable educational solutions that provide flexibility, technology, and a path that includes not only a career, but also one that incorporates and builds upon natural entrepreneurial skills.

In order to keep up with the vast changes and demands in higher education, traditional schools risk becoming obsolete if they don't make changes to accommodate the needs of the 21st-century learner. As a higher education institution, the keys to success must include the ability to provide real-world learning, listening to graduate student feedback, relevancy to the global population, as well as providing affordable options to the community. These factors better the chances for universities to thrive, while achieving profit at the same time.

Dr. Ron Wagner, CEO and President of Relearnit states, "By positioning yourself as an entrepreneurial institution that not only values a superior educational experience, but also provides first-rate student care, profit will be a natural byproduct."

Help Students Launch Their Own Businesses

According to Nation 1099, "Anyone following workforce trends will have seen eye-popping numbers about the gig economy along the lines of all workers are freelancers, or half of us will be in the gig economy by 2025."

Considering the rapid technological changes that took place over the past decade, nothing would be better than teaching, exposing, and helping students launch their own businesses. Universities, both large and small, can create community partnerships with local businesses and non-profits. They can also provide hands-on experiences by shadowing leaders, meeting with other student-entrepreneurs, and creating opportunities to learn from some of the most successful founders.

If universities can see life outside of their classrooms, they can create ways to build relationships with external entities such as the Small Business Administration. Students can learn how to file patents, create pitches, find funding, and network with people who can mentor and assist them.

Biomedical Business and Legal Management Essentials

As convergence of technologies enables the birth of avant-garde combination products or devices, the classical distinctions between what the U.S. Food and Drug Administration (FDA) considers a "drug," "device," or "biologic" begin to blend together. Envision, for example, a molecular machine programmed to "seek and destroy" cancer cells in the body. These machines would combine into one therapeutic product — a nanoscale device for delivering a payload of drugs, together with a biologic component that self-assembles into a protective capsule around the delivery site. The drugs would affect only the cancer site within this protective capsule, thereby improving efficacy and minimizing side effects. Just as a nanotechnology combination product unites these three physical components — drug, device, biologic — so too are the regulatory, intellectual property (IP), and business law issues increasingly related with regard to the legal aspects of these products.

To succeed in the marketplace, the innovators of combination products must be armed with an integrated legal strategy.

Managing and Leading Biotechnology Professionals

The roles of managers and leaders within biotechnology companies undergo constant change. Biotechnology manager and leaders must engage in new and innovative problem- solving strategies; lead a divers +e and global workforce;

develop partnerships with other businesses, customers, and competitors manage horizontally and across teams; and utilize technology a competitive advantage.

Biotech continuum

Two other factors play a critical role in forming companies that earn long-term success. First, the quality of the original idea and founding vision behind the company's formation must always remain constant—even when the business grows larger and adapts to change.

Second, the original founders and entrepreneurs should remain and lead the company through the inevitable peaks and troughs.

Although the founders' roles and responsibilities will no doubt change, founders tend to confer the same enthusiasm and passion that they did when they first set up their business, which keeps an entrepreneurial spirit at the heart of the company.

Timing: predicting the future

Some people argue that timing is luck and that you can't plan for things. They are wrong. You can plan, but only if you are open-minded and position your start-up correctly. For example, the Human Genome Project created huge excitement, and companies that were founded two or three years before the project were well supported by the market. Also, consider that in the early 1990s nobody was looking at antibodies, but from 1998 onward they became huge. Timing can be everything and a real determinant of success.

Good founders, entrepreneurs and management teams will be able to take a macro view and predict how the industry (or a particular sector) will develop and what it will look like in 5–7 years. The rule of thumb is that it is easier to predict how a market or sector will develop during the next few years than it is to predict the destiny of your drug or molecule. If antibodies are going to be valuable for the next decade, ask if your company should be developing alternative platform technologies, new delivery routes or generics. Always look ahead.

Cash: VCs equal success

Drug discovery and development is very capital intensive—companies need to invest hundreds of millions of dollars before they can start generating profits.

Unfortunately, financing is probably the greatest risk companies face in their early stages.

A common feature of successful biotechs has been their financing strategies and the investment from VCs. The earlier you can get VC backing, the greater your chances of success.

Serial entrepreneurs who have previously accessed venture capital recognize this and are more likely to look for venture capital earlier than first-time entrepreneurs.

Of course, it helps if your business generates cash, because that decreases the dependence on equity and/or debt financing.

Forming strategic alliances with corporate partners as soon as possible can provide valuable endorsement in addition to financial support.

Conclusions

Starting a sustainable biotech company means having the right blend of management, access to cash, adaptability, timing and location. By recognizing, leveraging and capitalizing on all the possible opportunities, you will give yourself a head start on the road to building a successful company.

Another biotech category exploding with opportunity is new medical devices.

A friend of mine, a distinguished physician and surgeon, happens to manage a small private investment fund seeking early-stage companies with new medical devices that have an established market. If you know a hot new startup in this area.

There's never been a more exciting time to be a biotech startup. People tell me that "Big Pharma" companies have nearly $100 billion in cash that will keep buyout offers large.

There are plenty of Holy Grail areas to focus on. How can you argue with this logic?

Now is the time to jump in.

What Savvy general counsels have learned

Savvy general counsels have learned that effectively communicating about the services and contributions of the legal function is almost as important as actually providing high-quality services. All inside lawyers should be sensitive to the need to convey the value of their work, communicate tangible results, and attempt to measure results in quantitative terms. Lawyers need to communicate in the language and methods employed by their clients, recognizing the substantive and stylistic differences that exist among financial, engineering, marketing, operational and other disciplines.

Following are examples of the contributions that inside bioscience and technology lawyers can make in the corporate environment:

- Develop a company-wide dispute prevention/resolution strategy and program.
- Promote effective intellectual property strategy, function, process and system to protect and enhance the intellectual assets of the company.
- Integrate document and contract production processes and systems.
- Integrate ethics, compliance and preventive law efforts.
- Establish a comprehensive record (including electronic) management program.
- Integrate legal and public relations.
- Support superior execution of deals and transactions.
- Support creative sales, marketing, and distribution programs.
- Contribute to new product ideas or design.
- Provide client coaching - deal making, negotiation skills, risk evaluation, judgment.
- Influence governmental and regulatory policy.
- Serve as internal early warning system in identifying potential risks to the company.
- Cut through toughest problems facing the company / crisis management.
- Supply leadership talent within the company

Law Firms and Millennial Attorneys: Strategies to Develop Leadership Pipelines for Smooth Firm Transitions

Next year millennials will make up one-third of the workforce. A recent study released by ManpowerGroup provides some compelling insight about millennials in the workplace. The study asked 19,000 Millennials and 1,500 managers across 25 countries how they viewed their careers and what were their career priorities, with the goal of offering practical advice for millennials and their employers in the quickly evolving work environment. The results offer some statistics and finding for employers generally, and law firms, specifically, have some lessons to take to heart.

According to the survey, 23% of the millennial respondents said making a lot of money is their main goal, 21% want to make a positive contribution and 20% want to work with great people. But only 22% of the millennials surveyed indicated an interest in growing into leadership roles and only 4% of millennial respondents valued "managing others."

These factors, when combined with the boomer exodus out of the workforce is pointing to a leadership vacuum across industries, with 84% of organizations anticipating a shortfall of leaders over the next five years. In fact, leadership transitions are becoming more frequent and complex, and developing a leadership pipeline in law firms needs to become a top priority.

Law firms, when working with millennial attorneys, would be well-served to find ways to incentivize leadership, increase transparency surrounding firm decisions, especially the partnership process in order to create a leadership pipeline to ensure successful succession planning and relationship management. To examine this issue, we spoke to several law firm consultants on the state of leadership in law firms, how firms can engage and cultivate their millennial talent to take on leadership roles, and how marketing and business development teams fit into this process.

Importance of Developing Millennial Leadership and Talent at the Associate Level

Jonathan Kirschner, CEO of AIIR Consulting, points to conditions in law firms, that may make developing leadership habits in millennial attorneys more challenging. In a traditional law firm structure, leadership at the associate level is not incentivized.

Associates are valued for their ability to work hard and long, creating a situation where young lawyers are not encouraged to reach out and develop leadership skills, but rather rewarded for keeping their nose to the grindstone. Kirschner says, "If a newly minted lawyer has to choose between a single billable hour and coaching a colleague or peer, the former is a much more useful currency in today's traditional firm."

Creating a Law Firm Culture to Develop Leadership Talent

According to Remsen: "There are things law firms can do beyond dollars to build a culture where young lawyers want to go and thrive." Law firms find extreme value in taking steps to craft a leadership pipeline, such as shifting the hierarchical structure to create a space for younger attorneys to flex their leadership abilities and shape the firm into a place where they want to be.

The Role of Business Development in Law Firm Leadership Development

Client relationship management is very important for a firm's bottom line, and the voice of the client--a voice that is increasingly demanding diversity from outside counsel can be instrumental in advocating for the kind of change many firms need to enact. Sutor says, "Marketing and Business Development folks can champion millennial participation by encouraging senior partners and law firm leaders to consider who may not be represented at the table in key activities like client pitches or network building activities."

Chapter 2

Creating a Biotechnology Enterprise

This book provides a foundation to start or help grow a young biotechnology company from inception through early growth. Topics include market assessment of innovative technology, patents and licensing, corporate law, preparing a business plan, raising money from angels and venture capitalists, government grants, strategic alliances, sales and marketing, real estate, human resources, and regulatory affairs. The course provides an overview of the key tasks and challenges typically faced by biotech entrepreneurs, their management team, and directors.

How to start a biotech company

Adriana Tajonar

With the current exuberant energy surrounding biotech entrepreneurship, it is hard to believe that the industry is close to 50 years old. Much has changed since Herb Boyer, a professor at the University of California, San Francisco (UCSF), and Bob Swanson, a young entrepreneur and aspiring venture capitalist, started Genentech in 1976, giving rise to the entire biotechnology industry. Back then, spinning out a company was limited to faculty members or experienced biotechnology professionals. Today, the democratization of life science entrepreneurship is allowing graduate students and postdocs to apply their scientific expertise toward the commercialization of newly developed technologies.

Much like the path of a PhD project, the life of a science startup is not straightforward, but there are some common milestones from birth to growth and success.

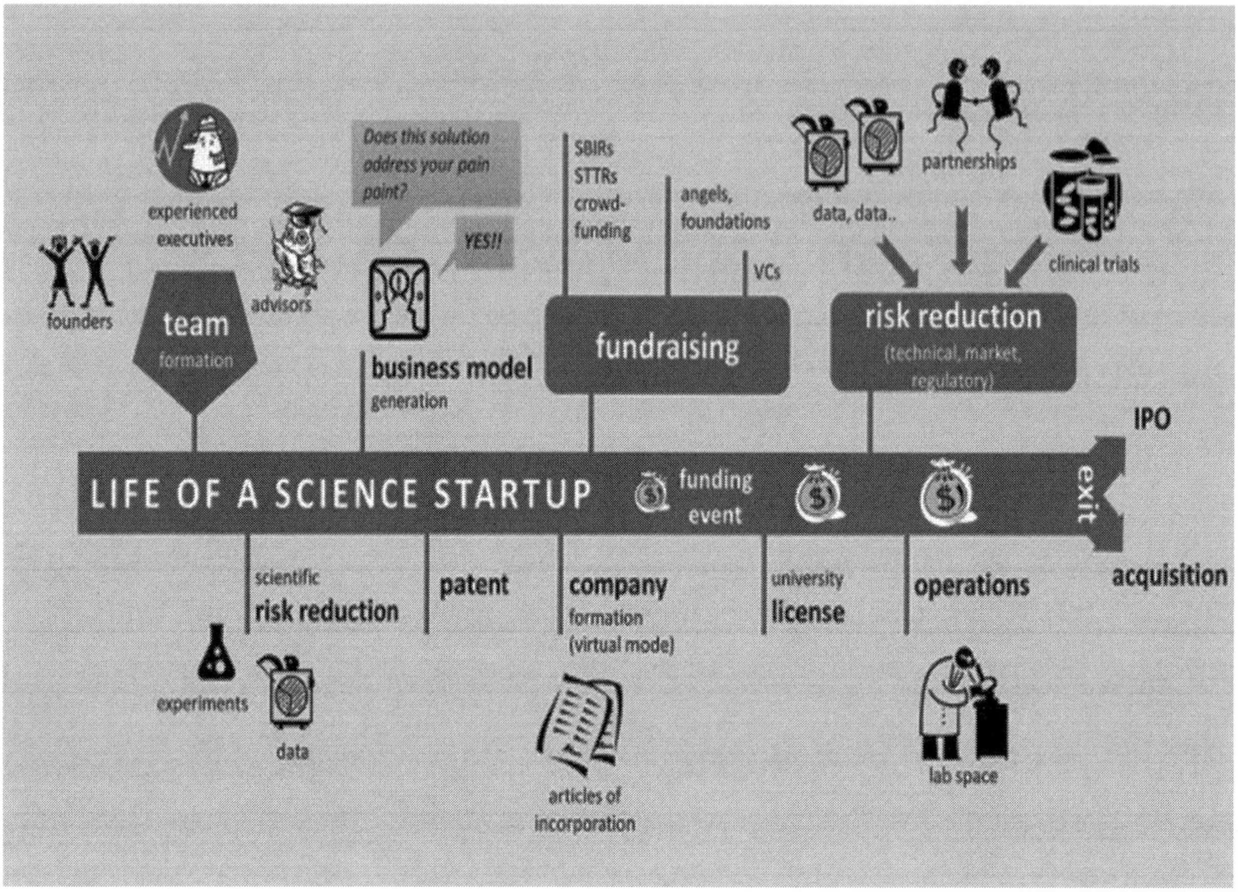

Life of a science startup.

The Birth of a Startup

In 2009, Dan Widmaier was a fifth-year graduate student at UCSF in the area of synthetic biology. His research was centered on engineering *Salmonella* to produce and secrete spider silk. Spider silk protein has incredible tensile strength, being stronger than steel and tougher than the body armor and tire material Kevlar. Despite these properties, the silk extraction process has remained incredibly labor-intensive for hundreds of years, limiting its use mostly to luxury textiles. Dan saw an opportunity to use synthetic biology to streamline the production and extraction of spider silk. He convinced his lab-mate and collaborator Ethan Mirsky and microfluidics expert David Breslauer, then a graduate student at the University of California, Berkeley, to join him in creating a new company, and Refactored Materials was born in 2009.

The team successfully applied for small business grants from the National Science Foundation and Department of Defense with their proposal for producing spider silk from engineered microbes for ballistic armor and medical device applications.

The company started their operations out of a single bench in an incubator space at UCSF called the QB3 Garage. Since then, Refactored Materials has successfully raised two venture rounds and is going after the textile market, a much larger market than originally anticipated that has seen little innovation since Lycra in the 1950s. In a few years, expect your athletic clothes to be more breathable, your socks to be softer, and your silk garments to be more durable, all thanks to three grad students with a vision to change the world, one spider dissection at a time.

Turning Research into an Agent of Change

There is no question that having a meaningful impact on society is a powerful driver for scientists. It is not surprising that so many of the discoveries that have improved our society by increasing efficiency, adding capabilities, and bettering health have come from basic research done in universities. Universities, however, are not equipped to fully translate technologies out of the academic lab into the market, and a separate vehicle is needed to truly fulfill the promise of societal impact. Certain efficiencies in the industry environment are rare in academia. This has been the case since Genentech's inception and remains true today, a reminder for young scientists and future entrepreneurs that industry is the conduit for translational applications.

Startups are the vehicle needed for this translation for three key reasons. First, startups can address key technical risks and arrive at go/no-go decision points with relatively low amounts of capital and close to no overhead. Of importance, thinly capitalized startups are incentivized to listen to their investors and advisors and act swiftly, a feat that is easily said but more rarely achieved in the academy. If the startup wishes to survive, the achievement of milestones is not optional. Thus, every experiment is tailored at answering go/no-go questions. Data must be not only publication worthy, but, more important, worth millions of investors' dollars and years of work.

Second, founders must constantly assess risk, and a thorough study is essential to select the best market for a technology with several potential applications. The selective pressures for an early-stage startup are extremely high when all the contributors to a viable business model are considered. These pressures enable a competitive marketplace for the best ideas. In such a marketplace, the startup structure allows for the ability to "pivot"—to remain nimble as the business model evolves. Startup founders can ensure that the technology has a viable market and create a validated plan to get there. Third, startups allow the correct alignment of incentives for their founders in terms of real-world impact and financial return. Students and postdocs are at a point in their careers at which they can dedicate the time to build this opportunity, something that faculty founders usually cannot do. Science startups often involve the original inventors behind the innovation—postdocs or graduate students who can easily address key proof-of-concept questions and develop the original technology.

In most cases, it was at the hands of these young scientists that the invention materialized, so the sense of ownership is strong, and they remain very passionate and motivated to see their work address a real-world need (and reap the benefits of their effort).

Advice Points

At QB3, the California Institute of Quantitative Biosciences, we have helped more than 200 teams of scientists start companies through the Startup in a Box Program. Of these teams, 65 have successfully raised funds within the first 18 months of coming to QB3 for help. Two-thirds of the teams come directly from academia, with postdocs or graduate students at the helm. Following are some lessons for the life science entrepreneur-to-be.

Identify the unmet need that your technology addresses

The best way to articulate your solution and the value of your approach is to clearly state the problem you are solving. It is important to solve a problem you are passionate about, but there must be a large enough market for this technology; in other words, make sure that there are enough people who care about this problem enough to pay for your solution.

Going after a small or niche market is acceptable, too, but your sources of capital will be fewer, and you will need to clearly articulate how your company can even recover its costs.

When looking for your market, "don't be a hammer in search of a nail"; that is, be objective when identifying a need instead of trying to make your special interest into a market that might never exist.

Build a high-quality, well-rounded team

No startup was ever created by a single person. When starting a company, find one or more cofounder(s) with complementary skill sets. For example, if you are a cancer biologist and your idea is to develop new cancer therapeutics, find someone with pharmacology or drug development experience. If you have a clinical background and want to develop a medical device, find an engineer. In the case of Refactored Materials, Dan had the chemistry know-how, Ethan brought in the electrical engineering and operational expertise, and David was able to spin fibers thanks to his microfluidics background. Having a cofounder has multiple benefits, from expanding the company's skillset, to having a sounding board and accountability partner, to showing investors that you can work with others.

Having a well-rounded team with the best people you can recruit is a key asset for a startup. Faculty cofounders commonly remain involved as advisors or board members. If your team is made up of academics, it can be extremely helpful to find an experienced entrepreneur or executive with startup experience. A youthful team is great, but an experienced person will help anchor the team and give you credibility in front of investors. The same goes for qualified mentors and advisors: everyone in your team should be passionate about the company's vision and mission.

Understand incentives, and use them to drive your company to success

Once you have put your all-star team together, make sure the people involved are incentivized to do their best work for the company. At the very early stage, you will not have the funding needed to steal your colleagues away from a salary in industry, consulting, or any salary for that matter. Therefore, you give equity or shares in your company tied to a vesting schedule, allowing your cofounders and early employees to participate in the ownership of your company.

Initially these company shares will be worth very little, but the idea is to incentivize high-quality work that will drive up the value of the shares with a large potential up-side to the shareholders.

Equity is the vehicle to recruit an experienced entrepreneur, senior advisor, or consultant with unique expertise to help your company.

Get quality legal advice

A good lawyer will become a key advisor in the early stages of your company, so it is crucial to seek out quality legal advice in the field of your startup (a lawyer with experience in real estate can help little when it comes to a company inventing cardiovascular implants). Yes, it is pricey, but you really get what you pay for, so it is worth spending slightly more to set up the foundation of your company correctly. Many large law firms have special incentives for startups, often with fees deferred until a funding event happens. In terms of company formation, make sure you choose the company structure that fits your business model best. For example, if you will need to incentivize early advisors with equity and if you will need to seek private capital to bring your product to market, a C-corporation makes more sense. If you will be operating as a service and do not depend on raising investor dollars, you might consider a Limited Liability Corporation (LLC). A "quick and dirty" online site to register your company may seem appealing now, but try to avoid it—fixing all the problems later will cost more money, and it will create unnecessary paperwork and transactions.

Your intellectual property (IP) is also one of your most valuable assets, so make sure you secure it early and well. If you are filing your own patent, craft the claims so that your technology is protected as broadly as possible; if you are licensing IP (for example, from a university), do this early and seek your lawyer's counsel to make sure the license terms are acceptable.

Money, money, money—search under every rock

There are many sources of early-stage funding: Small Business Innovation Research (SBIR)/Science and Technology Translation Research (STTR) and other federal grants, angels, venture capital (VC), foundations, crowd funding, friends, and family. Explore them all, but be prepared to roll up your sleeves and write some grants. SBIRs and STTRs are grants by any federal government agency that has an annual budget larger than $100 million.

Familiar sources such as the National Institutes of Health, National Science Foundation, Department of Defense, and Department of Energy participate and provide these types of grants.

The process is involved and competitive, but many successful companies, including Refactored Materials, started on the backs of these grants. Most VCs and angels have moved farther down the pipeline to where the technology has been de-risked, so government grants are certainly worth your time and effort. As an example, one-third of Startup in a Box graduates started operations on the back of SBIRs.

Finally, leave no rock unturned. It is always helpful to start building relationships with your potential future investors to understand what is needed for a "yes" later on and ask for advice before asking for money (the old adage, "if you want money, ask for advice," is certainly true in the early-stage investment world).

Research your investors before meeting with them.

Find out what their investment interests are and in which space they usually participate. This will help you spin your story appropriately in terms of specific application (if you have several possible ones), amount to ask for (some large investors cannot give you seed money), and your use of the funds.

Sooner or later, you will run into the rumor that you should not talk science with investors. Know that this is just a myth; sophisticated life science investors will want to understand the technology into which they are putting their cash. In the words of engineer and statistician William Edwards Deming, "In God we trust, all others must bring data."

Your investors will know more about the market than you will. This means that you do not need to dwell on the point that cancer is an important problem. Listen to your investors' advice even before they become your investors. Their insight can help you identify opportunities and refine your strategic thinking.

+

Learn to identify opportunities

This advice applies to technologies with more than one application, such as platform technologies; in such situations, it might be difficult to pick which application or market to pursue first. It is useful to think of having a strategy that includes an earlier or easier path to revenue.

Large markets may be alluring as a first battlefield, but they are often plagued with regulatory and market risks. Find out whether there is a better route to establish your proof of concept, even if it is in a smaller market. Having a direct path to market will allow you to move quicker on fewer funds; this will make it easier to tackle the larger and more challenging market later on. Refactored Materials realized that ballistic armor and medical devices would be challenging markets to crack, and they received much interest from the textile industry. The door is open to come back to the other applications in the future, but the silk textile market is primed for disruption.

Identify your white-hot risk, and use your time wisely

There are many risks in the way of taking a scientific technology to market: technical/scientific risk, regulatory risk, market risk. Higher risk in any of these areas correlates directly with the difficulty of getting money (since the uncertainty of return on investment for investors is higher). Convincing investors to accept these risks strongly affects early stage companies, as they have the largest number of unknowns. Your goal as an entrepreneur is to focus on answering the questions that will help you address and decrease those risks. Understand what the major risks are that stand between you and getting to market, and focus your time on them.

Test and build your business model

As a startup, one of your most important tasks will be to discover your business model, that is, how your company fits into the market. What is your value proposition? Who are your customers and partners? Do you understand how your product fits into the entire process or patient care procedure? If you are developing a diagnostic for a disease that has no current therapy, why will people be inclined to use (and pay for) your product?

You might have answers to all these questions, but at the moment they are really just hypotheses. The best way to validate these and develop your business model is to talk to relevant partners directly in a process.

The founders are the best people to do this validation, since they have a deep understanding of the technology and can make changes to the model (or pivot) if necessary. So, in Blank's words, "Get out of the building!"

Be lean

Money is the lifeline of a startup, and you will never have enough. You must use it wisely when you have it, and take it whenever you can. Make a budget and prioritize to ensure that your resources are going toward your key activities, and follow this plan with superb execution: in other words, be a *lean startup*. For example, you do not need to hire a full-time business person from the beginning; instead find someone who is willing to work with your company as an advisor or interim CEO in exchange for equity and reduced (or no) pay. If they believe in your company, they will be incentivized to help the company grow.

When being lean, you often need to find a middle ground that allows you to focus on your core skills. Trying to save some money by attempting to cram "Accounting 101" might not be a wise use of your time. Conversely, you do not need to hire a full-time accountant; outsource the company's accounting work, and pay by the hour or service.

Tell a story without giving away your secrets

An idea alone is not enough to make a company; you need execution and feedback from others.

You will need to learn how to talk about your idea without revealing the "secret sauce" with investors and potential partners: in fancy terms, this is called having a nonconfidential discussion. While you are in the process of filing a patent to protect your IP, it is useful to learn how to describe the problem you are solving and your approach without revealing confidential details. Being able to describe your idea in nonconfidential terms will also allow you to avoid having to ask for a nondisclosure agreement (NDA) when you have an introductory discussion with a potential partner.

Oh, and whatever you do, don't ask VCs for an NDA for an initial pitch: they will not sign them, and it makes you seem naive.

Staying informed is the key to success

Talk to entrepreneurs in the field, and find resources at your institution (career office, technology transfer office, entrepreneurship groups) that can help you learn about entrepreneurship and connect with alumni who have started their company or joined a startup. Reach out to faculty who have founded companies, and try to get connected with the entrepreneurs that drove their company.

Do not give up, and get ready for the best roller coaster ride!

Despite the plethora of (at times daunting) things to think about, I have not yet met a single entrepreneur who regrets starting a company. There will be ups and downs, much as in academic science, but as with any goal worth pursuing, it will all be worth it. In the case of Refactored Materials, it will be revolutionizing a centuries-old industry by enabling spider silk production for multiple applications at a large scale and in an environmentally conscious way.

ABBREVIATIONS USED:

CEO	chief executive officer
IP	intellectual property
LLC	limited liability corporation
NDA	nondisclosure agreement
QB3	California institute of Quantitative Biosciences
SBIR	Small Business Innovation Research
STTR	Science and Technology Transfer Research
UCSF	University of California, San Francisco
VC	venture capital, venture capitalists

References

- Blank S, Dorf B. The Startup Owner's Manual: The Step by Step Guide for Building a Great Company. Pescadero, CA: K&S Ranch Press; 2012.

- Articles from Molecular Biology of the Cell are provided here courtesy of **American Society for Cell Biology**

- **A successful founder off the beaten path**
- Ingmar Hoerr
- *Nature Biotechnology* **volume 35**, pages900–903(2017)

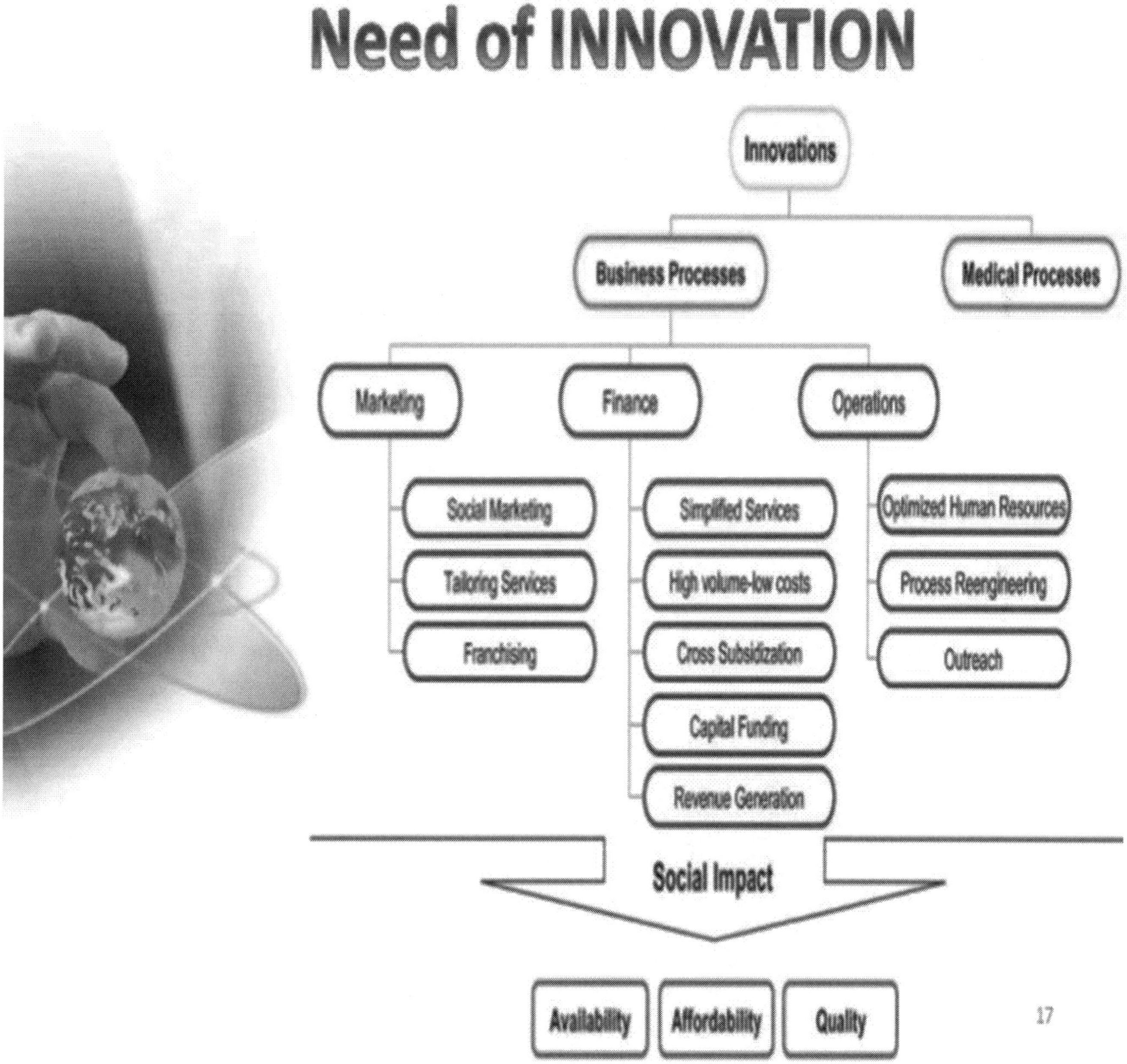

Chapter 3

How to develop a new vaccine or therapeutic modality in a skeptical environment, with little biotech experience, limited resources and limited capital.

Transitioning a biological discovery from bench to business is difficult enough for a well-conceived and researched technology or product in a traditional biotech hub. But what about companies seeking to develop a novel product outside of the United States, where experienced tech transfer advice, seasoned management and knowledgeable investors all come at a premium?

As a young and inexperienced CEO in Germany, I learnt many hard lessons as I built a startup, CureVac (Tübingen, Germany), from a doctoral thesis into what is now a company valued at more than a billion dollars.

In what follows, I provide an account of my experience building a company in Germany at the turn of the twenty-first century and the challenges I encountered. I conclude by providing some insights into how my experience can inform other entrepreneurs seeking to build a venture around an innovative new technology in a region not immediately recognized for its biotech prowess.

Early days

When I started my PhD in the mid-1990s, I was convinced that RNA could be a platform upon which a multitude of therapeutics could be developed, from prophylactic vaccines to immunotherapies. I was driven to make this vision a reality. However, as a scientist in academia with limited business experience, I knew there would be hurdles to overcome. What I did not realize at the time was how high or how many of these hurdles there would be.

CureVac was founded in a university based in Tübingen, Germany—where Friedrich Miescher discovered a substance he named "nuclein," later better known by the term deoxyribonucleic acid or DNA. Despite Tübingen's place in the history of science, it sits far outside the biotech hubs of Boston and San Francisco.

Yet this is where my colleagues and I launched CureVac with the ambition of changing the fabric of medicine. Though naive about the challenges of launching biotech companies, we, like many other young entrepreneurs, were undeterred.

In retrospect, I am grateful for our naiveté, because had we known what challenges lay ahead, we might never have taken that first step.

However, there I was in 2001 with an official certificate of incorporation in hand, sitting at a desk in my tiny apartment writing a business plan for CureVac's next five years with the goal of bringing the first therapeutic mRNA agents onto the market.

Like many scientists turned CEOs, I thought building a biotech required three simple steps.

1. Identify a groundbreaking scientific discovery.
2. Build a pipeline of products and execute a clinical trial program.
3. Raise financing for the company on the basis of its groundbreaking science.

To a scientist, steps 1 and 2 are familiar territory. Developing trial protocols and conducting experiments were second nature to me. Step 3 would follow easily enough, I thought. However, this seemingly straightforward process proved anything but.

Upon completing my doctoral studies, my colleagues and I approached the Federal Institute for Vaccines and Biomedicines in Germany and informed them we would like to begin clinical testing with our mRNA products. Not so fast, said the regulators.

We learned from our interactions with them that we needed to provide a data package and a clinical development strategy, and that good manufacturing practices (GMP) quality was required to even begin phase 1 testing. On top of that, we had yet to initiate (or complete) the preclinical animal models or provide clear statements about the pharmacodynamics, kinetics and toxicology of our mRNA technology.

The obstacles seemed insurmountable to us. We were left wondering how we could make progress with the technology and secure adequate funding and resources to move this project forward.

Incubating the technology

My colleagues and I—all without formal business experience—convened and mapped out plans on overcoming the various barriers to clinical testing. Remaining at the university became our goal, and we were fortunate to participate in a 'young innovators' program that allowed us to use the university's laboratories and infrastructure. Looking back, I can say with absolute certainty that staying close to the university saved CureVac, even though at the time we felt like college graduates returning to our parents' basement.

Hunkered down in the university lab, we were able to modify the immune response of our mRNA construct and test various formulations that became the basis of a patent-protected technology.

We also learned to prepare RNA with astonishing efficiency without RNase contamination and to develop a specific chromatographic purification process that would lead to one of our first production patents.

Despite lacking cash, we were nimble in the lab, which allowed us to keep our focus on the science, where we were comfortable, and enabled us to build confidence in our business strategy. However, each success in the lab reminded us that step 3 in building a biotech company, securing a financing, was becoming more and more urgent.

Finding a true believer

Attracting investors is perhaps the most challenging aspect of being a biotech CEO. Many groundbreaking technologies fall by the wayside because of a CEO's inability to fund their development. When we approached the first of many venture capital companies, we realized we had a difficult undertaking ahead of us. In the middle of 2000, Germany experienced the same technology bubble implosion that crippled the United States. And while CureVac was not a technology company in the traditional sense, we were lumped into the category of 'high risk, unproven' businesses.

For investors who had just lost tremendous amounts of money backing ideas that seemed sensible at the time, there was little appetite for risk, especially involving a scientific concept that, even with data showing its potential, read like pure science fiction.

Yet, there we were, emerging from academia as scientists in a geographic area where there were few biotech successes, with a team unfamiliar with ways to access capital, forging ahead with the aim of researching and developing therapeutic vaccines for cancer based on mRNA, a molecule that, at the time, was largely not considered a therapeutic platform.

Undeterred, we approached a multitude of investors. To our surprise at the time (but not as much in hindsight), we were repeatedly rejected, often before we had a chance to present our business plan. The specific reasons were many, but the consensus was the same. The risk of investing in an experimental technology being championed by a scientifically respected, but inexperienced management team, outweighed the high upside opportunity that mRNA represented.

As rational as this seems today, we were dumbfounded by the lack of interest.

How could they not see the same potential in mRNA that we did? The disconnect was maddening, but also motivating; and eventually we found a private business angel who wanted to help us find other investors. Our prayers had been answered—or so we believed.

Unfortunately, our business angel suddenly got cold feet when he realized how long the road ahead was going to be and how little interest other investors had in us or our technology. He abruptly withdrew all his money just a few months later.

Complete turnarounds like this are, unfortunately, all too common when raising capital. However, when you're in a fight for your company's life, calm, rational thinking is often replaced by desperation. But we remained persistent and tried to find one last lifeline.

We found one—our first true savior. The fund was Leonardo Ventures (Mannheim, Germany), a small venture capital boutique that was prepared to invest a little money so we could at least move from the university into the nearby technology park.

Leonardo Venture was very interested in biotech but had no expertise of its own. This gave us the opportunity to convince them without losing too much time in a drawn-out, science-driven due diligence process.

At the start of 2003, we secured €2.7 ($3.5) million, which enabled us to reach the next milestone: moving into the newly established technology park in the city of Tübingen.

Creating a flexible business model

While our operations were getting up to speed, our liquidity rapidly took a nose dive. We had difficulties convincing additional investors solely on the basis of our preclinical data. Simultaneously, the recession in German biotech was lingering and our existing investors did not have an adequate network to support us.

Although I would agree that biotech entrepreneurs require an unwavering belief in their vision and the potential of their technology, at times this zealousness must be tempered by practicality.

For CureVac, this meant switching to 'emergency mode' and taking on service tasks for clients in our key area of expertise, RNA.

This involved primarily manufacturing oligonucleotides (siRNA and antisense constructs) and making chemical modifications. We restructured our processes to meet these requirements.

Despite being disappointed in having to delay our own research and development, this period of time provided us with invaluable insights into our own technology and how we would want to eventually develop our own pipeline. When we were filling customer orders, we incorporated and tested a substantial number of different modifications using our technology.

This experience reaffirmed our understanding that CureVac's products should continue to use natural RNA bases, without chemical modifications. In retrospect, working with clients allowed us to de-risk our approach by attempting different combinations, which proved a key advantage from both a development and cost perspective in drug development.

While we were inadvertently broadening our knowledge base by working on projects outside of the focus of our clinical development programs to earn enough money to keep the lights on, it was a difficult period from a psychological point of view because we had to temporarily shelve our core programs.

A turning point

Thankfully, good fortune shined on us again, and we met Friedrich von Bohlen, the former CEO of LION Bioscience (Heidelberg, Germany), the 'biotech star' of Germany. He was searching for a suitable investment and a company with an innovative technology platform enabling the widest possible range of therapeutically relevant information to be delivered into the human body, a vision he had long pursued for LION.

We were once again able to talk about our actual approach. And von Bohlen quickly became enthusiastic when he heard what was actually possible with mRNA technology; within 30 minutes, he was convinced and decided to invest in our company. This was a turning point.

His interest in the company encouraged our existing investors to once again provide us with funds. By 2006, we were saved.

Reinvigorated with fresh capital, we revised our business plan, and with the help of von Bohlen, we were connected with Dietmar Hopp, the founder of European software giant SAP (Walldorf, Germany).

Known as the Bill Gates of Germany, Hopp was an investor we would have never considered given his primary interest in information technology. However, he turned out to be the perfect partner for CureVac because he could see what typical biotech investors could not. To Hopp, mRNA represented the computer code for the human body.

With Hopp's guidance, we chose our lead indication based on the size of the patient population and our knowledge about the relevant antigens. Hopp agreed to invest €35 ($38, at the time) million.

With this fresh influx of capital, we no longer needed our emergency plan of customer service and dedicated ourselves once again to our true goal of bringing our mRNA technology into clinical use. In January 2009, we successfully inoculated our first patient with our proprietary formulation.

Growing pains

After many years of trial and error, repeatedly networking ourselves and drawing upon the criticisms and advice of multiple experts, we were finally realizing our vision of transitioning from an academic concept to a viable biotech business.

For the first time, we could define ourselves as a living and breathing company with substantial capital in hand, a network of investors and experts within arm's reach, and a business and clinical plan to bring our vision to fruition.

However, as clarifying as this moment was for the stability of CureVac, it presented new challenges for the growth of the company. Namely, we would now be expected to use this capital to build a real, functioning biotech business.

For entrepreneurs, this realization can be even more daunting than the tooth-and-nail fight to raise capital because it requires the implementation of myriad operations and the management of numerous executives and employees.

Building the right team is ultimately the most important factor in a company's success, but it is particularly critical in the area of biotech. The complexity that defines the structure of a biotech company means that a single person can never cover all the expert skills needed.

It is important that people with the appropriate strengths are taken on in all the essential areas—science, processes, business planning and control, finance, business development and human resources.

As a scientist, I am accustomed to binary outcomes and data-driven results. But as a manager of people, such black-and-white assessments are vastly more challenging. Initially, we grossly underestimated what was required to manage the constant change within the company as it grew. Seemingly, each solution led to a new set of complications.

However, we came to the realization that the same scientific discipline we adhere to in the laboratory needed to be applied to the management of our company.

We determined that the individual interests of the various protagonists must be positioned within the context of the overall interest of the company. This also concerns the ongoing development of the founders who must continually adapt to the new circumstances. Just because we founded the company doesn't mean we're best equipped to handle every situation.

Five keys to flight

From this long process of building a company, I've come up with a handful of tips that can help innovative technologies get off the ground outside of a biotech stronghold. The five major ones are presented below.

First, for CureVac, incubating inside the university gave us a boost. Today, such tech transfer relationships are commonplace, as universities around the world recognize the value in aiding budding scientist–CEOs. Academic entrepreneurs should seek out these opportunities. Resist the desire to spread your business wings right away; stay close to the nest and investigate opportunities inside your university. It will allow you to grow in surroundings that are familiar, while giving you access to infrastructure that you'll only realize you need after you've begun your work.

The university network can also be very advantageous.

However, be careful not to hand over too many rights to the university. This could be toxic for further financing rounds. What's more, conflicts can arise between professors and budding executives, owing to the natural friction between academia and business.

If you find yourself challenged by your affiliated university, seek out others that might offer reasonable support for your startup, as this can not only help your bargaining power but also address conflicts with the institute to which you're currently affiliated.

Second, when we founded CureVac, we assumed that having a disruptive technology like mRNA would make finding investors easier. The opposite was true; disruption can be a distraction to more cautious investors. Therefore, you need to identify open-minded personalities who have a broad perspective on business and innovation. They often see the bigger picture, and can be a gateway to reaching other, like-minded influencers.

Unquestionably, the turning point in CureVac's growth was our relationship with Friedrich von Bohlen. Not only was he instrumental in facilitating a critical round of financing, but he also provided validation for us that paved the way to our meeting with Dietmar Hopp, our most significant benefactor.

Attracting an advocate like Friedrich von Bohlen can be the essential ingredient that brings you to success, but identifying such personalities isn't easy, and even once they're identified, there is strong competition for their attention.

The best way to start this process is to build your own network from scratch. Get to know as many relevant people as possible, and talk to them plainly without overselling. Be patient and focus on developing a growth strategy that differentiates your company from others. Be authentic; never pretend to be something or someone you are not. For those companies not in biotech hubs, don't immediately think you must travel far and wide. Travel may become necessary later, but start networking closer to home first.

Third, investors are by definition risk takers, but they take calculated risks. This dichotomy can make it challenging to convince investors to gamble on emerging companies, especially ones that lack the geographic or industry pedigree.

If you are a trailblazer in your field, as CureVac was in mRNA therapeutics, consider non-dilutive public funding programs. These programs usually are easier to access and will help you produce the meaningful data that can help secure investors. Valid preclinical data, and ideally broad patents, are essential. In addition, the personalities of the founding team play a crucial role. You need to be able to authentically demonstrate why your team will be successful. No investor will invest without strong confidence in the team.

Fourth, the adage in biotech, and all company formation, is to hire the best people you can. This can be hard outside of a biotech hub.

To quote Jianming Li and William E. Halal, "Many biotechnology companies fail not because of bad science, but because their management personnel did not have the knowledge or skill to design and guide a complex research organization effectively" (*Nat. Biotechnol.* **20**, BE61–BE63, 2002).

I frequently reminded myself of this as CureVac grew. I knew the key to success was going to be cooperation. When building a company, you will never have enough resources.

Consequently, you will be able to make progress only when cooperating intensively with other company members and external partners. This is why you need to hire people that share this cooperative spirit.

In the beginning, a startup company is not much different from an academic work group. You need to work with the team and elevate each member according to their respective strengths. In CureVac's early days, we had just a junior staff, hungry to build something 'big'. It was only after we had significant financing that we could acquire the knowledge of expensive experts.

When it is time to hire from outside, the solution *per se* is not to just bring aboard people with big pharma experience. They are accustomed to a work environment governed by process and protocol. That sort of steady hand needs to be balanced with the faster, more adventurous mindset of staff in biotech startups.

Be prepared to reinvent yourself several times as you grow; changes to the management team should be encouraged, not avoided. This can be difficult for entrepreneur CEOs to accept because of loyalties to original team members.

I have felt this myself. Instead, you must be objective in your assessment of your company, putting aside personal feelings. If personnel issues arise, act according for the needs of the company, not your wishes. You need to engage change and add new people to the management team. In these situations, it is important to communicate authentically and openly with all investors.

Once you reach a critical mass and validated technology, it is easier to find experts. One way to do this is by opening sites in hub cities.

In our case, we opened a site in Frankfurt to gain clinical experts and a site in Boston to find business development specialists. It is easy to keep communication open these days, with video conferencing.

Finally, if you intend to remain CEO after launch, you will need to change as your company grows. At the onset, you first need to decide which role you would like to assume within the company. For me, being chief scientific officer was never an option; my strength lay in being a CEO rather than leading research.

When you decide to be a CEO, delegate research-related topics to a dedicated colleague—heading research and being a CEO at the same time will not work out.

You might need training in management or leadership topics. Being a CEO primarily means delegating operative topics; founders that are not able to do this will fail.

Moreover, you need to be honest with yourself about your skill set and the areas in which there are better qualified people than you. You then need the courage to hire those people.

I always keep in mind that a certain type of CEO is needed for every development phase of a company, and it is important to verify from time to time whether you still fit the requirements of the current (and future) development phase. For me, an important indicator is whether you still enjoy being a CEO—if you don't enjoy it anymore for a longer time period and you face some sleepless nights, it is time to consider other options. Remember, as much blood and sweat as you put into your company, the company is more than you.

https://europepmc.org/article/pmc/6058957#free-full-text

Entrepreneurialism in the Translational Biologic Sciences: Why, How, and However.

ACC Basic Transl Sci. 2018 Feb; 3(1): 1–8.

Because they are perceived as distinct from the biological sciences, entrepreneurial pursuits may be daunting to the average researcher. In this report, we explain why academic scientists and in particular translational researchers should be naturally as well as rationally attracted to entrepreneurial endeavors. We go into some detail of how entrepreneurial achievements are actually accomplished and offer a few caveats for consideration when embarking down entrepreneurial pathways. We conclude that, although not for everyone, for translational investigators in the biologic sciences, entrepreneurial pursuits are desirable, accomplishable, and professionally rewarding.

The passage and signature into law in 1980 of the Bayh-Dole Act (1) is credited with transforming the U.S. economy from a manufacturing to an innovation-driven base (2). The basic thrust of the law was to transfer ownership of patents generated from federally funded research to the institutions under whose aegis the funding was awarded and where the work was conducted. The law was conceived and enacted in response to the recognition that taxpayer-supported research discoveries were not adequately benefitting the public, in a system where the federal government controlled patents and allowed only nonexclusive licenses to private sector companies seeking to develop the intellectual property (IP) 2, 3. The result of Bayh-Dole was an explosion in numbers of submitted and issued patents and their subsequent application 3, 4. Part of the impact of Bayh-Dole legislation was the establishment of the U.S. biotechnology industry. In 2016, there were 2,772 biotechnology companies in the United States, approximately 50% of the world's total (5).

Much of the industry is funded by venture capital (VC) investments in start-ups, the majority of which are scientifically founded by university-based researchers. Currently the U.S.-based biotechnology industry is at an all-time high in investment (6), and in terms of growth is outperforming the broader market (7). In this report, we discuss the basics of why faculty-based translational scientists may want to participate as entrepreneurs in the biotechnology innovation arena, and how this is typically done. We also describe some of the caveats or "howevers" that should be considered before embarking on such a journey.

Although academically generated IP can be licensed to a third party for development, the emphasis in this paper is on the application of IP to found start-up companies where the IP inventor or inventors are playing important entrepreneurial roles. In addition, we are using a more expansive definition of biotechnology beyond the original description of "the use of living organisms to make products or run processes" (8) to include any IP discovered by a translational researcher working in the biological sciences that is entered into commercial development by a life sciences company, defined by a focus on development of biotech, pharmaceuticals, or medical devices.

Creating a life sciences start-up provides the means of realizing the full potential of a discovery or a new technology, which generally cannot be achieved in an academic lab where direction is typically driven by trainees seeking to make open-ended new discoveries.

In this regard, it is worth highlighting the distinctions between the goals of academia and biotech. In academia, almost anything new can be interesting even when seemingly unrelated to a human disease or treatment, and the eventual connections between basic science discovery and a possible therapeutic might take decades to realize. In contrast, the primary goals of start-up companies are to optimize discoveries in a very directed way, which often translates into studies of toxicity, delivery, and pharmacodynamics. Such efforts are extremely important for therapeutic development and are not easily achieved in an academic laboratory.

Psychologica Belgica
Journal of the Belgian Association for Psychological Science

Psychol Belg. 2015; 55(1): 32–56.
Published online 2015 Jun 4.doi: 10.5334/pb.be

Explaining Entrepreneurial Status and Success from Personality: An Individual-Level Application of the Entrepreneurial Orientation Framework

Tim Vantilborgh,[1] Jeroen Joly,[2] and Roland Pepermans[1]

Introduction

The field of entrepreneurship has flourished in the past decades. It seems imperative to understand what drives people to become successful entrepreneurs, because entrepreneurs play a major role in economic development (Brandstätter, 2011). Many researchers therefore focused on the entrepreneurial orientation (EO) of firms.

This construct refers to the strategies, processes, and styles of firms (Lumpkin & Dess, 1996). A firm that is entrepreneurially oriented will act autonomously, be innovative, take risks, take a competitive stance towards competitors, and proactively pursue new opportunities.

Several studies have indeed shown that firms with a strong EO perform better than firms with a weak EO (e.g., Wiklund & Shepherd, 2005).

While EO was originally considered a firm-level characteristic, it has recently been argued that EO can be translated to the individual level (Kollmann, Christofor, & Kuckertz, 2007; Krauss, Frese, Friedrich, & Unger, 2005).

Yet, it remains unclear which traits would underly EO at the individual level and, more importantly, how EO at the individual level would relate to entrepreneurial status (i.e., being an entrepreneur or not) and to entrepreneurial success.

Our goal is to address this gap in the literature, by empirically examining how individual EO relates to entrepreneurial status and success.

We define individual EO as an entrepreneurs' tendency to desire autonomy, take risks, be innovative, take a competitive stance, and be proactive (Kollmann et al., 2007). It hence forms a constellation of five individual personality traits that drives entrepreneurial behavior (Kollmann et al., 2007). We make three major contributions to the literature. First, we focus on all five personality traits that form individual EO concomitantly. Although these five traits have been the subject of several studies on entrepreneurial personality, they have rarely been studied simultaneously. This nonetheless seems important, because the five traits likely relate to each other and share variance. Therefore, studying all five traits simultaneously is necessary to unravel the unique role of each trait. Second, we introduce venture life cycle as a moderator in the relationship between individual EO and entrepreneurial success. This is important because prior findings on the relationships between entrepreneurs' personality traits and venture performance have often been inconsistent (Rauch & Frese, 2007). Some studies found that personality traits indeed related to venture performance (e.g., Rauch & Frese, 2007), whereas others found no statistically significant relationships (e.g., Baum & Locke, 2004; Gartner, 1989). This inconsistency could be due to situational factors that constrain the relationships between personality traits and firm performance (Hmieleski & Baron, 2009; Wiklund & Shepherd, 2005).

One such situational factor is venture life cycle, defined as the various phases ventures go through as they grow and mature (Lester, Parnell, & Carraher, 2003). We propose that the relationship between the five individual EO traits and firm performance depends on the venture life cycle.

In other words, we propose that personality traits may predict entrepreneurial success, but not necessarily in all phases of the ventures' life cycle.

We hence acknowledge that researchers should incorporate factors at various levels:

(1) the environment in which the organization is active, (2) the organization itself, (3) the process or actions taken by individuals to start a new venture,
(2) and (4) the individual (e.g., the personality of the entrepreneur) (Kollmann, et al., 2007). These factors may interact, meaning that the influence of individual characteristics may be moderated by factors at other levels, such as the organization or the environment. Third, we focus on objective indicators of entrepreneurial success, namely growth in the number of employees and growth in revenue over a period of three years. We hence avoid issues associated with subjective indicators of entrepreneurial success, such as common method bias (Podsakoff, MacKenzie, Lee, & Podsakoff, 2003).

Individual entrepreneurial orientation

Previous research has given ample attention to entrepreneurs' personality. Not surprisingly, the five dimensions of individual EO have already been used as personality traits to explain entrepreneurial behavior, albeit most often separately. Therefore, we will discuss each of the dimensions of individual EO and their relationship with entrepreneurial status and success separately. We follow the recommendation by Kollmann and colleagues (2007) and operationalize individual EO as five personality traits: innovativeness, proactivity, risk taking, need for autonomy, and need for achievement.

We operationalize entrepreneurial status as being active as an entrepreneur or not. Entrepreneurial success is operationalized as revenue growth and employment growth (Murphy, et al., 1996). We develop hypotheses relating personality traits to entrepreneurial status and success, based on person-environment fit theory (Caplan, 1987) and the attraction-selection-attrition model (Schneider, 1987). According to these models, people become an entrepreneur because it matches their personality (Niess & Biemann, 2014). Moreover, these models suggest that some entrepreneurs will be more successful because their personality matches the activities and the entrepreneurial role and environment.

Innovativeness

Innovativeness is one of the oldest traits associated with entrepreneurs, reflecting a person's willingness to create and develop new products and processes (Schumpeter & Opies, 1983).

It is important to notice that innovation differs from creativity. Whereas creativity implies creating novel ideas, innovation also entails implementing or adapting novel ideas (Cromie, 2000). Given that innovation and entrepreneurship go hand-in-hand, it is not surprising that entrepreneurs are more innovative than non-entrepreneurs (Koh, 1996). In addition, entrepreneurs score higher on creativity tests than most other occupational groups, with the exception of teachers, lecturers and trainers (Cromie, 2000). While innovativeness can stimulate people to pursue an entrepreneurial career, hence acting as a motivator (Shane, Kolvereid, & Westhead, 1991), it can also enable entrepreneurs to perform better, thus acting as a facilitator. Successful entrepreneurs tend to more fluently produce original ideas than unsuccessful entrepreneurs (Ames & Runco, 2005).

This can help them come up with new venture opportunities or devise alternative solutions to existing problems, hence increasing venture performance. A meta-analysis by Rauch & Frese (2007) indeed demonstrated that innovativeness positively correlated with venture success.

We therefore propose:

Hypothesis 1a: Entrepreneurs score higher on innovativeness than non-entrepreneurs. Hypothesis 1b: Innovativeness positively relates to entrepreneurial success.

Proactivity

Entrepreneurs start their own business by seizing an opportunity. Hence they are very likely to display a proactive personality: a tendency to influence their environment by identifying opportunities and acting on them, showing initiative, taking action, and persevering until meaningful change occurs (Crant, 2000). Moreover, high proactive individuals have higher entrepreneurial intentions (Crant, 1996). A recent meta-analytic study also established proactivity as an important predictor of venture success (Rauch & Frese, 2007).

This comes as no surprise as proactivity has been associated with both objective and subjective career success, in a diverse set of occupations and organizations (Seibert, Kraimer, & Crant, 2001).

Proactivity might influence entrepreneurial success through the strategy chosen by the entrepreneur. For instance, proactive entrepreneurs tend to adopt a prospector strategy, intensively scanning their environment for new opportunities, and focusing on product development and market research (Kickul & Gundry, 2002). This in turn might give them an edge over competitors who adopt other strategies. Hence, we propose:

Hypothesis 2a: Entrepreneurs score higher on proactivity than non-entrepreneurs. Hypothesis 2b: Proactivity positively relates to entrepreneurial success.

Risk Taking

As entrepreneurs' function in an uncertain, unstructured environment, bearing ultimate responsibility for their decisions, they inevitably become exposed to a certain amount of risk. Consequently, several authors claim entrepreneurs are more risk-tolerant and differ from non-entrepreneurs in their propensity towards risks (Perry, 1990; Rauch & Frese, 2007; Stewart & Roth, 2001). Indeed, Niess and Biemann (2014) demonstrated in a longitudinal study that people who are risk tolerant are more likely to become self-employed. However, entrepreneurs are no gamblers: they take calculated risks (Stewart & Roth, 2001).

Moreover, a business opportunity might appear risky to outsiders but not to experienced entrepreneurs, as the latter possess more accurate knowledge and information to appropriately evaluate its risk (Chell, Haworth, & Brearley, 1991). This ability to properly judge and subsequently act, where others would not, on risky but rewarding opportunities can stimulate business growth and create a competitive advantage. Indeed, Krauss and colleagues (2005) demonstrated that entrepreneur's risk-taking explained business growth, although this effect disappeared when they added additional personality traits to their model. Interestingly, Niess and Biemann (2014) showed that entrepreneurs with medium risk-taking levels were most likely to remain as an entrepreneur. This suggests the potential existence of a curvilinear relationship between risk taking and entrepreneurial success, as taking too much risk may actually be detrimental for business survival.

We nonetheless propose and test a positive linear effect of risk taking on entrepreneurial success, given that Rauch and Frese's (2007) meta-analysis supported the presence of such a linear relationship and because curvilinear relationships are not the main focus of our study.

Hypothesis3a:Entrepreneursscorehigheronrisktakingthannon-entrepreneurs. Hypothesis 3b: Risk taking positively relates to entrepreneurial success.

Need for autonomy

People with a strong need for autonomy desire to have a high degree of autonomy in various aspects of their lives (Kollmann et al., 2007), which implies that they are motivated to independently take decisions and have control (Perry, 1990). Because people differ from each other in their need for autonomy, it can be considered an individual difference that is often studied from a trait perspective (e.g., Brandstätter, 2011). Entrepreneurs strive for control: they try to avoid restrictive environments (rules, procedures, social norms) and display a higher need for autonomy than other occupational groups (Cromie & O'Donaghue, 1992).

Need for autonomy is also a frequently mentioned key motive for starting a venture (Perry, 1990). However, there have been fewer studies that related need for autonomy to venture success. Overall, it has been argued that autonomous individuals may achieve their goals faster because their environment hinders them less. Perry (1990) indeed found that independence differentiated successful from failed entrepreneurs. Moreover, Rauch and Frese's (2007) meta-analysis found a positive relationship between need for autonomy and venture performance.

Hypothesis 4a: Entrepreneurs score higher on need for autonomy than non-entrepreneurs. Hypothesis 4b: Need for autonomy positively relates to entrepreneurial success.

Need for achievement

Not surprisingly, (global) competition forces entrepreneurs to take an aggressive stance towards rivals. Competitive aggressiveness indicates that entrepreneurs have a combative attitude and attempt to outperform business rivals (Lumpkin & Dess, 2001).

From this point of view, there is a clear link between competitive aggressiveness and need for achievement1 (Kollmann, et al., 2007).

People scoring high on need for achievement are more likely to "engage in energetic and innovative activities that require planning for the future and entail an individual's responsibility for task outcomes" (Collins, Hanges & Locke, 2004, p. 96).

Like need for autonomy, need for achievement can be considered an individual difference that is often studied from a trait perspective (e.g., Brandstätter, 2011). People with a high need for achievement also prefer tasks that require skill and effort, are challenging and provide immediate feedback. Hence, McClelland already suggested in 1967 that these people would be attracted to and perform well in entrepreneurial jobs. A recent meta-analytic study supported that need for achievement differentiates between entrepreneurs and non-entrepreneurs, although there were few differences between managers and entrepreneurs (Collins, et al., 2004). The characteristics of managerial jobs may also attract high need for achievement individuals (Cromie, 2000). The aforementioned meta-analysis also revealed that need for achievement differentiated successful from unsuccessful entrepreneurs (Collins, et al., 2004). Similarly, Krauss and colleagues (2005) demonstrated that need for achievement explained business growth, even when controlling for other personality traits. Hence, we propose that:

Hypothesis 5a: Entrepreneurs score higher on need for achievement than non-entrepreneurs. Hypothesis 5b: Need for achievement positively relates to entrepreneurial success.

The moderating role of venture life cycle

Previous studies on the relationships between entrepreneurs' personality traits and entrepreneurial success often led to inconclusive findings (Baum & Locke, 2004; Gartner, 1989).

For example, Rauch and Frese's (2007) meta-analysis demonstrated that innovativeness, proactivity, risk taking, need for autonomy, and need for achievement were positively related to venture performance. However, other scholars failed to find statistically significant relationships between one or more of these five personality traits and various indicators of entrepreneurial success (e.g., Begley & Boyd, 1987; Kraus et al., 2005; Zhao et al., 2010).

It has therefore been suggested that moderators need to be taken into account to explain these inconsistent findings (Hmieleski & Baron, 2009). We therefore focus on venture life cycle as a moderator in the relationship between individual EO and entrepreneurial success.

The underlying reason is that leaders require distinct characteristics along various stages of the venture's life cycle (Hmieleski & Baron, 2009). Smith, Mitchell, and Summer (1985) distinguished three distinct life-cycle stages. First, organizational inception and mobilization refers to gathering resources and getting the organization going. Second, growth refers to expanding the organization. Third, maturity refers to managing a status quo or restructuring for new growth. Based on the literature, we contrast two opposing perspectives on the potential moderating role of venture life cycle: a situation strength perspective and a differentiation perspective.

Based on *the situation strength perspective*, various venture life cycles may be characterized by different levels of situation strength, defined as "implicit or explicit cues provided by external entities regarding the desirability of potential behaviors" (Meyer, Dalal, & Hermida, 2010, p. 122). According to this perspective, one's personality will exert a stronger influence on one's behavior in weak, ambiguous situations. In contrast, strong situations have clear cues that signal how people should behave, meaning that personality will exert a weaker influence on one's behavior. It has been suggested that as organizations mature, they formalize their management and practices (Mintzberg, 1998), leaving less room for the entrepreneur to influence organizational processes. In other words, later venture life cycles may represent strong situations, whereas early venture life cycles could be considered weak situations. Organizations in an early life cycle operate in an uncertain, dynamic environment, lacking cues on the desirability of entrepreneurial behavior. Because these constitute "weak" situations, personality traits ought to have a strong effect on entrepreneurial behavior. In contrast, organizations in a mature life cycle are formalized and hence can be considered strong situations, possessing clear guidelines on how one ought to behave. In such situations, personality traits ought to have weaker effects on entrepreneurial behavior.

In contrast, *the differentiation perspective* suggests that an entrepreneur's personality may offer a competitive advantage in certain phases of the venture life cycle.

As organizations enter successive life cycles, isomorphism will cause them to gradually become more similar (Powell & DiMaggio, 2012). For organizations in a later venture life cycle, the entrepreneur's personality may help to differentiate the firm from other, similar organizations and, hence, offer a unique competitive advantage.

Indeed, Wiklund and Shepherd (2005) demonstrated that firm-level EO had a stronger positive relationship with firm performance in stable environments, compared to dynamic environments. Based on these findings, one might argue that individual EO has a stronger relationship with firm performance as venture life cycle increases.

In sum, we propose that venture life cycle will moderate the relationship between individual EO and firm performance. Hence, we take an exploratory stance and do not specify a direction for this moderator effect, because the situation strength and the differentiation perspectives suggest opposite effects. Whereas the situation strength perspective suggests that individual EO is more strongly related to entrepreneurial success in early venture life cycles, the differentiation perspective suggests that it is more strongly related in later venture life cycles.

Hypothesis 6. Venture's life cycle moderates the effects of individual EO on entrepreneurial success.

Why Should Translational Scientists Consider Engaging in Entrepreneurial Activities?

Potential positive outcomes

The reasons why academic scientists should consider becoming involved in entrepreneurial activities range from pursuit of positive outcomes to avoidance of some of the negative circumstances likely to be encountered in a typical career trajectory. **Table 1** lists some of these, in descending order of importance or encounter likelihood for positive or negative reasons, respectively. At the top of the positive list is to create a better chance of one's discoveries entering into commercial development, and ultimately being made available to improve human health. The alternatives to scientist-driven commercialization is to not have eligible discovery converted to IP, or to license IP to an outside organization such as a pharmaceutical or device company. In our opinion, it is the ethical if not legal responsibility of academic scientists to convert patentable scientific discoveries into IP that can potentially benefit the taxpayers who support research institutions and federally funded research. In other words, scientists should attempt to convert all eligible discoveries into IP.

Once that is accomplished, the very difficult challenge of trying to move the IP into commercial development begins. Here the choice is between licensing the IP to an outside interest, typically a biotechnology, pharmaceutical, or device company, or attempting to develop the IP oneself.

Benefits of Entrepreneurial Activities	
Potential Positive Outcomes	
Improving societal health, through increasing the probability of commercializing discovery	
Creation of additional sources of funding, allowing for grant-independent research support	
Potential of favorably influencing the scientific field	
Exposure to new research techniques and areas	
Opportunity to experience and learn nonscientific skill sets	
Job creation	
Generation of investor and institutional return on investment	
Positive effects on personal mental health through creation of an interesting, new challenge and an alternative career path.	

If a scientist is able to use IP to found a company and then attract start-up investment, this will ordinarily be accompanied by research support to consolidate and extend the IP, some of which typically is done in the founding scientist's laboratory. Depending on the strength of the IP, the licensing details of the IP, and the start-up characteristics, some of the funding may return to the scientist's laboratory for general research support, in exchange for a first option of review or license of any new IP related to the research support. In an age of near single-digit National Institutes of Health pay lines, any type of additional research funding is generally viewed favorably.

Another, less obvious potential benefit of successful entrepreneurial activity is that its recognition may influence other investigators or companies to invest in the research area, increasing the chance that something from the research sector will ultimately be available to society.

Regardless of the details of any entrepreneurial activity, once launched, the academic scientist will be exposed to new scientific and nonscientific perspectives and activities, none of which would likely have been encountered outside of the new venture.

For example, in the science arena, it is likely that techniques beyond the scientist's range of expertise will need to be employed, and to stay engaged in the IP development the founding scientist will need to become facile with them. Some of these might include high throughput screening and compound optimization, regulatory science, and clinical trial methodology. From the business side, the function of corporate governance, federal regulation, initial public offerings, and exit strategies will all become familiar to a scientist-founder.

Job creation, often reaching substantial proportions, will stimulate the local economy and provide further impetus to the local biotech sector. And not to be ignored is the local stimulus to the regional economy of a successful company exit, where employees, local venture investors, and other regional stockholders recycle profits back into the economy and the sector.

The last 2 entries on the positive side of **Table 1** relate to personal benefit to the scientist who successfully engages in entrepreneurial activity. The first (item 8 in the list) is based on our own anecdotal experiences, both personal and in observation of colleagues. There is a near-universal favorable effect of being involved in successful entrepreneurial activity that relates to its being interesting, challenging, and accomplishable.

Any equity-based revenue accruing to the scientist is welcome but should not be a motivating factor in engaging in entrepreneurial activity. In our collective experience, the benefit of such revenue is more to defray or decompress the need to raise full academic salary support than to create personal wealth. This in turn allows more protected time for the scientist to pursue purely investigational activities, as opposed to supporting salary from administrative or clinical sources.

The final point is that because most start-ups fail (see However section), the traditional pathway depicted in **Figure 1** is much more likely to result in economic gain. Stated succinctly, the gain of personal wealth is not a rational or valid reason to engage in scientific entrepreneurial activity.

Academic scientists are natural entrepreneurs

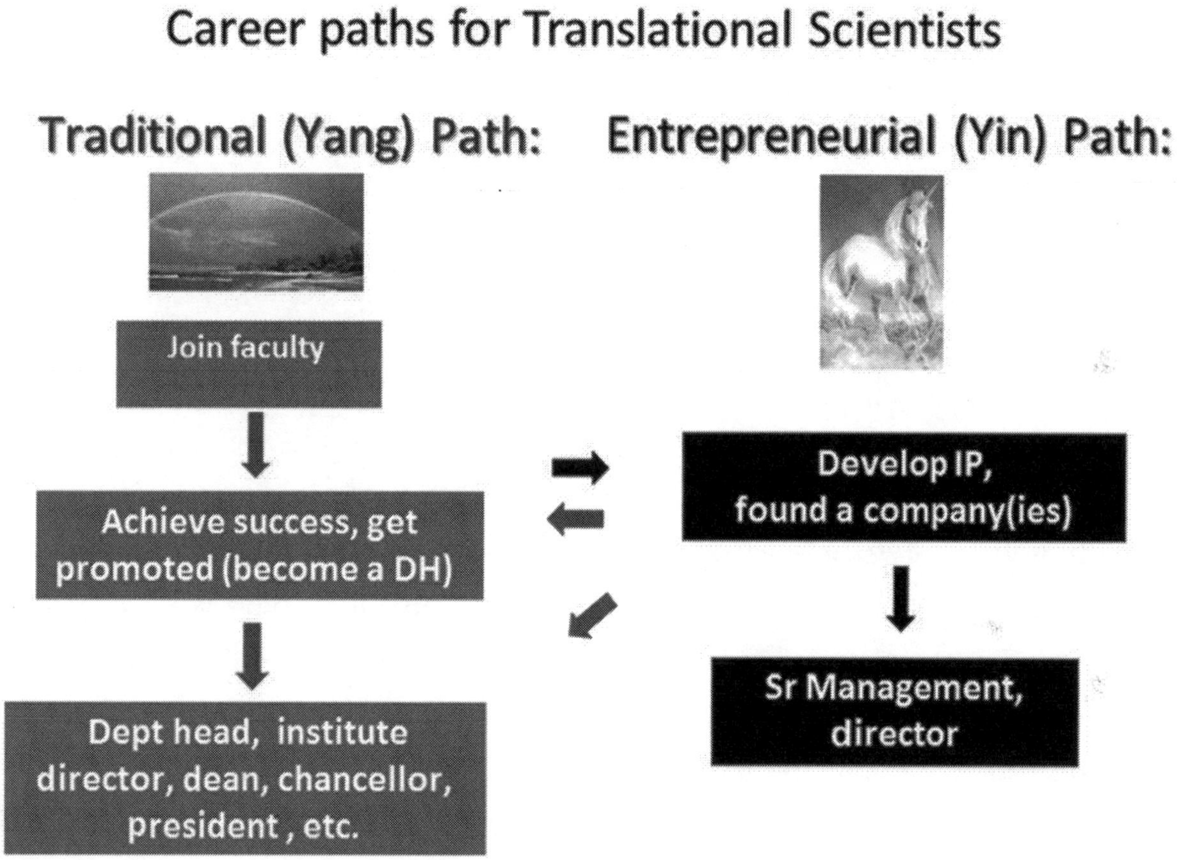

Translational scientists are ideally positioned to engage in entrepreneurial activity in the biological sciences, because they are likely to be proficient in both basic and clinical research concepts and methods. Work in human systems may be particularly valuable because it may allow for earlier patentability of IP, based on the direct connection to therapeutic outcomes.

Avoidance of negative career obstacles

On the negativity avoidance side of the ledger in **Table 1** are situations that may or may not concern an academic scientist. For some of us the “unicorn” career path portrayed in **Figure 1** is preferred to the standard academic career path, where after being a division or section director, one progresses to department chair, then dean, and so on, progressively gravitating away from personal research interests and activities in the process.

The crossover from the traditional to the entrepreneurial path typically occurs at mid-career after a scientist is well established, but it can occur at any time during career development.

The move into the entrepreneurial side does not have to be and typically is not permanent, and the scientist may return to the traditional academic track while maintaining contact with the start-up company in the form of scientific advisory or other consulting arrangements. However, to maintain a meaningful impact on IP development as well as to extract maximum benefit from association with the start-up entity, it is advantageous for the scientist to maintain a formal management association with the company. Some universities allow this and some do not, but we maintain it is in the best interest of a university to allow such arrangements.

Academic scientists are natural entrepreneurs

Potential benefits notwithstanding, another factor that should be considered when contemplating a move into or support of entrepreneurial activity is that by virtue of their nature (9), upbringing (10), scientific training and career experience, academic scientists are natural entrepreneurs (11).

An entrepreneurial venture is basically a high-risk test of a hypothesis, in concept not unlike what is typically done in scientific laboratories. **Table 2** lists some of the attributes that contribute to this natural entrepreneurial spirit. The typical academic scientist is comfortable with uncertainty, is capable of adapting quickly to a change in circumstances, and can function in the *Iron Chef* mode 11, 12 to produce results with a minimum amount of starting material. In our experience, academic scientists like to think big, as the discipline selects for individuals who want to make a difference in terms of improving societal health.

This is not simply a psychologically desirable trait, but it is also crucial to business tactics.

The potential value of a venture is determined by its upside, because downside risk tends to be roughly the same across value propositions (13).

The realities of scientific training and subsequent conditions for maintaining an academic laboratory eliminate pessimists and create an ecosystem where failure (of papers being accepted, grants being funded, and so on) is routine and is simply factored into tactics and strategy

And finally, because they have to balance budgets, hire and manage employees, and engage in high-risk and speculative discovery activities, academic scientists are essentially small businesspersons. All these factors favor a comfortable transition of academic scientists into entrepreneurial activities.

Why Academic Scientists Are Natural Entrepreneurs

Thrive on uncertainty, do not require predictability for optimal function

Not bound by rigid goals, able to quickly adapt to changing circumstances

Effective in the *Iron Chef*(12) mode

Like to think big

Inherently optimistic

Not afraid to fail

Are essentially small businesspersons living by their wits

Academic scientists are natural entrepreneurs

Chapter 4

How to Move Biologic Discovery Into Commercial Development

General process of converting scientific discovery and IP into a VCFU

The process of creating a minimum venture capital fundable unit (VCFU) of IP is straightforward (**Figure 2**), but execution of the component steps is not. The entrepreneurial "Valley of Death" for IP is the step of obtaining VC funding. VC groups vary tremendously in their appetites for investment, and if generally interested, all of them engage in extensive due diligence of variable quality.

The challenge of obtaining VC funding is to convince a single fund to invest, because that investor will typically make a seed investment and then recruit other members of a syndicate into the series A round, the first major round of funding.

The key to obtaining VC funding, assuming the IP has value and the founding scientist(s) are of high quality, is tenacity and willingness to continue engaging prospective investors in the face of serial rejection.

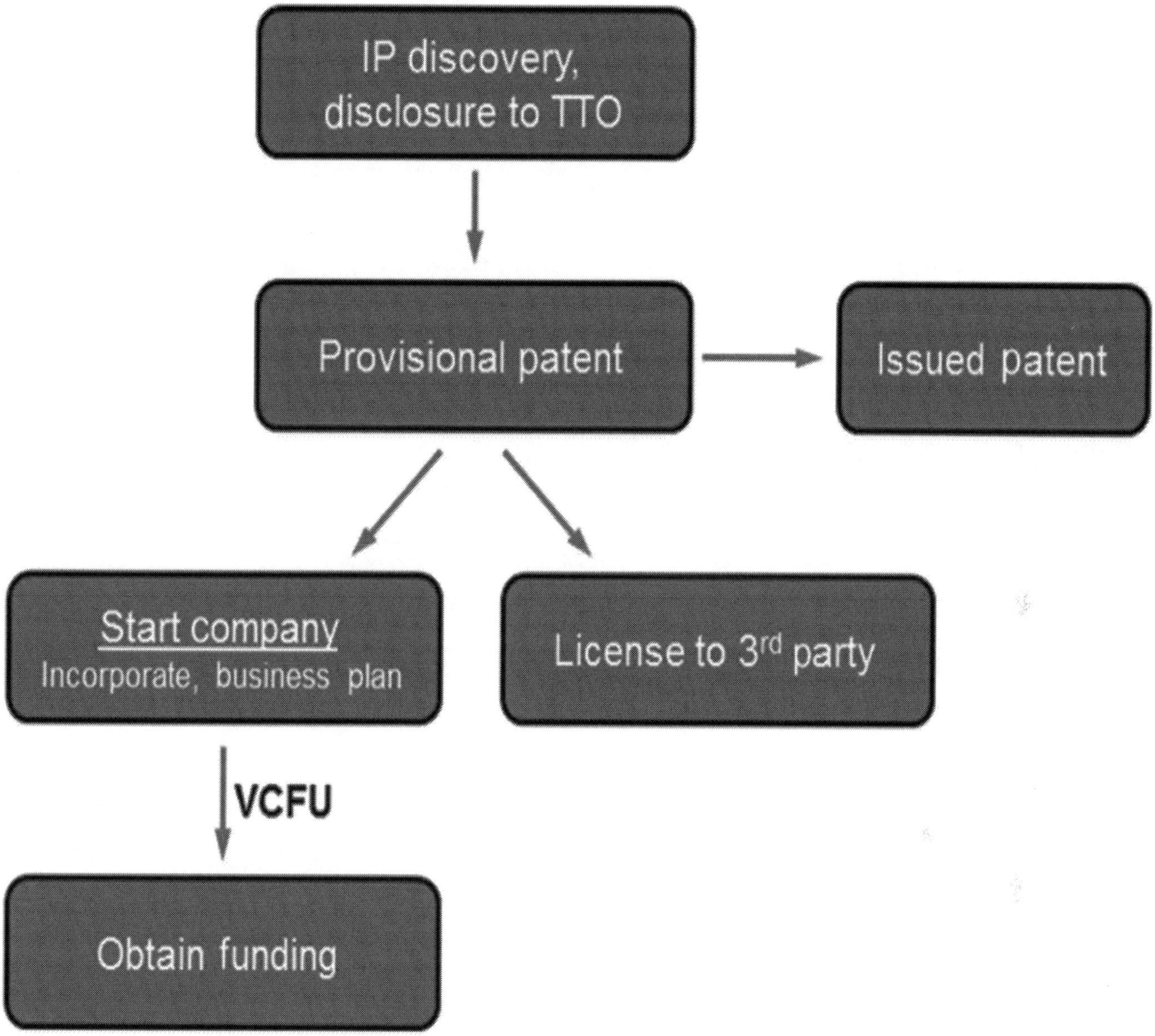

Figure 2

Major Steps in Formation of a Biotech Start-Up

General process of converting intellectual property (IP) to a minimum venture capital fundable unit (VCFU) capable of developing the IP. 3rd = third; TTO = Technology Transfer Office.

Determinants of success for biotechnology start-ups

Some major determinants of success for biotechnology start-ups are given in **Table 3**, in our estimated rank order.

Factors Influencing Success of Biotechnology Start-Ups

Intellectual property

Founders

Capital availability

Management and company strategy, including practicality of the scientific plan

Tactics and company execution

Geographic location

Sector and general economic cycles

Luck/serendipity

Intellectual property

Assuming the founding scientists have no disqualifying characteristics, the most important determinant of start-up formation is IP. To be of high value, the IP that serves as a platform for the start-up ("actionable IP") should be patentable, address an unmet medical need, have the potential for a large return-on-investment, and be amenable to a cost-effective and executable development strategy (14). Not only does IP need to meet these criteria, but the data and materials have to be developed to communicate these characteristics to potential investors.

Founder's qualifications

Scientific founders of life sciences start-ups are a diverse group who possess a wide array of backgrounds and strengths. Although the most important, critical path-enabling aspect of converting scientific discovery into successful entrepreneurial activity is the strength of the IP, the perceived quality of the founders is also heavily weighted by most investors.

For some VCs, the value of founders' qualifications exceeds that of the IP, termed "betting on the jockey, not the horse". In any event, there are a few founders' characteristics that bear consideration (**Table 4**). Although not all of the characteristics listed in **Table 4** are or need to be inherent in successful scientist-entrepreneurs, typically most of these attributes are present and major deficiencies in any of them are potentially disqualifying to astute investors.

Note that the career trajectory position is not listed as a factor; provided that criterion 1 in **Table 4** is satisfied, a founder may be an early-, mid-, or late-career investigator. Also, in device start-ups, criterion 1 is not applicable. For device development there is less of a funding requirement and a shorter development time, and it is not uncommon for cardiovascular junior scientists to found companies.

Favorable Characteristics of Academic Founders of Biotechnology or Device Start-Ups

Ideally should be at/close to the top or clearly headed for the top of their scientific field

Reputation for effective collaboration; should not be considered a difficult co-worker

Stellar ethical reputation; should not be controversial

Willing to commit long-term to the mission of the start-up

Open to sharing the responsibilities and recognition with co-founders and senior management; "team player"

Capital acquisition

There are 2 general strategies for ongoing capitalization of a start-up company. At 1 pole is a strategy typically favored exclusively by some founders and management, which can be characterized as "raise all the capital possible, all the time, from any source." This approach may allow for developing multiple assets, thereby hedging risk of failure of any 1 program. However, the additional capital in-flow dilutes out early-stage investors, who may prefer hedging their own risk through single-asset investment in other companies.

In addition, this model commits senior management to a continuous cycle of fundraising (15), which will necessarily be accompanied by less focus on the company's primary business.

An alternate model at the other end of the spectrum and favored by some VCs is the capital efficiency model (16), where investment is typically limited to the initial asset on which the company was founded and financing stages are dependent on valuation step-ups to reduce capital cost. The more realistic and usual approach is typically something in between these 2 extremes. The fact is that scientific founders are usually not in a position to select one model versus another, given the exigencies of fundraising.

Company direction

Once a start-up company is founded and has secured its series A funding, there are a few "good business practices" that deserve mention. The first is that capital is precious, and operations need to proceed on the most parsimonious course that allows for meeting program objectives in a timely manner. The second is that to be successful in the context of finite resources, mistakes in direction or execution must be avoided, which means experienced personnel must be brought into management positions ranging from directors to company officers. The choice of board members is another critical step. Here the blending of multiple backgrounds relevant to the company's mission is the major challenge, followed closely by the choice of individuals with track records of working effectively with others. The board and senior management are responsible for setting strategy, but equally important are the execution tactics that are the major responsibility of mid-level and project managers.

Geographic location

We believe it is important to consider where to locate a life sciences start-up. Among the important factors are: 1) proximity to a major research university, typically that of a founder; 2) a region with enough ongoing sector business activity to have created a pool of qualified potential employees;

3) a locally favorable cost of living/quality of life index; and 4) a favorable business climate. Collectively we have founded or co-founded companies in Northern

California; Boulder/Denver, Colorado; Boston, Massachusetts; and Dallas, Texas, all of which at the time of founding satisfied the above-mentioned criteria and were able to attract adequate human and financial capital.

External factors

Table 3 lists 2 factors beyond the control of founders, management, and directors; sector or general economic cycles; and good or bad fortune. For example, during the major recession in 2007 to 2008 it was not possible to raise capital, and creative financing instruments such as reverse mergers had to be resorted to in order to maintain start-up viability. Luck and serendipity are always factors, at all levels of scientific activity.

Serendipity plays a major role in scientific discovery as well as product development (17), and luck tends to favor a well-organized/opportunistic organization (18) as well as one that is unafraid of risk (19).

However, Entrepreneurialism in the Translational Sciences Is Not for Everyone

But there is another perspective on life sciences start-ups, from a founder's point of view. A <50% chance of success is factored into the calculus of venture investing, accepted as the cost of doing business. The VC perspective is that return on investment is not normally distributed, and they depend on the occasional large multiple (>5-fold) to generate net fund profit. For founders, a good analogy is major league baseball, where hitters fail at least 2 out of 3 times but sustaining this batting average over time qualifies them for the Hall of Fame. Although serial failure will lead to loss of investor confidence in founders, an early success will allow a certain degree of failure tolerance.

In any event, the most effective way to become proficient in entrepreneurial ventures is to participate in them, and the experience gained increases the probability of success for subsequent endeavors.

Failure to return a sufficient multiple therefore is not considered a disqualifier for future venture investment in founders and their IP, as long as the founder's participation in the start-up is viewed as positive.

Training and preparation for entrepreneurial activity

Most academic entrepreneurs are self-taught and do not have business backgrounds or formal business school training, which is certainly the case for us. However, some formal instruction in relevant topics such as IP process, patent law, finance and business tactics and strategy as applied to the life sciences sector may be available in academic centers. If research universities want to maximize their entrepreneurial potential, they should offer or have access to these types of didactic programs, if for no other reason than to raise the faculty level of consciousness for IP development. However, it should be emphasized that the steps involved in entrepreneurial activity can be self-taught or sought from more experienced individuals, who typically are willing to be helpful.

Conclusions

Participation of translational scientists in entrepreneurial activities can be effectively woven into an academic career without major difficulty.

Most technology transfer offices at research universities possess the expertise to assist investigators in these endeavors. However, successful outcomes in life sciences entrepreneurialism are low-probability events whose likelihood can be increased by the quality of the founding IP, the strength of the founding scientists, and other factors. By far the most compelling reason to engage in life sciences entrepreneurial activity is to attempt to shepherd one's discoveries into the marketplace, that is, to ensure that research progress translates into societal benefit. This principle is codified in U.S. federal law, and should also be considered a moral obligation of the research enterprise.

References

1. The University and Small Business Patent Procedures (Bayh-Dole) Act of 1980. Public Law 96–517, 96th Congress. December 12, 1980. 94 Stat. 3015.
2. Loise V., Stevens A.J. The Bayh-Dole Act turns 30. Sci Transl Med. 2010;2:52cm27. [Abstract]
3. Markel H. Patents, profits, and the American people—the Bayh-Dole Act of 1980. N Engl J Med. 2013;369:794–796. [Abstract]

4. Thursby J.G., Thursby M.C. Intellectual property: university licensing and the Bayh-Dole Act. Science. 2003;301:1052. [Abstract]

5. Statista. Number of Biotechnology Companies in the United States from 2012 to 2016. 2017. Available at: https://www.statista.com/statistics/197930/number-of-united-states-biotech-companies-by-type/. Accessed October 23, 2017.

6. National Venture Capital Association. Total Venture Capital Dollars Invested in 2017 on Track to reach decade High. October 10, 2017. Available at: https://nvca.org/pressreleases/. Accessed October 23, 2017.

7. PR Newswire. Biotech Sector Looking to Outperform in 2017. Available at: http://markets.businessinsider.com/news/stocks/Biotech-Sector-Looking-to-Outperform-in-2017-1002370082. Accessed October 23, 2017.

8. Investopedia. Biotechnology. 2017. Available at: http://www.investopedia.com/terms/b/biotechnology.asp. Accessed October 23, 2017.

9. Bergstrom T.C. On the evolution of hoarding, risk-taking, and wealth distribution in nonhuman and human populations. Proc Natl Acad Sci U S A. 2014;111 Suppl 3:10860–10867. [Europe PMC free article] [Abstract]

10. Haislip B. How to raise an entrepreneur. Wall Street Journal Online, June 13 2011. Available at: https://www.wsj.com/articles/how-to-raise-an-entrepreneur-1376593029. Accessed October 21, 2017.

11. Sarasvathy S.D. Edward Elgar Publishing; Northampton, MA: 2008. Effectuation: Elements of Entrepreneurial Expertise.

12. Hoketsu K. Diane Publishing; Darby, PA: 2004. Iron Chef: The Official Book.

13. Lapidus S. Bernstein report on biobusiness. BioCentury, October 23, 2006;14(47):A3.

14. Van Norman G.A., Eisenkot R. Technology transfer: from the research bench to commercialization part 1: intellectual property rights—basics of patents and copyrights. J Am Coll Cardiol Basic Trans Sci. 2017;2:85–97.

15. Shuster M. Always Be Raising: A Road Map to Getting Venture Capital Funding. January 17, 2012. Available at: https://www.fastcompany.com/1808985/always-be-raising-road-map-getting-venture-capital-funding. Accessed October 22, 2017.

16. Booth BL. Framing Up Capital Efficiency in Early Stage Biotech. Forbes Pharma and Healthcare, July 17, 2014. Available at: https://www.forbes.com/sites/brucebooth/2014/07/17/framing-up-capital-efficiency-in-early-stage-biotech/#7978788e10e5. Accessed October 21, 2017.

17. Merck GW. What the doctor ordered. Time, August 18, 1952.

18. Rickey B. Available at: https://en.wikipedia.org/wiki/Branch_Rickey#cite_ref-29. Accessed October 22, 2017.

19. Terence. Phormio. 161 BC:l. 203 ("fortis fortuna aduivat"). Wikipedia. Available at: https://en.wikipedia.org/wiki/Fortune_favours_the_bold. Accessed October 22, 2017.

20. Booth B.L., Salehizadeh B. In defense of life sciences venture investing. Nat Biotechnol. 2011;29:579–583. [Abstract]

21. Sanberg P.R., Gharib M., Harker P.T. Changing the academic culture: valuing patents and commercialization toward tenure and career advancement. Proc Natl Acad Sci U S A. 2014;111:6542–6547. [Europe PMC free article] [Abstract]

22. National Research Council of the National Academies . National Academies Press; Washington, DC: 2012. Research Universities and the Future of America: Ten Breakthrough Actions Vital to Our Nation's Prosperity and Security.

23. Harrison K.D., Kadaba N.S., Kelly R.B., Crawford D. Building a life sciences innovation ecosystem. Sci Transl Med. 2012;4:157fs37. [Abstract]

24. Stossel T.P. Regulation of financial conflicts of interest in medical practice and medical research: a damaging solution in search of a problem. Perspect Biol Med. 2007;50:54–71. [Abstract]

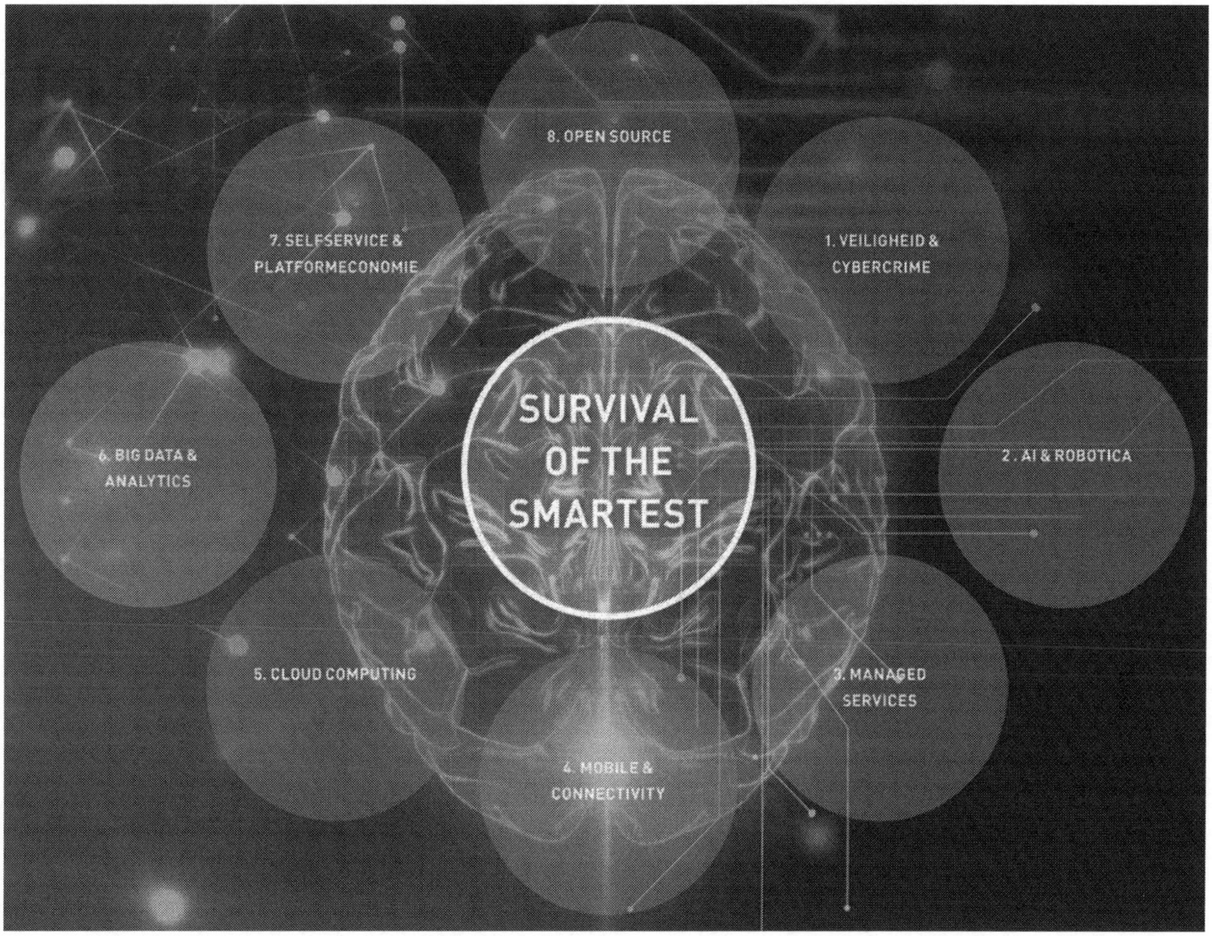

Survival of the Smartest: Funding Sources for Biotech and Life Sciences Companies

The proliferation of biotech and life sciences companies in the past decade has led to significant innovation in these fields. However, lack of access to reliable sources of adequate funding remains a key reason that new or emerging biotech and life sciences companies too often fail before reaching their potential.

What is apparent is that although there is no blueprint or one-size-fits-all path for capital formation, funding options available to businesses have evolved dramatically over the past decade, and biotech and life sciences companies have potential access to a wider than ever variety of funding options.

It appears this trend will continue in the next decade. For example, the US Securities and Exchange Commission (SEC) recently announced a proposed amendment to the definition of accredited investor that will significantly expand the range of individual and entity investors that will be able to participate in Regulation D offerings (the SEC's primary "private placement" exemption).

Below is a non-exhaustive list briefly discussing the funding options available to biotech and life sciences companies that are beyond the self-funded and "family and friends" funded capital-raising stages.

- ***Traditional Non-Dilutive Funding.*** Many businesses utilize traditional non-dilutive funding, if and when available, at some point during their existence, the most common being traditional bank loans or lines of credit. When a company has the balance sheet and/or assets to secure bank financing, such traditional non-dilutive funding is attractive because it does not require the founder or entrepreneur to surrender any ownership or control of a company in exchange for the funds. In addition, obtaining traditional non-dilutive funding is significantly less complicated than obtaining funding from other sources, which frees up management time to seek additional, potentially more permanent, sources of capital or to operate and grow the business. Traditional financing has its drawbacks, most importantly the need to make repayments on borrowed amounts. Lenders may also require collateral, guarantees, or other types of security before they will provide funding.
- However, depending on the source of the loan or line of credit and the business seeking funding, repayment options can often be negotiated and include terms that somewhat align the interests of the startup and the lender (e.g., revenue sharing).
- ***Non-Traditional, Non-Dilutive Funding.*** Beyond bank financing arrangements, yet still in the non-dilutive financing category, some biotech and life sciences companies are able to enter into revenue royalty financing arrangements whereby investors are entitled to receive a certain percentage of a company's revenue generated from specific products or operating lines or divisions of a company.

- As with traditional non-dilutive financing, royalty participation arrangements do not dilute the ownership percentages of founders or entrepreneurs, but they allow companies to raise capital without the drawbacks of borrowing money as noted above.
- ***Angel Investors.*** "Angel" investments are typically made in the development-to-early stage of a business. These investments are typically made by individual investors or groups of investors (often referred to as angel groups or networks). In exchange for the investment, angel investors will typically require a certain percentage of ownership of the company, a certain level of control (usually in the form of consent or veto rights) over the decision-making of the company, or some combination of both. Beyond simply providing funding, these relationships can be valuable for early-stage biotech and life sciences companies because angel investors often have the ability to provide invaluable expertise in a given field; can be useful mentors in areas such as capital formation, business development, and people and process management; and can provide access to networks of other investors.
- ***Venture Capital.*** Venture capital investments are typically made after the startup stage. Venture capital funding in the biotech and life sciences sectors typically comes from venture capital firms that specialize in, and have an understanding of, the biotech or life sciences industries. Venture capital investments are typically higher-dollar investments that are made with the expectation of high returns within a defined period of time.
- In addition, these investments typically require the business owner to give up a certain percentage of ownership and control of the business to the venture capital firm, and they also often come with restrictions on the ability to undertake certain corporate actions. Furthermore, these investments are often hybrid investments that include a combination of debt and equity features. However, specialized venture capital firms can provide invaluable expertise on operating and growing a Biotech or Life Sciences company, including access to networking opportunities within the industries and help with identifying executives with successful records in those fields.

- ***Federal and State Government Grants/Awards.*** Many US federal agencies provide grants to early-stage companies and startups in the biotech and life sciences fields, including Small Business Technology Transfer and Small Business Innovation Research grants. While these types of grants do not typically require the owners to surrender any ownership or control of a company, they often contain strict requirements with respect to the number of employees and the ownership and control of the grant recipient. These restrictions may limit the ability of a company to undertake certain actions or enter into certain strategic partnerships or ventures while the grant recipient is still using the funds.
- In addition, the grant process is lengthy and competitive and requires a significant amount of time devoted to grant writing. In addition to federal funding, many US states, cities, and regions have economic development agencies or public universities or institutions that provide grants, awards, or venture financing.
- ***Crowdfunding.*** In late 2015, the SEC adopted rules providing an exemption from SEC registration requirements to companies seeking to raise capital from the general public through "crowdfunding," which is a relatively recent, "virtual" method of effecting a private offering of capital (either debt or equity) via small investments from a large number of investors. These rules allow companies to raise up to a little over $1 million in any 12-month period. In addition, the company will not be subject to state "Blue Sky" requirements and is allowed to advertise about the offering on a limited basis.
- However, the rules cap the amount that individuals may invest in any 12-month period at $2,200 or 5% of the annual income or net worth of an investor for investors with annual income or net worth below $107,000, or 10% of the lesser of the investor's annual income or net worth up to a maximum of $107,000 for investors with annual income or net worth of $107,000 or more.
- The rules also require that crowdfunded offerings be made through a registered broker-dealer or through a registered "funding portal," that companies are required to disclose information to potential investors about their business

and the securities being offered, and that the company offering the securities be subject to certain ongoing reporting obligations with the SEC.

- ***Strategic Transactions and Outsourcing.*** In certain cases, the easiest way to obtain funding is for a company to align itself with another company that already has sufficient capital and liquidity to be a source of funding. Although not seen as a "traditional" source of funding *per se*, certain strategic transactions and the outsourcing of certain work can greatly benefit the bottom line of early-to-middle-stage biotech and life sciences companies. These transactions can take many forms, including joint ventures, mergers, or partnerships with similarly situated or larger Biotech or Life Sciences companies; utilizing shared spaces and incubators; and outsourcing certain work to contract research organizations (commonly referred to as CROs), which can provide certain scientific work for a fee at a much lower cost to a company than if the company had performed the work. However, in each such case, the party seeking funding should be prepared to surrender some degree of autonomy in exchange for access to the capital (e.g., ownership, control, and, in the case of outsourcing, exposure of potentially valuable intellectual property to third parties).
- ***Initial Public Offering.*** Middle-to-late-stage biotech and life sciences companies that have additional capital needs may also choose to conduct an initial public offering (IPO) of their capital securities, typically in the form of an offering of newly issued and previously issued and outstanding common stock. The principal reason that companies conduct an IPO is to raise a significant amount of capital.
- In addition to raising additional capital, an IPO can raise the public profile of a company, potentially leading to an increase in a company's goodwill or market share. Conducting an IPO is an expensive and time-consuming process that requires the preparation and filing of a registration statement with the SEC and applying to list the common stock on a national securities exchange. Furthermore, after forming the IPO, the company will be subject to ongoing ownership, quarterly, and annual reporting requirements with the SEC. The

SEC's rules and regulations governing public companies typically require significant upgrades to the corporate governance infrastructure of companies going public, which also cost significant time and money.

- With that said, IPOs have the potential to be lucrative exit strategies for founders and early-stage investors.
- While IPOs are a potentially lucrative funding option, IPOs are generally only conducted by relatively mature companies with demonstrable operating and financial performance histories (median annual revenue of companies conducting IPOs was $68 million and $101 million for 2018 and 2017, respectively). Additionally, IPOs are generally only conducted for large amounts of funding (the median offering size for IPOs has hovered around $100 million for the past 20 years).

Please note that any capital formation efforts will require a company's records to be in good order. Therefore, prior to seeking funding, companies should review their articles of incorporation/organization, bylaws/operating agreements, real estate property records, licenses, permits, and contracts with the assistance of counsel and other professional advisors, as necessary. Companies seeking funding will want to put their best foot forward to achieve their funding goals, optimize valuation, and attract the right kind of investors.

Please also note that many of the transactions related to obtaining the above-listed funding must strictly comply with numerous federal and state rules and regulations. These transactions will likely require the preparation and execution of numerous legally binding documents and may require the filing of certain documents with federal and state agencies, all of which should be prepared in consultation with legal counsel.

Curtis Hearn

Curt Hearn is the practice group leader of the Corporate & Securities Practice Group. He handles mergers, acquisitions, and divestitures, as well as capital raising transactions for a variety of publicly traded and privately held companies.

https://europepmc.org/article/MED/21144079

Venture capital on a shoestring: Bioventures' pioneering life sciences fund in South Africa

BMC International Health and Human Rights,

Share this article Share with emailShare with twitterShare with linkedinShare with facebook

BACKGROUND: Since 2000, R&D financing for global health has increased significantly, with innovative proposals for further increases. However, although venture capital (VC) funding has fostered life sciences businesses across the developed world, its application in the developing world and particularly in Africa is relatively new. Is VC feasible in the African context, to foster the development and application of local health innovation? As the most industrially advanced African nation, South Africa serves as a test case for life sciences venture funding. This paper analyzes Bioventures, the first VC company focused on life sciences investment in sub-Saharan Africa. The case study method was used to analyze the formation, operation, and investment support of Bioventures, and to suggest lessons for future health venture funds in Africa that aim to develop health-oriented innovations.

DISCUSSION: The modest financial success of Bioventures in challenging circumstances has demonstrated a proof of concept that life sciences VC can work in the region. Beyond providing funds, support given to investees included board participation, contacts, and strategic services. Bioventures had to be proactive in finding and supporting good health R&D. Due to the fund's small size, overhead and management expenses were tightly constrained.

Bioventures was at times unable to make follow-on investments, being forced instead to give up equity to raise additional capital, and to sell health investments earlier than might have been optimal.

With the benefit of hindsight, the CFO of Bioventures felt that partnering with a larger fund might benefit similar future funds. Being better linked to market intelligence and other entrepreneurial investors was also seen as an unmet need.

SUMMARY: BioVentures has learned lessons about how the traditional VC model might evolve to tackle health challenges facing Africa, including how to raise funds and educate investors; how to select, value, and support investments; and how to understand the balance between financial and social returns. The experience of the fund suggests that future health funds targeting ailments of the poor might require investors that accept health benefits as part of their overall "return."

Learning from Bioventures may help develop health innovation funding for sub-Saharan African that has combined health, financial, and economic development impacts.

Background

Since 2000, R&D financing for neglected diseases has increased significantly. In 2008, almost US$3.1 billion was invested in this area, with HIV/AIDS, malaria and tuberculosis initiatives comprising close to three-quarters of investment [1]. There have been innovative proposals for further development of funding mechanisms and sources [2]. However, although venture capital (VC) funding has fostered life sciences businesses across the developed world, its application in the developing world and particularly in Africa is relatively new. Is VC feasible in the African context, to foster the development and application of local health innovation?

VC funds invest in new enterprises, by providing financing and support that helps to scale up promising technologies and business ideas.

For decades, venture capital has been used in developed countries to move health technologies from idea to implementation and widespread adoption [3].

There has been discussion of funding for innovative health business models in the African context [4].

While South Africa is a relatively unfamiliar destination for investment from funds based in wealthier countries, it does have solid science, and more capacity and wealth than other countries in sub-Saharan Africa [5]. At the same time, it faces a number of significant health challenges including a high incidence of HIV/AIDS and TB, and its population displays a mix of developed and developing world health profiles.

This paper analyzes Bioventures, the first VC fund focused on life sciences investment in sub-Saharan Africa. Based in South Africa, Bioventures was headed from 2001 onward by CEO Heather Sherwin.

This 80-million-rand (~$US 12M) fund has invested in 8 home-grown companies since 2002, such as Disa Vascular, a creator of stents for coronary and peripheral artery disease (see Table **Table1).1**). Despite being a pioneer in the region, Bioventures achieved solid though not stellar returns.

We used a case study design. Our analysis is based on semi-structured interviews with key informants, site visits in Cape Town in South Africa, and analysis of peer-reviewed literature, news reports, government and NGO reports, and web sites. We conducted interviews with personnel of Bioventures and related organizations Acorn, Cape Biotech, Disa Vascular, and Real-World Diagnostics between October 2007 and June 2009. Bioventures was asked to fact-check the case study; the analysis and interpretation is our own. All quotes are from the interviews unless otherwise noted, and with permission. This study was approved by the Office of Research Ethics of the University of Toronto.

We begin by describing the formation and investment summary of Bioventures. The investment process is then discussed in detail, as this is a key function that venture capitalists must adapt to new settings. One investee, Disa Vascular, is considered in depth.

Finally, the challenge of bringing a "health return on investment" into the VC model is discussed, and lessons from the case as a whole considered, including adapting the VC model to work in lower-resource settings to help foster local health innovation.

Founding and investment summary

Formation of the Bioventures fund was begun in 2000 by Heather Sherwin who had completed her PhD in cell biology in South Africa followed by an MBA. As stated on its web site, "Bioventures believes firmly in the ability of South Africa to develop a quality biotechnology industry that consists of companies that compete with the best in the world [6]." A private placement memorandum to pitch the fund was produced in 2001 and marketed to various investors.

Both the International Finance Corporation (IFC) and South Africa's Industrial Development Corporation invested, attracted by both the developmental and financial potential of domestic biotechnology. According to Sherwin, the fund benefited from approaching investors in the middle of the dot com boom, since biotech was seen as being one of the next big investment areas.

The final trust deed was signed on November 30, 2001. Bioventures was formally established in late 2001, with a relatively small capital base of 80 million rand (approx $US 12 million).

As the CEO of the new fund, Sherwin (and the fund itself) was based in Cape Town, South Africa. Paul Miot of Johannesburg was brought in as the CFO; a chartered accountant with an MBA from London Business School, he had worked in banks and was already managing a general private equity fund, and his financial focus was complementary to Sherwin's scientific background.

Investments started in 2002, and by 2004 the fund had made all its investments. From 2002 to 2009, investments and results were as shown in Table **Table1.1**. Out of eight investments, final results once all investments were exited (estimated to happen in 2010) were projected to be two outright failures, two break-evens which returned only the initial investment, three which returned between 2 and 3 times, and one which returned between 5 and 7 times.

This represents a solid but not spectacular return – a proof of concept that it is possible to do life sciences investments in South Africa and make money.

Choosing investees

To choose its 8 investments, Bioventures had to go through over 300 proposals; some came from universities, others from local scientists and entrepreneurs. Bioventures benefited from having no local competitors in the sector of life sciences VC. The South African industry itself was small enough that Sherwin knew some of the investees beforehand. The early-stage R&D could require active involvement on the part of the investor, even to the extent of setting up a company to commercialize the science – indeed, Bioventures started three companies to commercialize good technologies.

Bioventures management reported that many proposals were poor quality, and many others too early stage. Although the fund's goal of investing in great science, developing it, and selling the investment for a good price was the same as with developed market funds, Sherwin notes it took more work to develop investees than a developed market fund might typically give: "The perfect business plan with the perfect management team and the perfect science all patented in the right countries just doesn't walk through the door...you've got to be entrepreneurial and create those businesses yourself."

Since it was difficult for South Africa to compete with India and China in manufacturing, R&D-based businesses were seen by Bioventures management to have more potential, with South Africa's regulatory environment and perceived quality advantages playing a supporting role. Proactively seeking out investments was necessary. The people involved in the investee companies were often PhDs who left university for the business world, and were sometimes proactively recruited to form companies directly from universities based on the potential of their research.

Supporting investees

Along with funding, Bioventures supported the companies it invested in with life sciences experience, a network of contacts, and value-added services.

Both Sherwin and Miot recalled significant value in simply "being there": staying in regular contact with investees, learning about human relations and management issues in investees during visits, and using this tacit knowledge to give better, personalized advice and guidance to its investees.

As Sherwin put it, "A lot of what I look for when I go visit the businesses – and this is why it is so important in VCs to be on the ground, because you couldn't manage a VC fund remotely – it's the atmosphere in the business...You see how people are relating to the bosses....If there is a secretary, you know everything in the business from them, and you see the relationships. It's subtle things, it's part of the due diligence that you do on a business..."

A particular challenge for a small fund is spending time on management, investee support, and investment analysis – all activities that may increase overhead costs and thus reduce the fund's return on investment.

This has been identified as one barrier to smaller funds that would invest in global health innovation [7]. For Bioventures, Sherwin had to balance business support and development activities with making a return, yet knew she didn't have a choice about providing companies with the support they needed – if the support wasn't provided, the return wouldn't be made.

As a small fund, overhead had to be kept to a minimum. CFO Paul Miot managed a separate private equity fund and had his own fund management company, which gave him the financial flexibility to become involved part time at Bioventures.

As the only full-time employee, Sherwin worked on potential deals and investee interaction full time; Miot became more involved when new opportunities came along.

Although this lean cost structure was essential to making the fund viable, Miot felt that future funds should be larger, to benefit from economies of scale and get the human resources necessary to fully realize opportunities. Sherwin did note one upside: she thought her investees appreciated the fact that "we live the same lifestyle as our entrepreneurs do".

Valuing and exiting investees A key step when investing into an R&D based business is coming up with a valuation (i.e. estimated worth) of how much the business will be worth in 3, 5, or 10 years.

When valuing more mature companies, many valuation methods are used, such as estimating future income streams which are discounted appropriately for risk. But since venture firms like Bioventures invest into new companies, projecting future income is difficult – especially in new sectors as biotechnology was in South Africa.

One method Bioventures used was to agree with an investee company on figures for investment required and future sales. However, two mechanisms were then used to mitigate risk. The investment might be made in parts, with later investments depending on milestones being hit after earlier investments. And if income figures were not hit, then Bioventures would take more shares. (Some caution was required in taking additional shares, in order not to de-incentivize investee management by reducing their ownership stake too far.)

Bioventures aimed to make much of its money back on "exits," when investments are sold off to purchasers. A key exit strategy was to create IP (Intellectual Property) that would be valuable enough for a US or European company to purchase. These equity exits differ from the debt financing route used to grow a company into a large manufacturing entity; Bioventures perceived this to be a lower-return option in most cases, and one with time scales longer than might be suitable for the fund.

Sherwin reported that an IPO (initial public offering) on local stock exchanges would have been challenging, as local investors tended to be risk averse and less familiar with R&D based health businesses.

Another exit strategy was to do an IPO on foreign exchanges, with the Swiss exchange being explored for investee Disa Vascular due to Swiss investors' long history with healthcare.

Two other investees, PlatCo and Shimoda, were sold to Abraxis Bioscience – a biotechnology company trading on the NASDAQ exchange in the US that has cancer therapeutics as one focus. According to Reuters, Abraxis acquired the full equity of both Shimoda and Platco for an initial payment of US$15 million, plus potential additional payments if specified milestones were met [8].

Disa Vascular: the investee point of view

Disa Vascular, mentioned in the previous section, was one of Bioventures' more successful investees – a stent company that built itself from an R&D operation into a full-scale medical device manufacturer.

Gregory Starke, CEO of Disa Vascular and co-founder with Damian Conway, studied orthopedics and cardiology at the University of Cape Town, whose faculty member Christiaan Barnard performed the world's first heart transplant in the late 1960s. After several years of consulting for local orthopedics companies, he and colleagues decided in late 1999 to develop their own coronary stents, with savings from their consulting work followed by a small angel investment (i.e. small initial investment) in 2000. As Starke recalled, "It was a much bigger leap then we realized...we had a lot of cardiology expertise around that we could get hold of.

But on the commercial side, both the production and the ultimate selling of the implant, we were extremely naive and really had no idea of the massive challenges that faced us on actually producing an implant, getting the various certifications etc. and then commercializing it in a professional and normal manner."

Disa's management decided early on to pursue European regulatory approval for their coronary stent product, wanting to differentiate themselves in terms of quality perception. Although the device's South African origins did not in itself pose difficulties for European regulators, Disa Vascular's management did find it difficult to find local people experienced in taking a new biomedical device through the regulatory process, and later developed this expertise in-house.

Receiving European regulatory approval opened more doors for Disa in international markets, which Starke noted had the unanticipated side effect of causing them to lose focus on the South African market.

In practice, they did not have sufficient funds to go to trade shows, do marketing, follow up on leads, and otherwise break into competitive international markets.

An experience with an Irish company that licensed the product also turned out poorly, with the Irish company reneging on the agreement once they saw that Disa didn't have the resources to pursue legal action.

Disa's management rethought their strategy, and came back with new products and investment from Bioventures, and a more mature understanding of markets, branding, and working with distributors.

With a better understanding of "what all the rules were and the ways to get a product to market," Disa Vascular has had a more typical sales operation for the past several years, with distribution in about a dozen countries in Latin America, Europe, and Asia. As of June 2008, Disa had sold about 6000 stents, with a product line focused on technology for the treatment of coronary and peripheral artery disease, including bare metal stents, catheters, and angiography accessories; the stents had received European certification, and were structurally designed to reduce restenosis (re-narrowing of the artery after stenting due to a buildup of scar tissue). A new coated and drug-eluting stent was also undergoing clinical trials [9].

According to Starke, he first met with Heather Sherwin when Bioventures was still in the process of raising funds. In 2002, Disa made an offer to its angel investors that was underwritten by Bioventures, thus enabling the exit of the angel investors while bringing new money into the business. Bioventures invested approximately $2 million, with about $1.3 million coming into the company, and the remainder going to the angel investors. Disa subsequently got another investment of a little less than $US 1 million along with a loan for capital equipment purchase, both from South Africa's Industrial Development Corporation.

Although these investments let the company survive and grow, and do development and marketing locally, Starke found them to be insufficient to travel to big congresses or take the business global, thus hampering access to new markets.

Our analysis revealed other challenges to be getting partners such as cardiologists involved in the testing and development of the stents, doing sales effectively in an organization filled with engineers, coming to terms with 'soft marketing' aspects of medical device sales, and a lack of mentorship and local industry experts to network with.

Fund performance

The distribution of returns on the investees of the Fund as of 2009 is shown in Table **Table1.1**. Overall, Sherwin reported that the Fund made money overall, earning a modest but not stellar rate of return from 2001 to 2009 (the exact figure is proprietary).

PlatCo, the investment with the best returns at 7 times initial investment, reportedly made roughly an 80% internal rate of return over the life of the investment. Based on public statements, PlatCo's buyer Abraxis Bioscence was willing to pay for it because the anti-cancer health technology was seen as having huge potential [8].

Sherwin and Miot felt that in principle Bioventures itself could have taken those products into clinical trials and perhaps made a 20x return instead of 7x, but it didn't have the time or the money available. PlatCo was almost a virtual company, composed of one researcher, several students, and space rented from a university; as such, its overhead was extremely low.

Bioventures was faced with a landscape in South Africa where there were few established life sciences innovators, be it in biotechnology or in non-generic pharmaceuticals. All of its investees were early stage R&D companies.

Challenges included dilution due to inadequate capitalization, investment choices, a fund lifespan which was short for doing biotechnology in a new location, and operating in a challenging environment. The Fund's short lifespan of only 7 years nominally ended in November 2008, though Sherwin had arranged for a two-year extension period to wind down some investments such as Disa Vascular in a more measured way.

Balancing financial and social return on investment

Given the overhead and risks involved, Sherwin was ultimately forced to consider whether a typical high "VC rate of return" was achievable, or even a desirable goal to aim for.

Despite Bioventures' location in South Africa, financial pressures necessitated a focus on developed-world diseases. Diseases whose patients are mostly poor don't represent attractive financial investment opportunities, absent third-party financial support for innovation.

One investee of Bioventures in drug discovery started an HIV program along with a pain treatment program, but was forced to cancel the HIV program for perceived insufficient payback. As Sherwin said, "If you follow your pure VC mandate, you cannot be invested in TB companies, in HIV companies – you're just not going to get your returns."

Both Sherwin and Miot had thoughts on this balance. Sherwin suggested one analogy for future funds would be microfinance funds, which have pooled investment capital into fund structures, invested the funds into a portfolio of microfinance enterprises, and rewarded the original investors with a combined financial return and social impact return.

This "mixed model" investment fund for healthcare companies might invest in those African countries with political stability and populations which can pay for better health care. Such a fund would focus on shorter-term investments that scale up existing health delivery models. For example, investing into a clinic might have a 5 to 7 year time frame to get a loan paid back, as compared to a risky new drug which might require a 10+ year time frame. At least one such fund has been started since Sherwin made this suggestion [10].

Lessons learned Appreciate scales of time and money

After running Bioventures, Sherwin better appreciated the time and money it takes to see investments through to success: "Timeframe and quantum of money I think has just surprised everyone, and not just in South Africa, but everywhere – just how much money it does take to get it there, to get biotech there."

Miot felt that access to larger amounts of capital for highly promising investments would be a key feature to be built into future local funds.

He suggested partnering with a fund overseas which had more money, so that the local fund would find and grow the investment initially and then exit to the overseas partner fund, which in turn would benefit from a risk-mitigated series of high-quality deals in an emerging market.

Comparing a fund with $10 million to invest against one with $100 million to invest, the overhead as a fraction of funds under management is typically higher for the smaller fund. The smaller fund thus finds it more difficult to provide value-added services, as they may come out of the core bottom line. While investees such as Starke felt that Bioventures had added value, addressing the issue of overhead is essential to making smaller funds work, such as through technical assistance or mentoring provided by third parties on a non-profit basis. Similar issues are likely to arise in the establishment of any large Southern fund focused on investing for health impact.

Educate investors about life sciences and emerging economies

Sherwin noted that the IFC (International Finance Corporation), as a large, sophisticated, global investor into Bioventures, had a good understanding of what biotech is and what it requires. This was not the case with some other investors, who compared the performance of Bioventures unfavourably with that of funds in other areas such as IT. Sherwin suggested "I think part of it is us educating them in the beginning, to what they're getting into...in raising [future funds], even if we end up turning down investors or we lose investors, we know that the investors we have really understand what they're doing. It makes a big difference."

With the above in mind, potential investors from Europe and North America may see risks in investing in emerging economies. However, the solid performance of Bioventures is a positive proof point, and Sherwin believed political and currency risk would be low for offshore investors. Such investors might also be motivated by greater upside potential, given the growing scientific and entrepreneurial strengths of the South. If and when future funds are set up which directly target local health impact, they will be able to benefit from past fund experiences in the region.

Summary

While Bioventures has been a modest and not stellar success financially, it represents a significant accomplishment: creating a life sciences investment fund in Africa, which has shown proof of concept for investing into R&D based health technologies and creating viable businesses on the ground.

Although South Africa is more economically developed than the rest of sub-Saharan Africa, the fund faced several challenges common to the region, including local capacity constraints and developing IP in the global economy. At the same time, it benefited from positive aspects of the South African context, such as entrepreneurs with personal initiative, private and institutional investment, a positive economic climate, availability of skilled personnel, and a reasonably stable financial and legal climate.

In transplanting the venture model elsewhere in Africa, the presence or absence of such factors must be taken into account.

Beyond providing funds, the support given to investees included board participation, contacts, and strategic services.

Bioventures had to be proactive in finding and supporting good R&D, and not merely wait for the ideal company to walk through the door. Providing hands-on support to early-stage health ventures posed problems – due to the fund's relatively small size, overhead and management expenses were tightly constrained. Bioventures sometimes wasn't able to make follow-on investments, being forced instead to give up equity to raise follow-on investment capital.

Being better linked to market intelligence and other entrepreneurs was seen as an unmet need – to "people who have done it before." The experience of the fund also suggests that future health care technology funds targeting ailments of the poor might require investors to accept health benefits as part of their overall "return."

While not yet targeting the tougher health challenges facing the continent as a whole, BioVentures has learned lessons about how the traditional VC model might change to tackle those health challenges, yet still retain the risk-accepting spirit that has turned promising ideas into reality in other technological fields.

Lessons learned include how to raise funds and find "educated investors"; how to select, value, and support investments; and how to evaluate different models for investment funds targeting health products and services.

Similarly, funds which have already been started on the health delivery side suggest the potential viability of co-investing in health technologies along with health delivery systems. The challenge facing those who would invest in health innovation in Africa is to learn from examples like Bioventures, and develop viable health innovation funding that combines health, financial, and economic development impacts.

Masum H,

Singer PA

BMC International Health and Human Rights,

Acknowledgements

This work was funded by a grant from the Bill & Melinda Gates Foundation through the Grand Challenges in Global Health Initiative, and supported by the McLaughlin-Rotman Centre for Global Health, an academic centre at the University Health Network and University of Toronto. We are grateful for comments from Justin Chakma, Jocalyn Clark, Abdallah S Daar, Sarah Frew, and Ronak Shah.

References

1. Moran M, Guzman J, Henderson K, Ropars AL, McDonald A, McSherry L, Wu L, Omune B, Illmer A, Sturm T, Zmudzki F. G-FINDER 2009: Neglected Disease Research & Development: new times, new trends. Sydney, Australia: The George Institute for International Health; 2009.
2. Hecht R, Wilson P, Palriwala A. Improving health R&D financing for developing countries: a menu of innovative policy options. Health Affairs. 2009;28(4):974–85. doi: 10.1377/hlthaff.28.4.974. [Abstract] [CrossRef]
3. Ackerly DC, Valverde AM, Diener LW, Dossary KL, Schulman KA. Fueling innovation in medical devices (and beyond): venture capital in health care. Health Affairs. 2009;28(1):w68–75. doi: 10.1377/hlthaff.28.1.w68. Jan-Feb, Epub 2008 Dec 2. [Abstract] [CrossRef]
4. International Finance Corporation. The Business of Health in Africa. Washington D.C.: The World Bank Group; 2007.

5. Al-Bader S, Frew SE, Essajee I, Liu VY, Daar AS, Singer PA. Small but tenacious: South Africa's health biotech sector. Nature Biotechnology. 2009;27(5):427–445. doi: 10.1038/nbt0509-427. [Abstract] [CrossRef]

6. Bioventures Web site. 2010-05-06. http://www.bioventures.co.za/index.php (Archived by WebCite® at http://www.webcitation.org/5pWqdtQFa)

7. Bailey E, Wirth M, Zapoi D. Venture Capital and Global Health. Brookline, MA: Commons Capital; 2005.

8. Abraxis BioScience Acquires Shimoda Biotech and Platco Technologies (Reuters, 2008). http://www.reuters.com/article/pressRelease/idUS109171+04-Apr-2008+BW20080404 (Archived by WebCite® at http://www.webcitation.org/5kwjtcW7A)

9. Jabara R, Chronos N, Conway D, Molema W, Robinson K. Evaluation of a novel slow-release paclitaxel-eluting stent with a bioabsorbable polymeric surface coating. JACC Cardiovasc Interv. 2008;1(1):81–7. doi: 10.1016/j.jcin.2007.11.009. [Abstract] [CrossRef]

10. Health in Africa Fund - African Development Bank. http://www.afdb.org/en/topics-sectors/initiatives-partnerships/health-in-africa-fund/

11. Chakma J, Masum H, Singer PA. Can incubatory work in Africa? Acorn Technologies and the entrepeneur-centric model. BMC International Health and Human Rights. 2010;10(Suppl 1):S7. [Europe PMC free article] [Abstract]

12. Novogratz J. Meeting Urgent Needs with Patient Capital. Innovations Journal. 2007;2(1-2):19–30. doi: 10.1162/itgg.2007.2.1-2.19. [CrossRef]

13. Masum H, Daar AS, Al-Bader S, Shah R, Singer PA. Accelerating Health Product Innovation in sub-Saharan Africa. Innovations Journal. 2007;2:129–149. doi: 10.1162/itgg.2007.2.4.129. [CrossRef]

14. Masum H, Chakma J, Simiyu K, Ronoh W, Daar AS, Singer PA. Venture funding for science-based African health innovation. BMC International Health and Human Rights. 2010;10(Suppl 1):S12. [Europe PMC free article] [Abstract]

Chapter 5

The Societal Benefit of Nonprofit Biotechnology Companies

Rena M. Conti, PhD,

H&O What is the unmet need to which nonprofit biotechnology companies could respond?

RC Biotechnology investments are risky due to significant scientific and regulatory uncertainty. The high failure rate of oncology drug development has concentrated investor enthusiasm toward later stages of development in biotechnology, even as venture capital investment in the industry overall remains high.

Uncertain regulatory enforcement, increasing political scrutiny of the prices of novel treatments and company profits, and the recent economic downturn appear to be operative in the stagnation of venture capital investment in biotechnology. Taken together, these forces push biotechnology research and development into areas meeting specific investment criteria.

By necessity, for-profit biotechnology firms that are primarily financed by external funds require the expected profit associated with innovative product development to be large enough to cover research and development (R&D) expenses and the opportunity costs of capital investment, both in a timely way.

Consequently, for-profit firms tend to focus efforts on the development of drugs or small molecules where the protection of intellectual property is clearly defined and legally defensible, the target population is large enough to potentially benefit from treatment and willing and able to pay for treatment innovation, and scientific uncertainty is minimized to the extent possible.

Taking scientific uncertainty in any R&D endeavor as a given, it is believed these incentives result in a variety of challenges: the ability of individuals and/or governments to pay for new therapies at a rate that rewards the risks taken in producing them; the distribution system for getting therapies to needy individuals; the protection of intellectual property rights, particularly in the developing world; the size of the target population; and the nature of insurance coverage and reimbursement policy.

H&O How would nonprofit biotechnology companies be organized?

RC In essence, the nonprofit model is an integrated market-based approach to address the market failures engendered by current financing incentives through the efficient integration of financing with drug development. The non-profit biotechnology model capitalizes on existing tax-code structures—the 501 (c) (3) charitable organization model—successfully used by all private academic institutions in the United States, existing nonprofit biotechnology firms, and nonprofit venture capital firms. The charitable 501(c)(3) organization model is also widely used in the healthcare market to deliver services. The nonprofit biotechnology model requires a leadership team with substantial expertise in clinical pharmacology and therapeutics, the design and implementation of clinical trials, and fundraising and regulatory affairs.

Deep relationships with the for-profit industry and academia are critical in identifying middle- and late-stage products in development that may be donated or licensed to the firm. Finally, a commitment to furthering the social good and passion for pursuing the values of the firm through product development and approval are critical for success.

H&O Does the nonprofit model suit either the developed or the developing world better?

RC Current financing incentives appear to adversely affect R&D for technologies that would have significant societal benefit in the developed world but little opportunity for a high return on investment: treatments for pediatric patients with little adult analog, diagnostics to better guide use of existing medications, and therapies that are available generically or over-the-counter applied to alternative illnesses or populations.

There has been a tendency to rely upon public policy to help guide the for-profit industry to undertake socially valuable R&D that does not meet investment criteria, but assessments have found them to be mixed in effectiveness and associated with unintended consequences. The Best Pharmaceuticals for Children Act and the Orphan Drug Act are prominent examples. The 2007 US Food and Drug Administration (FDA) priority voucher policy provides a direct financial incentive for the development of therapies for tropical diseases primarily affecting the developing world, with a strong emphasis on early-stage investment. To what degree this incentive spurs significant investment in R&D, translating into novel product development and approval, is uncertain at this time. Importantly, this incentive does not address financing problems in the developed world.

Nonprofit ventures are increasingly being established to address these concerns. Prominent example focus on the financing and/or development of global health products, such as the nonprofit biotechnology firm the Institute for One World Health (iOWH; www.oneworldhealth.org) and the nonprofit financing firm BlOVentures for Global Health. Both have been generously supported by the Gates Foundation, the biotechnology industry itself, and private individuals. Given the market failures in the developed world, there is no a priori reason why the nonprofit biotechnology firm model in use for the developing world would not also work in the developed world.

We already see a number of firms aiming to complete product development for neglected developed-world populations.

H&O What current examples demonstrate the nonprofit model's success?

RC There are numerous firms that focus on coordinated financing and development of single agents, but it is believed firms with a portfolio strategy based on neglected diseases, populations, or technologies are the future. For example, the iOWH is perhaps the most successful example of a nonprofit pharmaceutical company devoted to the development of anti-infectives for the developing world. The company started with a low-risk project, resuscitating a drug that had gone off patent and was no longer available. Paromyocin for the treatment of visceral leish-maniasis was approved by the Drug Controller General of India last year. iOWH has been extremely successful at raising money to support its efforts; the Gates Foundation granted the organization $42.5M in 2002. Already, iOWH is acting as an alternative funder for external ventures: Berkeley-based Amyris Biotechnology received $12M last year for the development of an antimalarial product when it could not raise private financing.

The Alfred E. Mann Foundation for Biomedical Engineering (www.aemf.org), founded in 1986, is perhaps the most successful nonprofit focused on the development of innovative technical solutions for persons suffering from debilitating medical impairments largely in the developed world. The Institute for Pediatric Innovation (IPI; www.pediatricinnovation.org) is a new venture dedicated to the development and reformulation of drug-based treatments and devices for children, particularly the neonatal intensive care unit and pediatric cardiology. IPI shows much promise, given its leadership team, partnerships with the leading children's hospitals in the United States, and focus on clinical areas where product development means literally the difference between life and death for children. For these companies, a focus on a set of neglected diseases, populations, and technological strategies allows for coordinated efforts to fundraise and identify, prioritize, and invest in complementary scientific efforts dedicated to maximizing social value.

H&O What are the next steps for the community at large toward more broadly adopting the nonprofit model?

RC It is believed the establishment of more nonprofit biotechnology firms focused on the development of diagnostics and therapeutics for illnesses that primarily affect the developed world is an idea worth further testing in the marketplace.

The establishment of more nonprofit biotechnology firms would provide alternative partners for academic researchers focused on translational treatment development in consonance with the FDA's Critical Path Initiative, while removing increasing public concerns about improper influence associated with profit motive. There are reasons to believe that cancer may be a good area for the future establishment of nonprofit biotechnology firms focused on promising but neglected R&D. In recent years, there has been substantial for-profit investment in the development of cancer therapeutics. However, translational cancer therapy is arguably the most expensive and scientifically uncertain area of R&D.

The development of pharmacogenomic diagnostics for personalized oncology treatment may be a critical focus of a new nonprofit biotechnology firm. There are a handful of approved diagnostics on the market and promising pharmacogenomic diagnostic candidates in the middle and later stages of development in academic medical centers and for-profit firms. It is clear that the potential health benefits and cost savings derived from the validation and use of these tests in oncology practice may be substantial.

In addition to the potential morbidity and mortality gains accrued from their application to guide oncology treatments for individual patients, it is believed the development and use of these tests may have significant social value from cost savings through the reduction of misused or overused treatments. Still, there has been little investment by for-profit firms in pharmacogenomic diagnostics to date, possibly explained by the fact that diagnostics have traditionally been difficult to legally protect against competition because their intellectual property protection is based on use patents and insurance reimbursement for them has traditionally been low relative to therapeutics. Furthermore, pharmacogenomic diagnostics are ordered only once in a person's lifetime but may have implications for the treatment of other cancers and medical illnesses. The willingness to pay for these tests by any individual insurance company may not reflect their aggregate social value across all health benefits or any potential cost savings, given the fractured coverage system of the United States.

Like iOWH, a firm could enter the pharmacogenomic diagnostic development process at the point at which for-profit firms find it unprofitable to continue R&D or when academic researchers have found no willing government or for-profit firm to partner with for further investment.

Scientific and business leadership could be marshaled toward this purpose. There are many individuals in the for-profit industry and academia with significant expertise in clinical therapeutics and pharmacology and a commitment to translational oncology product development. The public is rich with individuals with a deep personal commitment to finding effective cancer therapies. Almost one sixth of health philanthropy in the United States is devoted to cancer research; consequently, funding for a cancer-based nonprofit biotechnology firm maybe relatively easy to raise.

In sum, a nonprofit oncology biotechnology firm would allow for the leveraging of existing investment in the early stages of R&D by for-profit companies and academia, provide an infrastructure for technology transfer for these partners, and provide private donors the unique opportunity to commit directly to translational R&D (in contrast to existing cancer charities), with the goal of serving the public's interest.

Ultimately, this focus would establish proof of principle for the establishment of nonprofit biopharmaceutical firms focused on other socially important, but neglected, areas for investment by for-profit firms in the future.

. https://www.ncbi.nlm.nih.gov/pmc/articles/PMC6249613/

Non-profit drug research and development: the case study of Genethon

Free PMC article

Abstract

Non-profit drug research and development (R&D) has the potential to deliver innovative treatments at affordable prices. Using the case study methodology, we discuss some ethical and economic issues, including the possible impact of non-profit companies on innovation efforts from for-profit firms.

Like other non-profits, Genethon is willing to adopt an ethical attitude toward their donors by pricing their products affordably. It remains to be seen if the approach to internalize the marketing authorization, manufacturing and distribution activities prove to be efficient and sustainable.

Also, the firm faces an ethical dilemma because lower prices of innovative drugs can dry the for-profit R&D in the area and prevent patient access to future innovations.

ABSTRACT

Introduction

Non-profit drug research and development (R&D) is of growing attention worldwide [1–3]. In affluent societies, the exorbitant cost of advanced treatments, particularly in the segment of rare diseases, has placed increasing strain on the budgets of health care insurers and patients [2,4–10]. Even in European healthcare markets where national payers employ value-based frameworks to assist drug pricing decisions, orphan drugs achieve prices which fall much above typically used cost-utility thresholds [11]. Further, orphan drugs in Europe are purchased at a higher relative cost in lower income countries, due to differences in gross domestic product per capita [12]. Particularly, the for-profit sector has little interest in developing treatments for the so-called ultra-rare diseases which affect less than 150 patients across Europe due to small market size. Non-profit drug R&D has the potential to deliver innovative treatments for rare diseases at affordable prices [4,5].

Further, non-profits have been pioneers in the fields of gene therapies and rare diseases. From 1990 to 2010, the field of gene therapy was investigated almost exclusively by non-profit organizations. In Europe, the two major companies were established: Genethon in France and the San Raffaele Telethon Institute for Gene Therapy (SR-Tiget) in Italy. The development of the field was largely supported by donations from the society and patient organizations. The first sign of interest in the field from the for-profit sector was marked by a 2010 deal between SR-Tiget and GlaxoSmithKline PLC [13].

Today, many gene therapy products in pipelines of major biotech and pharmaceutical companies can be traced back to non-profit organizations.

For example, GlaxoSmithKline's Strimvellis was initially developed by SR-Tiget.

Further, AveXis' spinal muscular atrophy AAV9 vector, Audentes' AT132 for X-linked myotubular myopathy, Gensight Biologics' GS010 for Leber Hereditary Optic Neuropathy (LHON), Bluebird bio's childhood cerebral adrenoleukodystrophy and beta-thalassemia, sickle cell anemia programs and Orchard Therapeutics' X-linked chronic granulomatous disease program are fruits of the collaboration between the companies and Genethon.

Here we analyze Genethon, a French non-profit biotherapy R&D organization established in 1990. Genethon's mission is to 'design gene therapy products for rare diseases and to ensure their pre-clinical and clinical development in order to provide patients with access to these innovative treatments.' [14] Genethon is conducting four Phase I/II clinical trials as a sponsor or partner and is leading a dozen projects at various stages of preclinical development.

Using the case study methodology, we discuss some ethical and economic issues, including the possible impact of non-profit companies on innovation efforts of for-profit firms.

Origins and current challenges of genethon

Genethon was founded by the French patient support organization called Association Against Myopathies (Association Française contre les Myopathies, AFM-Telethon) [15]. Genethon's roots stem from its successful efforts to map the human genome in early 1990 and identify genes involved in several hundred genetic disorders [16–19]. In 2015, Genethon had a budget of €42 million, and in 2016, of €38 million; of which, nearly 60% was collected during fundraising events organized by AFM-Telethon. Currently, the company has 6,000 m^2 of laboratories and the largest Eropean bank of DNA and cell lines from humans with genetic disorders [14].

However, like many other non-profit R&D organizations, Genethon may face important challenges [1,4]. For instance, small ventures which are often established around a focused R&D program may not have the expertise or resources that are needed to develop medicines from discovery to commercialization.

Even if the clinical development program for one of Genethon's products is successful, the company may struggle to obtain the necessary marketing authorization (MA) or to subsequently manufacture and distribute the product, because of funding and human resource shortages [1]. In the following section, we discuss how Genethon has tackled these issues.

Securing resources for the entire value creation chain

The owner of Genethon has decided, at least for some of its inventions, to manage internally the regulatory activities, as well as manufacturing and distribution of its innovative products so that it can maintain the control over the supply and a 'fair and controlled price' for the products.

In 2016, AFM-Téléthon and the SPI fund (supported by the French government investment program), founded a firm called YposKesi [15]. The mission of the company is to obtain MA for Genethon's products and to ensure their manufacturing and distribution. AFM-Téléthon contributed to R&D assets by investmenting €37.5 million; the SPI fund invested €84 million. Because AFM-Téléthon has the majority holding in the venture, and thus, it can control prices of the marketed products.

However, even if YposKesi hires experienced talent from the largest pharmaceutical companies, it takes time to build effective teams in new functional areas. This may translate into delays or even limitations of patient access to Genethon's innovative therapies, as compared to more established organizations.

Possible alternatives to internalization of all activities while still avoiding monopoly that can lead to high prices include outsourcing activities to contract organizations or licensing the new product to multiple for-profit companies in order to encourage price competition [4]. While these approaches have proven useful in the developing world context, it remains to be seen if they can be effective in wealthy markets.

Issues with affordable pricing

Various non-profit R&D programs have adopted two general approaches to pricing their products: a) setting an affordable price that ensures sustainability of the drug supply by the company and b) forgoing price control by licensing products to for-profit entities, likely leading to a very high price [4]. The affordable pricing model would result in prices that fall significantly below the typical price range in the orphan drug segment. Therefore, the affordable price is lower than prices typically accepted by health care payers for such therapies.

The former approach to pricing is exemplified by Genethon through its affiliate YposKesi. Whereas the company has not marketed any drugs so far, it is strongly committed to affordable pricing, at least for some of its products.

The latter approach is exemplified by the US Cystic Fibrosis Foundation (CFF), which spent $150 million to develop ivacaftor – a cystic fibrosis medication – and subsequently sold the sales rights to a private company for $3.3 billion. Ivacaftor was one of the most expensive drugs available at that time, priced at $300,000 per year. Although CFF expressed concerns regarding the drug's price, it could not affect it once the deal was accomplished [20].

More recent examples of costly drugs whose discovery was funded by public funds at academia include voretigene neparvovec for the treatment of Leber's congenital amaurosis and tisagenlecleucel for the treatment of B-cell acute lymphoblastic leukemia priced at $850,000 per patient and $475,000 per treatment, respectively [4].

Further, Genethon has entered into exclusive licensing agreements for two of its products for an undisclosed genetic target and spinal muscular atrophy with Spark Therapeutics and AveXis, Inc for unrevealed amounts of money [21,22]. Consequently, it is likely that the company will not be able to influence the price of the licensed products and that their prices will be very high.

Whereas these prices may seem unethically high, the substantial royalties obtained by the non-profits from the transaction could be re-invested into research on novel drugs or used to support patients, depending on the profile of the organization. Because the royalties exceed by far the sums donated, more money will be invested back into R&D than the donors had provided [4]. However, such high prices bring about a risk related to delaying patient access due to possible unfavorable reimbursement decisions of insurers.

The 'affordable pricing' model and internalization of the value creation chain adopted by Genethon for some of its products have some ethical issues. Firstly, public donations collected for R&D are spent on commercial sale activities, but with a return-on-investment potential below that of the for-profit sector [4]. Secondly, building new infrastructure instead of using resources of established companies can delay or jeopardize patient access to products [4]. Thirdly, it remains to be seen if lower drug price tags will ensure commercial sustainably for the company, given the small sizes of target patient populations and high manufacturing costs for the innovative therapies.

Another possibility would be to price drugs differentially so that they are cheaper in low-income countries [23]. This approach has a limited value in the case of advanced treatments because they are deemed costly even in the wealthiest nations.

Further, differential pricing in Europe or Africa could result in parallel import of the drugs from countries where they are cheaper to countries where they are more expensive, possibly leading to stock outages in the source countries [24,25].

Incentives for future innovation

The absence of R&D on unprofitable diseases and the increase in R&D on selected rare diseases was observed after the US Orphan Drug Acts suggested that high drug prices create an actual incentive for R&D investment by the for-profit sector [4,26]. Therefore, the 'profit-maximizing pricing' of innovative products seems to maintain the traditional incentive for the pharmaceutical industry, because of the high potential for large revenues from the sales of expensive novel treatments.

However, this incentive could be compromised if a non-profit organization sells an innovative product at a relatively low price. Since innovative drugs are typically priced above previously used treatments in the same therapeutic area, the revenue prospects for a new product in the same pharmaceutical segment would be relatively low. This means that R&D on future products in the same area, which may be significantly better than the existing ones developed by non-profits, could be abandoned by the for-profit organizations for commercial reasons. This backlash in innovation may potentially limit the range of therapeutic options available to patients.

Conclusion

Like other non-profits, Genethon is willing to adopt an ethical attitude toward their donors by pricing their products affordably. However, the antitrust law does not permit them to impose prices on potential licensees. Possibly, the company chose to diversify their revenue by licensing certain products to for-profit firms and losing price control over the inventions and preserving exclusive rights to other products that are commercialized at affordable prices internally.

The licensing route will likely accelerate and optimize market access for the products, but it will lead to very high prices. It remains to be seen if the approach to internalize the MA, manufacturing and distribution activities for other gene and cell therapy products prove to be efficient and sustainable. Although it will allow maintaining price control, it may delay access and induce collateral damage.

Indeed, the firm faces an ethical dilemma because the lower prices of innovative drugs can dry the for-profit R&D in the area and prevent patient access to future innovations.

References

1. Hale VG, Woo K, Lipton HL.. Oxymoron no more: the potential of nonprofit drug companies to deliver on the promise of medicines for the developing world. Health Aff. 2005;24(4):1057–4. [PubMed]
2. Maxmen A. Busting the billion-dollar myth: how to slash the cost of drug development. Nature. 2016;536(7617):388–390. [PubMed]
3. Butler D. Neglected diseases fund touted. Nature. 2010;465(7296):277. [PubMed]
4. Jaroslawski S, Toumi M, Auquier P, et al. Non-profit drug research and development at a crossroads. Pharm Res. 2018;35(3):52. [PubMed]
5. Conti RM, Meltzer DO, Ratain MJ. Nonprofit biomedical companies. Clin Pharmacol Ther. 2008;84(2):194–197. [PMC free article] [PubMed]
6. Dougherty G, Harjivan C. Drug development for government, nonprofit, and developing-world markets. Pharm Technol Sourcing Manag. 2011;7:3.
7. Murteira S, El Hammi E, Toumi M. Fixing the price of the orphan drug siklos®: the council of state takes over the decision. Eur J Health Law. 2014;21(5):505–515. [PubMed]
8. Meekings KN, Williams CS, Arrowsmith JE. Orphan drug development: an economically viable strategy for biopharma R&D. Drug Discov Today. 2012;17(13–14):660–664. [PubMed]
9. Morel T, Arickx F, Befrits G, et al. Reconciling uncertainty of costs and outcomes with the need for access to orphan medicinal products: a comparative study of managed entry agreements across seven European countries. Orphanet J Rare Dis. 2013;8:198. [PMC free article] [PubMed]

10. Jarosławski S, Auquier P, Toumi M. No correlation between the prices of oncology orphan drugs in the US and their patient population sizes. Journal of Cancer Policy. 2017;14:1–4.

11. Medic G, Korchagina D, Young KE, et al. Do payers value rarity? An analysis of the relationship between disease rarity and orphan drug prices in Europe. J Mark Access Health Policy. 2017;5(1):1299665. [PMC free article] [PubMed]

12. Young KE, Soussi I, Toumi M. The perverse impact of external reference pricing (ERP): a comparison of orphan drugs affordability in 12 European countries. A call for policy change. Journal Market Access Health Policy. 2017;5(1):1369817. [PMC free article] [PubMed]

13. GSK, Fondazione Telethon and Fondazione San Raffaele to collaborate on gene therapy for rare diseases [press release]. London: 2010.

14. Genethon website. Available from: http://www.genethon.fr/en/about-us/profile-and-key-figures/.

15. AFM-Telethon website Available from: http://www.afm-telethon.com.

16. Cohen D, Chumakov I, Weissenbach J. A first-generation physical map of the human genome. Nature. 1993;366(6456):698–701. [PubMed]

17. McPherson JD, Marra M, Hillier L, et al. A physical map of the human genome. Nature. 2001;409(6822):934–941. [PubMed]

18. Bellanne-Chantelot C, Lacroix B, Ougen P, et al. Mapping the whole human genome by fingerprinting yeast artificial chromosomes. Cell. 1992;70(6):1059–1068. [PubMed]

19. Butler D. Genethon builds up 'genetic valley'. Nature. 1994;370(6484):4. [PubMed] [Google Scholar]

20. Pollack A. Deal by cystic fibrosis foundation raises cash and some concern. The New York Times. 2014.

21. Genethon Available from: http://www.genethon.fr/en/2018/03/13/avexis-enters-into-licensing-agreement-with-genethon/. 2018.

22. Genethon Available from: http://www.genethon.fr/en/2017/09/20/spark-therapeutics-enters-into-licensing-agreement-with-genethon/. 2017.

23. Danzon PM, Mulcahy AW, Towse AK. Pharmaceutical pricing in emerging markets: effects of income, competition, and procurement. Health Econ. 2015;24(2):238–252. [PMC free article] [PubMed]

24. Siringi S. Kenya allows parallel importation of drugs. The Lancet. 2001;357(9273):2034. [PubMed]

25. Rémuzat C, Urbinati D, Mzoughi O, et al. Overview of external reference pricing systems in Europe. Journal of Market Access & Health Policy. 2015;3(1):27675. [PMC free article] [PubMed]

26. Goldman DP, Jena AB, Philipson T, et al. Drug licenses: a new model for pharmaceutical pricing. Health Aff (Millwood). 2008;27(1):122–129. [PMC free article] [PubMed]

Non-profit Drug Research and Development at a Crossroads

Szymon Jarosławski [1], Mondher Toumi [2], Pascal Auquier [1], Claude Dussart [3 4]

Abstract

In wealthy nations, non-profit drug R&D has been proposed to reduce the prices of medicines.

We sought to review the ethical and economic issues concerning non-profit drug R&D companies, and the possible impact that their pricing strategy may have on the innovation efforts from for-profit companies targeting the same segment of the pharmaceutical market. There are two possible approaches to pricing drugs developed by non-profit R&D programs: pricing that maximizes profits and "affordable" pricing that reflects the cost of manufacturing and distribution, plus a margin that ensures sustainability of the drug supply. Overall, the non-profits face ethical challenges - due to the lack of resources, they are unable to independently commercialize their products on a large scale; however, the antitrust law does not permit them to impose prices on potential licensees. Also, reduced prices for the innovative products may result in the for-profit R&D in the area.

A biotech startup launches with unusual goal: invent new drugs, and sell them for less

Ned Pagliarulo

A new biotech startup launched Monday with an unorthodox and ambitious mission to undercut the makers of high-priced drugs by developing similar, but sharply lower-priced medicines.

EQRx, led by veteran biotech venture capitalist Alexis Borisy and backed by $200 million in initial funding, isn't setting out to make generics or biosimilar copycats.

Instead, Alexis and his co-founders believe there's a growing opportunity for a company committed to inventing and introducing new drugs at "radically different" prices than what brand-name drugmakers typically charge today.

"There's this larger disconnect from the ever-increasing prices we, as an industry, are charging for great new medicines and, at the same time, the technological base that is allowing us to rethink, reimagine, re-engineer and remake the whole process of how you make a drug, prove it and sell it," Borisy said in an interview.

Borisy, who left the venture capital firm Third Rock to start EQRx, aims for his new company to develop "equally as good, or better" versions of drugs already known to work. But rather than pricing such "me-too" medicines at par with on-market competitors, and striving through vast marketing efforts to convince insurers, physicians and patients to use its product, EQRx will compete on price.

"Our price is going to be much lower — so much lower that it's not about a rebate or a discount, it is a fundamentally lower price," said Borisy, referring to the payments drugmakers offer to insurers from a therapy's list price to secure coverage.

EQRx can do that, Borisy claims, because the current moment in medicine allows for drugmakers to move faster and more reliably through preclinical and clinical testing.

And, by going after known disease targets and established drug mechanisms, EQRx can sidestep some of the biological risk that can doom biotech endeavors.

Price competition, of course, is not a new concept in business, nor is it in the world of off-patent pharmaceuticals and biologics. Branded drug markets work differently, however, with few novel drugs introduced at a discount to their marketed rivals.

Instead, drugmakers engage in a opaque game of negotiation with insurers, trading rebates for formulary placement and wielding clinical trial data to carve out less contested slices of markets for themselves.

There are some examples of new drugs being launched at lower-than-market prices, such as Roche's multiple sclerosis drug Ocrevus, but they are typically the product of unique circumstances in an individual therapeutic area.

EQRx, by contrast, aims to replicate its vision at scale, with a grand goal of launching one new drug in five years and 10 in a decade. The company didn't disclose what disease and drug targets it will go after, but Borisy said they'd likely focus on oncology, immuno-inflammation and rare disease — categories that both command high prices and account for large chunks of healthcare spending on drugs. "He's trying to develop a business model for a market that doesn't currently exist," said Scott Gottlieb, former Food and Drug Administration Commissioner and now a partner at venture firm New Enterprise Associates, in an interview.

"He may well have an opportunity to do that because I don't think the status quo — in terms of the business model where companies use rebates to buy formulary access — I don't think that lasts," added Gottlieb, who is familiar with EQRx's approach.

Borisy's ambition is backed by his track record of successfully launching biotechs, including Blueprint Medicines, which last week won its first drug approval, and Foundation Medicine, bought out by Roche a year and a half ago for $2.4 billion. All told, Borisy has founded or had a hand in launching 15 companies.

At EQRx, Borisy will be joined by Melanie Nallicheri, former chief business officer at Foundation. Robert Forrester, who previously led Verastem Oncology, will be CXO.

Joining them as co-founders and advisors are Peter Bach, an oncologist and drug pricing expert at Memorial Sloan Kettering, and Sandra Horning, formerly chief medical officer and R&D head at Roche's Genentech.

The company will have $200 million in funding to start its work, raised in a large Series A round led by GV, ARCH Venture Partners, Andreessen Horowitz, and Casdin Capital, among others.

If EQRx is able to make it to market with new medicines quickly, winning market share away from well-resourced pharma companies will also be difficult, even with a lower price. Makers of biosimilars, low-cost copies of biologic drugs, could offer a case in point. While legal hurdles have held up many of the biosimilars approved in the U.S., those that have launched have entered at prices between 15% and 35% discount to the branded drug's price. Results have been mixed, sparking debate this year about whether the biosimilar market can succeed.

EQRx's Nallicheri acknowledged the challenges faced by biosimilars, but argued the U.S. experience to date could offer lessons for EQRx.

"If you want to change the trajectory on pricing, going about it in a timid way is not going to change the game," she said.

Crowdfunding for non-profit biotechs

Crowdfunding is a logical addition and practical next step for the various types of dreams that need financial support. Such as people who want to produce products, start businesses, or fundraise for non-profit or charity efforts around a cause they are passionate about.

Crowdfunding in its current form has been a game-changer, creating a more level playing field for both projects and investors, and the industry is only expected to continue its massive growth.

A new form of crowdfunding called an Initial Coin Offering took the tech world by storm with over $5.6 billion USD raised in 2017, attracting investments from both VC firms and individuals alike.

According to Fundly, crowdfunding has created 270,000 jobs and has contributed over $65 billion USD to the global economy. As an entrepreneur or creator, building a community of users/supporters while raising funds at the same time is pure gold.

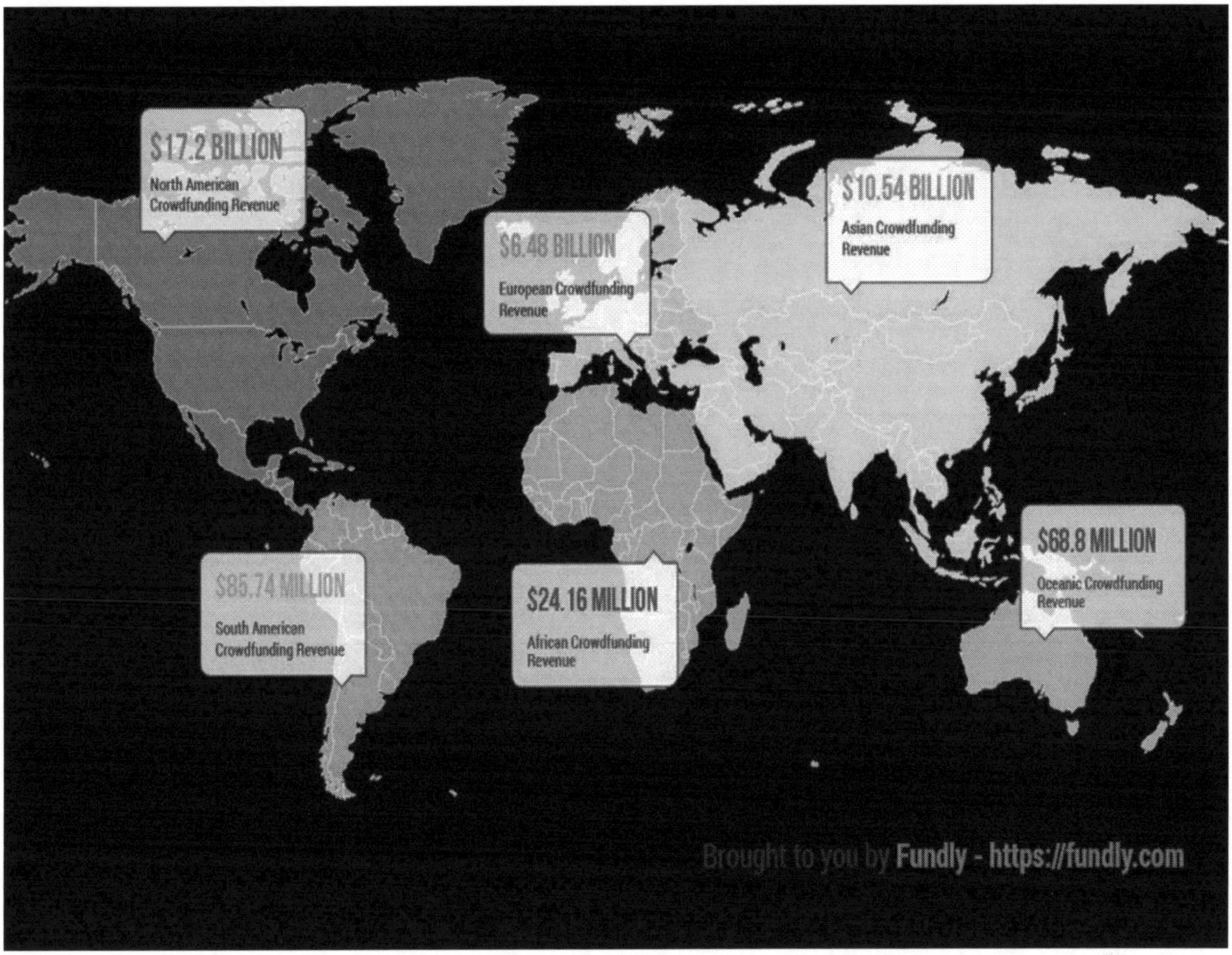

https://blog.fundly.com/crowdfunding-websites/

CROWDFUNDING: THE BASICS

Crowdfunding is a popular fundraising strategy used to raise more for medical expenses, artistic projects, scientific research, business startups, nonprofit organizations, and more.

Different crowdfunding websites vary in terms of fundraising guidelines, platform and payment processing fees, and so on, so it's a good idea to keep an eye out when considering your options.

For example, some crowdfunding sites follow a "Keep it All" (KiA) method of fundraising, while others opt for an "All or Nothing" (AoN) approach.

Essentially, organizers of KiA fundraisers receive funding regardless of whether they meet their fundraising goal. On the other hand, organizers of AoN fundraisers can only collect if they reach their goal.

With a solid understanding of key crowdfunding concepts, you're ready to dive in. Let's get started!

CROWDFUNDING WEBSITES FOR INDIVIDUALS

1. Fundly

- **THE BASICS**

Fundly's crowdfunding platform allows individuals (and nonprofits!) to raise money for nearly any kind of cause, project, or event. Fundly is a "Keep It All" (KiA) platform, which means that fundraisers don't have to reach their goal in order to receive the money they raise. They get to keep whatever donations they receive (minus a platform fee of 4.9% and a credit card processing fee of 2.9% + $.30/transaction).

- **STANDOUT FEATURES**

Fundly is incredibly easy to use and has a blog-like feel to it. Fundraisers can easily add images and videos, customize their fundraising pages with their personal stories, and share their campaign with their friends and family members via email, Facebook, and Twitter.

A fundraising thermometer shows each fundraiser's progress, and each page can be customized with colors, logos, and even background images.

- **FINAL THOUGHTS**

Fundly is one of the best crowdfunding platforms out there. It's easy to set your campaign up and start raising money. Plus, their support team is always there for you if you run into any problems during your campaign.

Click here to start a Fundly campaign

Raise money for your cause, project, or event.

Fundly Pro

- **THE BASICS**

Fundly Pro starts with the basics of the Fundly crowdfunding platform. Plus, it has added peer-to-peer fundraising capacity specifically crafted for nonprofits. With

Fundly Pro, organizations can set up a beautiful and brand-cohesive fundraising page in mere minutes.

From there, nonprofits can use Fundly's tools, such as social sharing options, to spread awareness and take their campaigns to the next level.

- **STANDOUT FEATURES**

Fundly campaigns are meant to be highly shareable and visibly stunning, both of which work in a nonprofit's favor. Additionally, nonprofits can set up their fundraisers as peer-to-peer pages to reach an even broader audience.

- **FINAL THOUGHTS**

Between cost-efficiency, ease-of-use, and dedicated fundraising features, Fundly Pro is the best choice for nonprofits that are looking to start a crowdfunding campaign.

Example Campaign

2. GoFundMe

- **THE BASICS**

GoFundMe was one of the first crowdfunding platforms to really take off. Since its initial launch several years ago, GoFundMe has helped individuals raise money for medical expenses, educational costs, memorials, and funerals among other causes.

- **STANDOUT FEATURES**

GoFundMe has a mobile app and boasts five-minute email support for users who run into issues. Like Fundly, GoFundMe is a "Keep it All" platform, and fundraisers will never incur a penalty for not reaching their fundraising goals.

- **FINAL THOUGHTS**

GoFundMe's platform is trusted by thousands of people. They guarantee that donations are safely processed and will give fundraisers a full refund if anything *does* happen.

- **THE BASICS**

It's free to start a crowdfunding campaign with MyCause, an Australian-based crowdfunding platform. They offer both a flexible and a fixed crowdfunding model, though they give fundraisers the choice of which campaign they'd like to run. Individuals can raise money for any cause, whether it's for personal medical expenses, adoption fees, scientific research, or something else.

- **STANDOUT FEATURES**

MyCause has a variety of social sharing options. Fundraisers and donors can share the crowdfunding campaign via Facebook, Twitter, email, LinkedIn, Pinterest, etc. This feature allows fundraisers to spread the word about their crowdfunding campaign far and wide, reaching as many people as possible.

- **FINAL THOUGHTS**

If you're looking for a beautiful crowdfunding website to help you raise money for a medical expense or healthcare cost, MyCause is a great option. Their simple layout and easy-to-use tools make it simple for anyone to fundraise!

Millennials want to donate to charities, save the world. Really

Nimble charities and philanthropists are instead discovering crowdfunding as an effective, efficient tool for collecting money from the masses. The digital platform is attracting younger do-gooders, in particular, who are tech savvy and would no more write a check for a charity than use snail mail.

"It's just a different game, when you're dealing with this generation," said Dave Boyce, founder of Fundly, a crowdfunding site devoted to helping nonprofits raise money. Philanthropists used Fundly immediately after the Boston bombings in April to collect funds.

"It's a foreign concept for them to pull out a checkbook, find an envelope," Boyce said. "They don't even trust the U.S. mail."

Why Millennials Like Donating Through Crowdfunding

Founded in 2009, Fundly says roughly 77 percent of its users are 44 or younger. And 58 percent are 34 or younger, Boyce said. "They'd much rather do it [donate] online," he said.

Why?

Younger do-gooders naturally feel comfortable with technology and online payment systems.

Crowdfunding websites, including industry behemoth Kickstarter, allow site users to seek donations (not loans)—usually nominal amounts—from family, friends and strangers. Projects range from artistic ventures such as films to shoring up small-business projects.

To be clear, Fundly supports nonprofits and charities. Meanwhile, Kickstarter is devoted to helping raise money for creative endeavors—not causes, according to Kickstarter guidelines.

Of course, it's easy to poke fun at philanthropic millennials—those between the ages of 18 and 34. The generation has been getting a bum rap lately. Human resources professionals say they've seen recent college grads text or take calls during interviews. *Doh.* (*Read More*: Texting? Pets? Millennials Are Flunking Job Interviews)

But crowdfunding for causes among millennials is serious business.

Fundly's younger users have enabled groups and individuals to raise more than $305 million since the site's launch. Jokes aside about living on mom and dad's couch, younger do-gooders are donating to causes.

The Creation Of Biotech Startups:

The startup paradigm for the creation and funding of new biotech companies has evolved enormously over the past two decades. Recently there's been a pair of articles from Tech VCs about applying alternative models of company creation to the world of biotech, so thought it was worth reflecting on the prevailing venture formation landscape and offering up some counterpoints.

When I first started in the venture business fifteen years ago, founding biotech entrepreneurs would often prepare pitch decks and then shop them around to different VCs as part of the typical "dog and pony" show. Sometimes those were academic professors or post-docs, sometimes they were entrepreneurs leaving existing biopharma jobs to do the startup thing. They'd often propose to build or lease a standalone bricks-and-mortar lab, hire 15-20 scientists, and advance an academic observation into *bona fide* drug discovery during the Series A round. Sometimes it would take $15M or more just to figure out whether the initial academic insight was reproducible and generalizable as a therapeutic approach.

Often the initial premise wouldn't survive these killer experiments, but because "real" capital had already been invested these companies would frequently try to "pivot" to other programs or approaches. Sometimes, albeit rarely, these pivots worked in biotech. But with fixed infrastructure and sunk cost, it was hard to just walk away. Returns suffered in this model.

Our 2006 vintage "prove-build-scale" model of biotech investing emerged from this world and was an attempt to change the paradigm. During the "prove" seed phase, the aim was to demonstrate the scientific robustness of the founding concept as cheaply as possible. This model was largely enabled by the emerging "virtualization" of the ecosystem.

Virtual drug discovery startups that leverage CROs and partners from around the world, assembling expertise on an as needed basis, became a realistic operating model about a decade ago. With the rise of biotech wet-lab launchpads like LabCentral, hybrid modelswith both in-house labs and heavy virtual outsourcing emerged, and are a common feature today. For novel areas of biology, some internal lab footprint is often critical.

Enabling technologies certainly helped (and continue to help) create the virtual infrastructure that powers up many biotech startups: computational drug design with partners like Schrodinger, in vitro safety screening, cheaper DNA sequencing and bioinformatics, lab automation, etc... Even virtual team management platforms like Slack for global remote project efficiency have helped.

I'd also argue the post-merger dismantling of Big Pharma's R&D footprints has had as much to do with the rise of virtualization as these enabling technologies: when large and small R&D sites around the world were shut down to reduce R&D footprints, many of these teams/facilities formed into new specialty CROs or were absorbed into existing ones. Europe and the Midwest have a huge number ex-Pharma sites that became CROs.

Further, the massive expansion of offshore medicinal chemistry services as China and India liberalized their business approaches also played a key role.

The venture-backed biotech ecosystem was embracing this virtually-enabled drug discovery model a decade ago, and that trend has just accelerated since – and will likely continue to.

We've evolved our strategy over the past 15 years to what we call our **seed-led venture creation model**.

During the setup and creation "prove" phase, we partner with our scientific and business co-founders to create new companies. We generally write small checks initially (from $100Ks to a few $1Ms) to do the seed-stage validation work, deliver the killer experiments, or assemble the right science/IP. But we also look for other signals – like whether the entrepreneurs involved in the startup have the savvy execution and strategic thinking required to launch and scale a young drug company (i.e., a "talent signal").

Another important variant of that talent signal is if experienced skilled entrepreneurs raise their hand to want to put their careers behind the idea during the seed phase. We also socialize the concepts with downstream Pharma and future funding partners during the seed to characterize the market interest in the approach (i.e., a "market signal"). This seed-led approach, and integrating these various signals, helps to bend the risk curve in our favor by weeding out the ideas/startups earlier with a high degree of signal stringency.

This in-house venture creation model helps bring the right elements together that were hard to assemble in traditional "pitch-deck" venture formation: rigorous and objective exploration of the founding science, enough capital to do the key early work, and, most importantly, the ability to attract and retain the right talent. Experienced drug R&D veterans and senior business talent can often better stomach the career risk of jumping out of bigger companies by joining not just one isolated high-risk startup in a random office park, but by joining an in-house startup community of other entrepreneurial executives within an incubator-like model. Most are mid-career by definition – in order to have assembled the requisite experience set.

To align interests and motivations, founder-EIRs know that if the scientific premise doesn't reproduce or validate, that we'll do well by them - often by recruiting them to other projects.

As company creators, we often shared a piece of the founding stock pool, which financially aligns us with the entrepreneurial team (as our ownership goes down, not up, with larger capital raises and lower valuations).

Today there are many flavors of this in-house venture creation model at different firms: some more artisanal and bespoke, some more systematic and formulaic. There used to be only a few firms doing this type of work 10 years ago – but the venture creation model has delivered stellar returns in the last decade for founders, employees, investors, and patients.

We went from tombstones hailing the death of life science venture capital in 2011 to being one of the star-performing sectors in the venture capital industry. And with that success, today we're seeing lots of VC firms talking about doing their version of in-house company creation. And seeing lots of tech VCs move into biotech. As they say, imitation is the sincerest form of flattery.

But as the biotech venture ecosystem continues to change, we will need to continue to evolve our model, of course.

A big change today is that the world is awash in capital. The tsunami of funding into private biotech firms in the last few years has led to the rise of the Series A mega-round: go big or go home. Some of these have been successful, but many others won't be. Along with more funding at the company level, VC fund sizes have also gotten bigger across the board, which means more capital has to be put to work per deal, worsening the venture capital math problem.

Series A sizes are way up, as are later rounds, and it seems like every week there's another $100M+ mega-round. There's also just more capital going into the same number of startups, in general. According to Pitchbook's data, the number of therapeutic biotech firms getting their first financing remains largely flat for the past 5+ years despite overall venture funding numbers being 2-3x greater. I've written on this paradox many times in the past (here is one example), which differs greatly from the tech space where the number of startups exploded with more fund flows.

This concentrated allocation of capital is potentially troubling, as it could presage that smart de-risking decisions aren't being done with discipline. Over-funding and crowding in 'hot' spaces like I/O and gene modification will likely dampen returns. I worry a great deal that in a world of capital abundance we will lose stringency as a sector. Two truisms come to mind today: more startups have died of indigestion than starvation; and, the average fitness of the herd goes down with abundance. We are at risk for this in biotech today.

We've tried to stick to our capital efficient startup model of seed-led venture creation, augmented by what we think is an optimal fund size configuration, without being dogmatic or formulaic about it. Some science deserves to be in an asset-centric focused startup, and other science requires a full and expansive platform build.

We added an Opportunity Fund to power up our more capital-intensive companies, and to secure additional positions in follow-on financings.

But in general, we're still starting companies that have a "prove" seed phase: whether it's a standalone seed investment, or a first "seed-tranche" of a more significant Series A, we remain firm believers that de-risking should be done before a large amount of capital gets deployed. It's the essence of the value-creating, positive aspects of equity capital efficiency.

Prove-Build-Scale was a mantra both the tech and biotech side we embraced for years.

The cost curve of drug R&D hasn't meaningfully changed with virtualization or new enabling technologies. Drug R&D is hard, and the typical program costs a lot to bring it through initial hit finding, hit-to-lead, lead optimization, preclinical, and early clinical testing.

Those phases - what I would call drug discovery and translational research - cost on the order of $25-50M per program, take 5+ years, and face high failure rates (with expensive false positives accruing spend over time).

Sadly, more virtual R&D models, even those enabled by computation, in our experience aren't fundamentally cheaper or faster over this entire multi-year translational period.

However, they are often more strategically flexible to respond to changes in the program (the benefit of variable vs fixed costs), and that flexibility allows for less expensive "down time" as well as earlier kill decisions on programs (and companies) than in prior biotech operating models.

Translating novel biology into real drugs is complex and still consumes everything else in the R&D process; it's the biology that takes so long and costs so much to unravel. While the cost to get a startup formed and initial experiments going may be cheaper than it was 15 years ago (when you had to build your lab), that's generally not the big cost over the 5+ years of moving from taking a "hit" into patients. And, frankly, we've been doing this model for a while: it's not a novel idea to do lean seed-stage experimentation in the process of starting biotech companies.

1. **Seed-stage capital in biotech doesn't bring a product forward, it just starts the long journey**. In the tech world, a seed stage investment can help a startup assess product-market fit questions and perhaps even get early revenue traction with consumers/users; that's just not the case with therapeutics.

2. This model may fit with other areas of "biotech" like research tools, synbio service companies, or B2B life science businesses, but making drugs for patients isn't weeks or months but many many years away from revenues. Given the timelines, and the reality that a biotech will burn cash without any top line for 10+ years, you can't "just" be a seed investor.

3. You have to keep investing capital until real inflection points happen, typically human proof-of-concept in the clinic (leading to an M&A event or an IPO). If you are only a seed investor, you will undoubtedly be massively diluted in the process.

4. That's why we, and most other biotech investors, tend to participate in all the private financings of our companies – you typically have to be there for the entire journey to make returns in biotech.

5. **Disruptions in regulated businesses where lives are at stake necessitate deliberate evolution not revolution.** Mark Zuckerberg's idea that success requires startups to "move fast and break things" doesn't apply to therapeutics companies.

6. We are making bioactive substances to put into patients, maybe even permanently engineer their genes. This isn't to be taken lightly or haphazardly. Regulators need to be brought along with new innovations. Iteration cycles are long. Safety and toxicology studies need to be thorough and take a certain immutable amount of time. Patients need to understand the risks, as people die because of drugs in clinical trials. Further, as an animal lover, think about the hundreds of animals we expose in our preclinical experiments in each drug program: the idea of animal models as things to "break" by moving programs faster doesn't seem right. Doing well-controlled, scientifically-justified experiments is not only smart business, but it's the right moral thing to do. Drug R&D, unlike many of the areas that tech VCs invest in, isn't the place for rapid iteration where it's ok to have a sloppy beta-test product hit the market (or go into the clinic, by analogy).

7. Deliberate, thoughtful advancement of optimized drug candidates that *could* go the full distance to approval is not really a choice but an axiom.

8. The therapeutics R&D model has evolved over the past few decades, and I'm sure it will continue to do so. But it won't change overnight as "do no harm" (i.e., "don't break things") is an important guiding principle in bringing new medicines to market.

9. **Experienced executive talent is critical to success in therapeutics.** CEO inexperience, naivety, and poor judgment have destroyed a ton of value over the past 40 years in biotech. In light of this history, we and other veteran VCs generally favor executives who have honed their skills running R&D programs or closing BD deals, and already demonstrated some level of judgment, credibility, and, frankly in light of Theranos, business ethics. I've written on this extensively – but the idea that a recent PhD or post-doc who has studied a narrow piece of biology for 5+ years is ready to run a

multi-disciplinary drug R&D organization powered with $10Ms in their first job out of academia seems far-fetched.

10. We do, however, back first-time CxO's all the time (most of our CEOs are first-timers), including lots of folks who've never "made money" for themselves or investors before. We are constantly adding talent to our network from biotech, pharma, and academia.

11. **Founders, entrepreneurs, and early-stage company-creation VCs frequently have the same interests**. As company formation focused investor-entrepreneurs, we are hurt by onerous VC terms too. In general, we try to increase the alignment between our interests and that of our other co-founders – and most VC financial terms don't tend to do this. Large liquidation preferences sitting on top of the cap table affect my early stakes much like a founding management team. I often have proposed "call-able" future tranches of funding if milestones are met, rather than "put-able" future tranches (the latter enable investors to buy up at their discretion at pre-agreed lower prices vs keeping options open for better cost-of-capital outside financings). One big difference in alignment arises with anti-dilution: generally early founder-investors don't get reloaded with fresh stock or options the way management teams do (without investing more capital).

12. I'm very sensitive to teams that are indifferent to dilution, just as most founders are. As for "control" protections and the most important decision of a Board – which is the hiring and firing of a CEO – I do think investors who've significantly financed the enterprise should have a big say in this decision. Further, as a general observation, biotech VC terms have actually become more startup-friendly in recent years.

13. Those counterpoints aside, I eagerly await the verdict on whether these new tech-oriented, young founder models for biotech venture formation deliver value for their teams, investors, and patients.

14. Unfortunately, given the nature of drug R&D, we won't know that verdict for a long, long time.

Finance for Biotechnology

Build an understanding of the basic essentials of financial management. This chapter will include a means to develop a working knowledge of the critical financial factors for decision-makers from the perspectives of key stakeholders.

This is designed to provide readers with limited or no background in finance an opportunity to establish a means to understand financial basics and communicate clearly in financial terms when conducting business. This review is uniquely designed to meet the current needs of those leading the global life science industry.

A Crash Course in the Basics of Finance in Biotechnology

Alex Dale

Getting your head around intricate biotech research and technology can be difficult enough, without having to contend with financial figures and jargon.

With news coming out thick and fast, you might be switching from the first market approval of a **CAR-T therapy** to the latest strategy to **protect crops** from pests to a new **anti-Parkinson's drug**. It can be hard to keep up with all the science, let alone all of the business and finance terminology too.

Biotechnology harnesses **powerful biological processes** to develop products that improve our lives and the planet we live on. But, of course, the time, money and effort that goes into developing these potentially life-changing products deserve a **financial reward** – and that is where business and finance come in.

Here, we have put together a **crash course** to help you understand any financial terms you might come across in our articles, allowing you to relax and enjoy our wonderful content.

Fundraising Series

Split into 3 main rounds – A, B and C – fundraising series really are **as easy as 1, 2, 3**.

Series A fundraising is used to **'optimize'** the product that is being developed. Series A often raises **$2-15M (€1.7-12.8M)**, but biotech 'unicorns' can achieve higher than this, as **Bayer** and **Ginkgo Bioworks** did when they raised **€84M** for their plant microbiome technology. At this stage, the main investors tend to be **venture capitalists (VCs)**, who generally receive their money from wealthy investors, investment banks and other financial institutions.

Series B helps the company to reach the **next level**. Typically, it will help a biotech to conduct Phase II studies, but also to look at another cancer indication in the case of **Genenta** or to complete a Phase III trial in the case of **Iterum Therapeutics**.

At this stage, companies generally raise between **$7-30M (€6-26M)**, with money again coming from VCs.

Series C comes when a company is ready to **scale up** its business. The company will be established, meaning investment is relatively **low risk**, so hedge funds, investment banks and private equity firms will now be willing to get involved, taking over from venture capitalists.

But fundraising doesn't necessarily stop there! It can continue all the way up to **round G** depending on the route taken by the company.

Fundraising series can also be a good indicator of a company's value. A **pre-money valuation** does not include money raised during the latest round of financing, while a **post-money valuation** will take this into account. A successful fundraising could give a company's value a particularly big boost, whereas a company could be **damaged** if it struggles to reach its fundraising goal.

Return on Investment

Return on investment, or **ROI**, measures the **amount of return** that an investor receives in comparison with their **initial investment**.

This gives an idea of the **efficiency** of investment, which helps investors to compare different investment options. ROI can be calculated simply using the equation below:

ROI = (Gain from Investment – Cost of Investment) / Cost of Investment

Although ROI is very popular thanks to its **simplicity**, it does have a number of **limitations**, including being unable to take into account the duration of the investment.

Stocks

A shareholder buys stocks in a company to become the **owner** of a part of it and have **rights** to its assets and earnings.

As the shareholder buys more and more shares in a company, they begin to have a bigger say in its actions. There are **two main types** of stocks:

1. **Common stocks** allow the owner to attend and vote at shareholder meetings and receive dividends.
2. **Preferred stocks** do not give buyers the right to vote at meetings, but instead, gives them a higher claim on assets and earnings.

The value of a biotech's stock is **volatile**, going up or down following <u>clinical trial results</u>, major <u>investment</u> in the field or even <u>political unrest</u> in the company's country.

Market Cap

Market capitalization or 'cap' is the **total market value** of a company's outstanding shares. It is calculated by multiplying the number of shares that the company has on the market by the price of a single share.

It is often used to determine the **size of a company** and helps investors decide which companies to spend their hard-earned cash on, as company size helps to determine **investment risk and return**.

Initial Public Offering (IPO)

An IPO signals a company's switch from being **private to public**, as it places its first set of stocks on the financial market.

The stocks will be available on one of the global markets, for example, the London Stock Exchange, Brussels Euronext, or even across the pond in the US on Wall Street or Nasdaq. This will determine who invests in the company and the capital made available to it.

But, before going public, the company must tick a few boxes:

- A strong team in place ready to go public.
- Audited financial statements using IPO-accepted accounting principles.
- Anti-takeover strategies.

- Independent board of directors.
- Appropriate timing of going public.

Dilutive and Non-Dilutive Funding

Funding often comes in exchange for stocks that the investor will receive in return. This is **dilutive** funding as the owners of the company will see their equity diminish. In contrast, **non-dilutive** funding sees a company receive financing but the owners do not see their pieces of the company get smaller. This often comes in the form of **business loans or government grants**.

Crowdfunding Case Study: How to build a $710 Million Biotech in Silicon Valley?

Richard Swart, PhD, Research Director, Program in Entrepreneurial and Social Finance

Crowdfunding has moved from a tactic used by smaller firms who could not raise capital by any other means, to an accepted, if not required part of the funding process for many firms.

Entrepreneurs have realized the value in mobilizing social and financial resources in a single, coordinated campaign.

There are literally dozens of business models within the field of crowdfunding – but we must ask whether the model used by Sanovas is a novel model of crowdfunding, or if it represents a traditional capital raise with a strong social component.

Self-Directed IRA's

Sanovas was started in 2010, during the great recession and at a time when capital markets essentially dried up. As a result, Sanovas was bootstrapped through its initial growth phases – which is nearly unheard of for biotechnology firms. Nevertheless, Gerrans could not escape the inevitable day when Sanovas had burned through available cash.

So Gerrans approached his family, friends, and former colleagues and found that despite being connected to a fairly successful network of high net worth individuals, nearly none of their friends had the capital to make investments. Many had their funds in 401k programs, and had no liquidity.

Gerrans moved his money out of his Traditional 401k into a Self-Directed IRA program and bought 120,000 shares of stock in a life science company where he knew the founders and their technology well. That firm went public at $13 a share and has traded as high as $27 a share. This experience taught Gerrans that wealth comes from early access to private companies and that Traditional 401k programs do not allow investors the opportunity to invest in companies they happen to know well.

Based on this personal experience, Gerrans shared his example with potential investors, and has so far raised over $30 million from his personal network. He and his team have singlehandedly helped hundreds of his friends and family extract over $20 million from their Traditional 401k accounts and redirect them to Self-Directed IRA Trusts to invest in Sanovas and to take control their retirement futures. He has developed systems and processes to help potential investors through the laborious and often intentionally opaque processes of transitioning a Traditional 401k and creating a self-directed IRA.

Self-Directed IRA – Process and Syndication Model

United States law allows private citizens to create a Self-Directed Investment Retirement Account (IRA) and to control the assets held in that account. This little utilized provision is now receiving significant attention within crowdfunding as a potential source of investment capital.

Traditional IRA companies generally try to prevent their investors from doing private placements with their IRA accounts.

They employ procedural tactics that makes the process very difficult, since their business relies on the management of the IRA funds through their own vehicles. There are a few 'Retirement Trust' companies who specifically focus on serving as 'Custodians' to private investors.

These Self-Directed IRA companies enable private investors to 'Roll Over' their individual retirement accounts from the Traditional IRA companies and are generally more accommodating to their clients wishing to make private placement investments.

Gerrans created a customer service process to help his investors manage the administrative and compliance issues involved with rolling into a Self-Directed IRA and then making the investment into Sanovas. Through the process of syndicating investors through their personal IRAs, Sanovas has raised $20 million out of a total of $30 million raised.

They have full time staff members dedicated to managing investor relations for over 300 investors who made 589 investments in Sanovas as of August 1, 2014.

Sanovas Capital Structure

Sanovas first started raising capital in 2010 with an $8.5 million convertible loan. As of June 2012, Sanovas converted that note into 10 million shares of equity at a $60 million valuation. This valuation was based on one subsidiary company and 25 patents.

Today the valuation of the whole portfolio of 12 companies and 90 multi-national patents/patents pending is expected to be more than $500 million, largely based on the value of the first six (6) business units, with a total of $30 million of equity invested. Sanovas has a cost of capital of 12% that includes 5% of equity, 2% of overhead, and 5% in warrants.

Equity crowdfunding promises to 'break the monopoly of the rich'

Can equity crowdfunding change the world?

Visit a site like Wefunder.com — one of the first registered equity crowdfunding portals — and you'll start thinking it can.

"It's time to save capitalism together," one slogan reads. "Break the monopoly of the rich. Invest in your local community. Invest in startups and help save the American Dream."

What are they talking about?

Up to now, the opportunity to invest in startup companies has been limited to "qualified investors" — in other words, wealthy people.

The crowdfunding you've heard about — Kickstarter and the like — is a form of donation: You may receive a product or service in return, but basically, you're giving money to help support an initiative.

Equity crowdfunding is different. Now you're buying a share in the enterprise — giving you the opportunity to earn big returns if it succeeds.

"It opens up an opportunity for the average investor," Millersville University economics professor Mike Gumpper said.

Test case review:

Med-X, Inc. Qualified by the SEC to Launch Second Crowdfunding Offering in Conjunction with Investment Banking Firm NMS Capital Advisors, LLC

LOS ANGELES, Aug. 15, 2019 /PRNewswire/ -- Med-X, Inc. -- On August 12, 2019, the Securities Exchange Commission (SEC) qualified Med-X, Inc. (Med-X) to begin the company's second Regulation A+ Equity Crowdfunding Offering. This time Med-X will be working with a Broker/Dealer, NMS Capital Advisors, LLC ("NMS Capital"), in selling the offering which is now live on the crowdfunding portal StartEngine.com.

The company plans to also link and use its own web site resources which include, Med-X, Inc. the official company website, as well as placing links and information regarding the company's offering on its divisional and subsidiary web properties, such as Thermal-Aid, Nature-Cide, The National Investor Network, Malibu Brands and The Marijuana Times.

"Regulation A+ allows us to advertise and reach out to all investors, not just wealthy accredited investors who comprise the top few percent of the country. While we do have a large number of the wealthy accredited investors, it is our philosophy to let all of our customers who use our products and or services, our small business partners, friends, family and fans to all participate in our company mission," explained Med-X President and COO, Matthew Mills.

For this offering, while allowing the "Working Class American" to buy Med-X shares for as little as $420 for 525 shares, Med-X management and NMS Capital are working together to create a syndicated network of Broker/Dealers to accelerate the offering. This will provide Med-X with the ability to execute on immediate key growth strategies.

For example, Med-X is in the midst of discussions and negotiations with multiple like-minded Eco-friendly pest control service companies, for strategic acquisition and or partnerships within the Nature-Cide's Service Division. This strategy is expected to fast-track the use of Nature-Cide's environmentally friendly and effective products within residential and wide-spread commercial applications nationwide. Other growth opportunities for Med-X divisions include adding new products to Nature-Cide's product line up, while expanding Malibu Brands new Pacific Pain Relief Cream to include a legal hemp CBD infused formulation version of the product, along with Thermal Aid's product lines and the Media Divisions, which includes the Marijuana Times and the new National Investor Network.

DISCLAIMER AND FORWARD-LOOKING STATEMENTS

The securities offered by Med-X, Inc. hereby are highly speculative. Investing in shares of MED-X, INC. involves significant risk.

Chapter 6

Starting a Biotech Company

1. **Nucleation of the team.** The team is key, and the initial team is the cornerstone of it all. Without a good nucleus, the company won't go anywhere. The team should initially consist of 2-3 individuals that are aligned in vision and outcomes. The team must work well together, have complementary skill sets, and "talk a good game." Mike recommends that the team should initially include a visionary, a science-minded individual, and a specialist.
2. Notably, the team must have an upfront conversation about his or her goals and vision for the company; this will help avoid future complications and potential conflicts that waste money and time.
3. **Raising seed money.** "Before seeking funding, ask yourself if you really want to do this." Biotech startups are only successful if they are 100X better than current technology and get customers to change behavior. When you are ready to commit to the company, the internet, crowd funding, federal funding, foundations, and investors are examples of various sources of funding.
4. **Always ask for money**. Moreover, many universities throw out old equipment that still works. "We use functional spectrometers from the early 1990s that were free and free to repair." If the team works well, the idea is solid, and "the pitch is packaged to perfection", seed money will hopefully be raised and the company may begin to prove the technology. This transition takes around 1 – 2 years.
5. **The product is the measure of success.** Technology is proven in (A) Productize, (B) Roll out to market, and (C) Break even cycles. Work hard. Work fast. Be flexible. Be quick at failing and succeeding.

6. "<u>There are no excuses for a startup to fail - it all depends on you.</u>"

What to do First? 7 Steps to Starting a Biotechnology Company

Beginning a company requires significant planning and many events must simultaneously converge in order to be successful. Some people describe the successful convergence of timing and opportunity as "serendipity", others call it "chance" or "luck". Whatever you call it, heed the words of Louis Pasteur who said, "chance only favors the prepared mind". Knowing what to do first can be most challenging since there are so many things that must be accomplished. Here is a checklist of 7 steps that are essential for starting a biotechnology company.

Step 1. Make absolutely sure the idea has a true market need

Good ideas are just that...good ideas, however, not all good ideas produce needed products.

Recognize that there are many exciting technologies still in search of a market need. Be absolutely sure that there is a real market need for your future product. Also, be sure that the technology of interest is protected by intellectual property (IP).

Next, secure the assets, IP rights and commitments from the inventors and key personnel (if you are not one) who have the know-how required for making the technology successful.

Step 2. Identify Founders and Key Personnel

Good people are critical to any company's success. Carefully identify these individuals and understand their interest and commitment to the future organization. Not all individuals with interest at this stage should be founders of the company; nor should all founders be equally compensated with identical amounts of stock unless all intend to work full time in the organization once it is funded. Determining percentage ownership is a difficult issue. You do not want one founder receiving identical equity ownership who will not be working with the new organization yet keeps a secure position receiving a good paycheck and rides on the coat-tails of other founders.

Step 3. Find a Good Attorney

This individual is a key partner. Your attorney will be the individual you go to for advice, guidance, counsel, and of course, legal answers. They will help you navigate through the corporate and business issues during all stages of establishing and growing your company. Within the first week of starting your company, you will have this person's phone number committed to memory. Therefore, they need to be someone you trust and someone with whom you work well, and above all, a professional with many years of expertise in advising start-up biotechnology companies.

Step 4. Incorporate your company as a C Corporation

Your next objective will be to raise money and/or secure federal SBIR (Small Business Innovative Research) grants.

Without an incorporated company you won't be able to do either.

There are many reasons to incorporate early, one reason is that you can then issue founders stock without having to pay exorbitant sums of money for shares (or incur large tax consequences) since the valuation of the company at this stage is extremely low. The majority of all biotech companies should be C Corporations rather than S Corporations or LLCs. Serious investors know this and decline to invest because they do not want to go through the trouble of changing an inappropriate business structure.

Step 5. Conceive a well-planned marketing and business strategy

It is impossible to raise money without a well-written business plan that clearly describes: the market problem and need, how your product will solve it, how much money your product will generate, what you intend to do with the cash, what the return and exit is for the investor, and who the key personnel are within the company. Write your business plan with the guidance of your attorney. They will help convert this into a fundraising document (private placement memorandum).

You will then seek an audience with the appropriate investor groups interested in your stage and sector of industry.

Step 6. Operate as a virtual company

Keep your day job! Build the company carefully while minimizing your risk. At this early stage, brick and mortar are not necessary when you possess a computer, a cell phone and have an internet connection. However, be sure to have access to a conference room or meeting room but don't spend money on rent at this stage. As you work on your new enterprise, be careful about performing any work for the new enterprise while employed at your current place of business. There can be legal issues with ownership if you use company time and/or facilities while starting your new business venture.

Be sure to discuss these issues with your attorney.

Step 7. After raising seed capital, advance the technology consistently through successive product development milestones

Be sure to outline the key value-increasing product development milestones throughout the entire product development pathway. Then demonstrate consistent progress by meeting these projections for the first few of these milestones.

All investors like to hear about companies making steady progress along a planned development pathway. By timely meeting key milestones, you will increase the value of your company and decrease the investment risk. Consistency in meeting planned milestones increases the likelihood of securing subsequent funding.

Tips for Raising Startup Capital in Biotech

Sell the science, because that's what we're buying in early stage startups. Too many pitches waste a ton of time trying to tell us that Alzheimer's is really big disease, heart failure kills more than cancer, and Genzyme made big markets out of orphans. Yes, we all know that. Focus instead on the crux of the investment decision in early stage: is the scientific thesis compelling and are we likely to have real impact on patients.

Make sure your team has some grey hair, but not so much as to lack youthful enthusiasm. A clear pairing with the exciting, credible science outlined above is the need for solid, backable team.

Talent is essential.

In some ways it's chicken and egg with great science: great talent rarely jumps at crappy science, and great science is what it takes to recruit great talent.

Importantly though, biotech startups work in a highly nuanced, regulated, and complex science-driven world that isn't well taught in books – its best practitioners have learned through years of apprenticeship, project leadership, and portfolio learnings.

Make sure your team has some of this deep experience on its roster. This is where a carefully crafted SAB might be helpful.

But you can't start a new biotech company with a team of Medicare-eligible former industry executives at its helm; make sure you've got a good blend of grey-haired experience and "youth" (under 50?).

Don't skimp on legal advice as you lay out the foundations of a startup. Nothing hurts a startup fundraising's early momentum more than poor corporate fundamentals: odd structures, cap tables, huge but useless boards, lack of IP or Freedom to Operate, or a poorly drafted academic option/license agreement.

Find a good counsel with experience in biotech and get to know them.

Crank up the energy – the time is now. Be psyched about "doing well by doing good".

Tell the vision of how you will impact patients and change medicine for the better. Be excited and share your infectious passion.

Seven Expert Tips on How to Grow a Successful Biotech Startup

The journey to create and grow a successful biotech startup is long and carries a high risk of failure. I decided to explore the main pitfalls that biotech entrepreneurs find and how to avoid them.

Biotech startups can bring solutions to some of the biggest problems in the world, making some bucks along the way. But few biotech startups make it to the finish line, a process that, unlike for a software startup, can easily take a decade before the company makes any profit.

Even the company with the most promising technology can end up failing because of many other factors external to the core science, such as finances, regulations, partnerships, manufacturing, scaling up, investor relations, and many others.

And most importantly, these challenges can vary wildly from the early to mid and late stages until a biotechnological product makes it to the market.

For those starting a new company, these challenges may seem insurmountable, but they are not alone. Many others have been there before and we can learn from their experience.

1. Getting the word out

"I think the main challenge as a young startup is you're trying to develop your compound and raising funds but you're also educating the world of your presence," says Thomas de Vlaam, CEO of Amylon Therapeutics.

He founded the company less than a year ago and has just started communicating to the world his goal of treating CNS disorders using RNA technology.

"That becomes a whole paradigm shift," says de Vlaam. *"From having everyone around you believing 100% in what you are doing to going out into the public and facing a lot of new opinions and also a lot of skepticism."*

Except for companies working on cancer and other well-known areas, in many cases the general public is not even aware of the problem that a biotech startup is trying to solve. And even when the problem is known, in the early stages of a startup the resources and data to back up the science behind the company are limited.

A young biotech startup therefore needs to work on the story from the very first moment in order to get experts, investors and even employees on board. *"For me, it is not about what we have as much as about what we could be,"* says the Vlaam.

2. Building a dream team

"I've made some shocking mistakes with hiring people, probably too much based on technical skill versus fit," says Ajan Reginald, CEO of Celixir. His company has been working for over eight years in the cell therapy space and is now in late development.

"You're always tempted by someone that has brilliant technical skills, and in the back of your mind you think actually I'm not really sure this person really is going to have the risk tolerance the ambiguity tolerance, he's going to play nice with the other super smart people. But you kind of go through it and then very quickly you realize oh my god this is a disaster."

Replacing someone that doesn't fit well in a company has a huge cost both in terms of money and time. Hiring the right people is one of the most important things to get right from the beginning. In addition, as the biotech startup grows and faces new challenges, the team and skills it needs can change radically.

At first you might just need some scientists and technicians, but later you'll need people that can run clinical trials, scale up the manufacturing or deal with regulations. And the talent pool can be limited.

"If I had to do it all over again, I would start building the team on day 1, looking for the best people, "adds de Vlaam. *"Once you hit the point where you need them, that's too late."*

3. Raising the cash

"There is a lot of capital in Europe, but people remember the failures, not the successes," says Ajan Reginald. *"In an environment like Europe where we don't have a lot of success stories people tend to be more risk-averse."*

As Reginald points out, the dynamics of risks can be different depending on where you are. While in Europe a good first round is €20M, in Boston that number is closer to $200M. *"In Boston, if you're not getting into the next best thing — CRISPR, synthetic biology, whatever it is — people come to you [saying] 'why are you not in this?'"*

The management of a biotech startup needs to be aware of the culture according to their location and play with it.

For example, some companies in Europe start searching for US investors early on if they are anticipating they will need a lot of cash to get their science rolling.

4. Honing your decision-making skills

"Not taking decisions quickly enough, I think that is the biggest mistake that you can make as a CEO," says Shelley Margetson, CEO of Gadeta, whose immuno-oncology company is now about to start its first clinical trial.

She's also had a lot of experience in biotech finances in her previous position as the CFO of Merus, during which she led a Nasdaq IPO that raised almost $50M.

"When we ultimately decided to start preparing for an IPO, I think we waited a little bit too long to take that decision, but once we did, we realized we should have

started six months earlier," says Margetson. *"That is a mistake I did I would have done differently. Don't be afraid to make decisions."*

Taking a decision at the right time can prevent significant delays anywhere. If you don't raise the money or start a clinical trial when you need to, it can significantly delay the whole pipeline. And, as de Vlaam highlighted: *"For us, time is more expensive than money."*

5. Engaging with regulators

Biotechnological products are strictly regulated. The FDA in the US and the EMA in Europe have guidelines that biotechs need to follow to provide data backing the safety and efficacy of their product. Engaging early on with the regulators can help a company get on the right track to receive the approval they need to market a product.

"It's so much better if you talk to the regulators yourself," says Reginald. *"Both the EMA and FDA are very supportive, as long as you really understand what you are talking about. They are scientists, basically, and they want to understand from you — the people who did the work — what you are doing."*

"They are much more helpful than I would have anticipated beforehand," agrees Margetson. So don't get scared and go talk to them.

6. Preparing for the finish line

The ultimate goal of a biotech startup is to get their product on the market. And Reginald believes a biotech startup should start preparing for it from the very beginning. *"We build a target product profile for everything in preclinical, in discovery, and we kill things early if we think it's not going to have a target product profile that we like. We've got six products in the public domain and we've killed about 30."*

It might seem difficult to predict the success of a product years before, especially when new technologies are continuously changing what is possible. *"Technology will evolve, of course it will, but commercial markets evolve much more slowly,"* says Reginald.

"It's so easy to predict where there's going to be gaps in pipelines. Pharma analysists do it all the time."

He points out to a study by The Boston Consulting Group that establishes the percentage of the market that a new product captures based on how many others have been launched before and whether it has a therapeutic advantage over them.

7. Setting a consistent strategy

"There is no one reason for success, but you have to choose one and hope it's the right one," says de Vlaam, pointing out at the two opposite models followed by US biotech's Denali and Moderna. *"They are two sides of the same coin; one is momentum and the other is science."*

While there is not a single strategy to success, creating and making it consistent is essential. As Reginald says: *"The problem you have in a company, or in any project, is when you're not clear what success versus failure is and if you punish people for failure."*

"Typically, medical device startups were built around one medical device, so you had the entire team working on one device, one regulatory pathway, one go-to-market," Gura said.

So what can traditional healthcare players do to achieve the same type of out-of-the-box thinking? Don't look at the stats pharma has "on any challenge they would like to solve," Davidson said. And "pull in talent from completely other disciplines," he recommended, adding, "that's what worked for us."

How Employee Stock Options Work In Startup Companies

Thousands of people have become millionaires through stock options, making these options very appealing to employees. (Indeed, Facebook has made many employees into millionaires from stock options.)

The spectacular success of Silicon Valley companies and the resulting economic riches of employees who held stock options have made Stock Option Plans a powerful motivational tool for employees to work for the company's long-term success.

Employee stock option

An employee stock option is commonly viewed as a complex call option on the common stock of a company, granted by the company to an employee as part of the employee's remuneration package. Wikipedia

What is a 'Stock Option'

Stock options are sold by one party to another, that give the option buyer the right, but not the obligation, to buy or sell a stock at an agreed-upon price within a certain period of time. American options, which make up most of the public exchange-traded stock options, can be exercised any time between the date of purchase and the expiration date of the option. On the other hand, European options, also known as "share options" in the United Kingdom, are less common and can only be redeemed at the expiration date.

Breaking Down the 'Stock Option'

Stock options normally represent 100 shares of an underlying stock. Therefore, if the premium (cost) of an option is $0.10, buying one contract costs $10 ($0.10 x 100 shares), plus any fees or commissions.

Put and Call Options

A call is when the buyer has the right to purchase stock at a specified price before the option expires. A put option is when the buyer has the right to sell stock at a specified price before expiration.

The purchaser of a call option believes that the underlying stock will increase in price, while the seller of the option thinks otherwise.

The option holder has the benefit of purchasing the stock at a discount from its current market value if the stock price increases prior to expiration.

For example, if the strike price of an option is $10, the trader buys the option for $0.50, and the underlying stock increases to $12 at expiration, the traders nets $1.50 per share, while only have put up $0.50 of capital per share. The amount paid for the option is the most the option buyer can lose.

If the option buyer believes a stock will decline in value, they buy a put option as this gives them the right to sell the stock at the strike price before expiration. If the underlying stock loses value prior to expiration, the option holder makes money. For example, if the strike price of a put option is $50, the trader paid $1 for the option, and the stock falls to $45 by expiration, the trader nets $4 per share.

On one contract that is $400, and the trade only cost $100 to make. In this case, if the stock goes up instead, the cost of the option is the most the option buyer can lose.

The strike price, relative to the current price of the underlying stock, is what dictates whether or not an option is valuable. The strike price is the predetermined price at which the underlying stock can be bought or sold. Time value and volatility also play a significant role in the price of an option. High volatility increases the cost of an option, as does the amount of time until expiry. Since more volatility and more time mean an increased chance the price could move through the strike price, this will make the options more expensive than options with lower volatility and less time till expiration.

Writing Options

While some traders buy options, others need to write them. The writer is on the opposite side of the trade as the buyer. The writer receives the premium for writing the option. This is their maximum profit.

In exchange for receiving the premium, the writer takes on the risk of having to buy or sell shares from/to the option buyer at the strike price. This could mean large losses. For example, if a trader writes a call option the option buyer has the right to buy at the strike price. Say the strike price is $10, but the stock price shoots up to $30. The option writer is still responsible for providing the shares to the option buyer at $10.

This means, if the option is exercised, the writer will need to buy shares at $30 only to sell them to the call buyer at $10, a loss of $20 per share.

Writers can protect themselves by writing covered calls. This is a common strategy. An investor already owns shares of a company.

Instead of selling the stock directly, they write call options for a strike prices above the current stock price. For this they receive the premium. If the stock does rise above the strike price, they simply sell the call buyer their own shares.

Option writers can also use puts to accumulate a stock position they want. For example, if a stock is trading at $15, but a trader wants to buy it at $13, instead of waiting for the price to drop they can write put options right now with a strike price of $13. For this they receive income/premium. If the stock drops below $13, they buy the shares they wanted anyway. If the strike price stays above $13 they keep the premium and can continue to write puts until they get the stock position they want.

Employee Stock Options

Employee stock options are similar to call or put options, with a few key differences. Employee stock options normally vest rather than having a specified time to maturity. This means that an employee must remain employed for a defined period of time before they earn the right to purchase or receive their options. There is also a grant price that takes the place of a strike price, which represents the current market value at the time the employee receives the options.

Stock Option Plans are an extremely popular method of attracting, motivating, and retaining employees, especially when the company is unable to pay high salaries. A Stock Option Plan gives the company the flexibility to award stock options to employees, officers, directors, advisors, and consultants, allowing these people to buy stock in the company when they exercise the option.

Forbes Magazine:

Stock Option Plans permit employees to share in the company's success without requiring a startup business to spend precious cash. In fact, Stock Option Plans can actually contribute capital to a company as employees pay the exercise price for their options.

The primary disadvantage of Stock Option Plans for the company is the possible dilution of other shareholders' equity when the employees exercise the stock options.

For employees, the main disadvantage of stock options in a private company—compared to cash bonuses or greater compensation—is the lack of liquidity.

Until the company creates a public market for its stock or is acquired, the options will not be the equivalent of cash benefits. And, if the company does not grow bigger and its stock does not become more valuable, the options may ultimately prove worthless.

Thousands of people have become millionaires through stock options, making these options very appealing to employees.

(Indeed, Facebook has made many employees into millionaires from stock options.)

The spectacular success of Silicon Valley companies and the resulting economic riches of employees who held stock options have made Stock Option Plans a powerful motivational tool for employees to work for the company's long-term success.

How Does a Stock Option Work?

The following shows how stock options are granted and exercised:

- ABC, Inc., hires employee John Smith.
- As part of his employment package, ABC grants John options to acquire 40,000 shares of ABC's common stock at 25 cents per share (the fair market value of a share of ABC common stock at the time of grant).
- The options are subject to a four-year vesting with one year cliff vesting, which means that John has to stay employed with ABC for one year before he gets the right to exercise 10,000 of the options and then he vests the remaining 30,000 options at the rate of 1/36 a month over the next 36 months of employment.
- If John leaves ABC or is fired before the end of his first year, he doesn't get any of the options.
- After his options are "vested" (become exercisable), he has the option to buy the stock at 25 cents per share, even if the share value has gone up dramatically.
- After four years, all 40,000 of his option shares are vested if he has continued to work for ABC.
- ABC becomes successful and goes public. Its stock trades at $20 per share.
- John exercises his options and buys 40,000 shares for $10,000 (40,000 x 25 cents).
- John turns around and sells all 40,000 shares for $800,000 (40,000 x the $20 per share publicly traded price), making a nice profit of $790,000.

Why Do Companies Issue Stock Options?

Companies issue options typically for one or more of the following reasons:

- Options can be used to attract and retain talented employees.
- Options can help motivate more dedication from employees.
- Options can be a cost-effective employee benefit plan, in lieu of additional cash compensation.
- Options can help smaller companies compete with larger companies in attracting great employees.

Key Issues in Stock Options

A company needs to address a number of key issues before adopting a Stock Option Plan and issuing options. Generally, the company wants to adopt a plan that gives it maximum flexibility. Here are some of the important considerations:

- **Total number of shares**:

The stock option plan must reserve a maximum number of shares to be issued under the plan. This total number is generally based on what the board of directors believes is appropriate, but typically ranges from 5% to 20% of the company's outstanding stock. Of course, not all options reserved for issuances have to be granted. Also, the investors in the company may have some contractual restrictions on the size of the option pool to prevent too much dilution.

- **Number of options granted to an employee**:

There is no formula as to how many options a company will grant to a prospective employee. It's all negotiable, although the company can set internal guidelines by job position within the company. And what is important is not the number of options, but what the number represents as a percentage of the fully diluted number of shares outstanding.

For example, if you are awarded 100,000 options, but there are 100 million shares outstanding, that only represents 1/10 of 1% of the company. But if you are awarded 100,000 options and there are only 1 million shares outstanding, then that represents 10% of the company.

- **Plan administration**:

Although most plans appoint the board of directors as administrator, the plan should also allow the board to delegate responsibilities to a committee.

The board or the committee should have broad discretion as to the optionees, the types of options granted, and other terms.

- **Consideration**:

The plan should give the board of directors' maximum flexibility in determining how the exercise price can be paid, subject to compliance with applicable corporate law. So, for example, the consideration can include cash, deferred payment, promissory note, or stock. A "cashless" feature can be particularly attractive, where the optionee can use the buildup in the value of his or her option (the difference between the exercise price and the stock's fair market value) as the currency to exercise the option.

- **Shareholder approval**:

The company should generally have shareholders approve the plan, both for securities law reasons and to cement the ability to offer tax-advantaged incentive stock options.

- Right to terminate employment: To prevent giving employees an implied promise of employment, the plan should clearly state that the grant of stock options does not guarantee any employee a continued relationship with the company.

- **Right of first refusal**:

The plan (and related Stock Option Agreement) can also provide that in the event the option is exercised, the shareholder grants the company a right of first refusal on transfers of the underlying shares. Doing so allows the company to keep share ownership in the company to a limited group of shareholders.

- **Financial reports**:

For securities law reasons, the plan may require that periodic financial information and reports are delivered to option holders.

- **Vesting:**

How do options vest? Most companies provide a vesting schedule, where the employee or advisor has to continue to work for the company for some period of time before the optionee's rights vest. For example, an employee may be awarded options to acquire 10,000 shares with 25% vested after the first full year of employment, and then monthly vesting for the remaining shares over a 36-month vesting period.

- **Exercise price**:

How much does the optionee have to pay for the stock when he or she exercises their option? Typically, the price is set at the stock's fair market value at the time the option is granted. If the stock's value goes up, the option becomes valuable because the optionee has the right to buy the stock at the cheaper price.

- **Time to exercise**:

How long does the optionee have the right to exercise the option?

The Stock Option Agreement typically sets a date when the option must be exercised (the date is usually shortened on termination of employment or death). Most employees only have 30-90 days to exercise an option after their employment with the company has terminated.

This can be burdensome, particularly since the optionee may not have been able to sell any of the underlying shares to help pay the tax resulting from the exercise of the option.

- **Transferability restrictions**:

What restrictions apply to the transfer of the option and underlying stock? Most Stock Option Agreements provide that the option is nontransferable. The agreements also state that the stock purchased by exercising the option may be subject to rights of purchase or rights of first refusal on any potential transfers. Increasingly, companies desire to implement more robust restrictions on both the options and the shares received upon exercise of the options to limit trades in the secondary market that may cause practical concerns in managing holders of the company's stock.

- **Securities law compliance**:

The issuance of options and underlying shares requires compliance with federal and state securities laws. Experienced corporate counsel should be involved here.

- 409A valuation: The company needs to make a determination of the fair market value of its common stock in order to set the exercise price of the option, pursuant to Section 409A of the Internal Revenue Code. This is often done by hiring a third-party valuation expert.

- Cash usually needed: To exercise an option, the option holder typically has to pay cash out of pocket for the exercise (very few companies allow "cashless exercise").
- ISOs: An employee holding tax advantaged Incentive Stock Options (ISOs) does not have a tax (or tax withholding) event upon exercise. You report taxable income when you sell the stock, but will need to include the difference between the exercise price and the current fair market value at the time of exercise (the "spread") in income for purposes of calculating any additional tax obligation under the alternative minimum tax rules. If certain holding periods are met before selling the stock, all of the gain (back to the exercise price) may be taxed at the more favorable long-term capital gain rates.
- NSOs: If the options are not tax advantaged ISOs, they are "non-qualified stock options" (NSOs), and the spread upon exercise will be taxed at the more unfavorable ordinary income rates (as opposed to the capital gains rates).

Additionally, as the exercise date is a taxable event, the company will have to report the spread as taxable income on the employee's Form W-2 in the year of exercise and withhold applicable taxes on the amount of the spread, which generally means that the employee will have to write a check to the company to cover the tax withholding liability.

- **Illiquidity**:

Stock in privately held companies is typically not liquid and is difficult to sell.

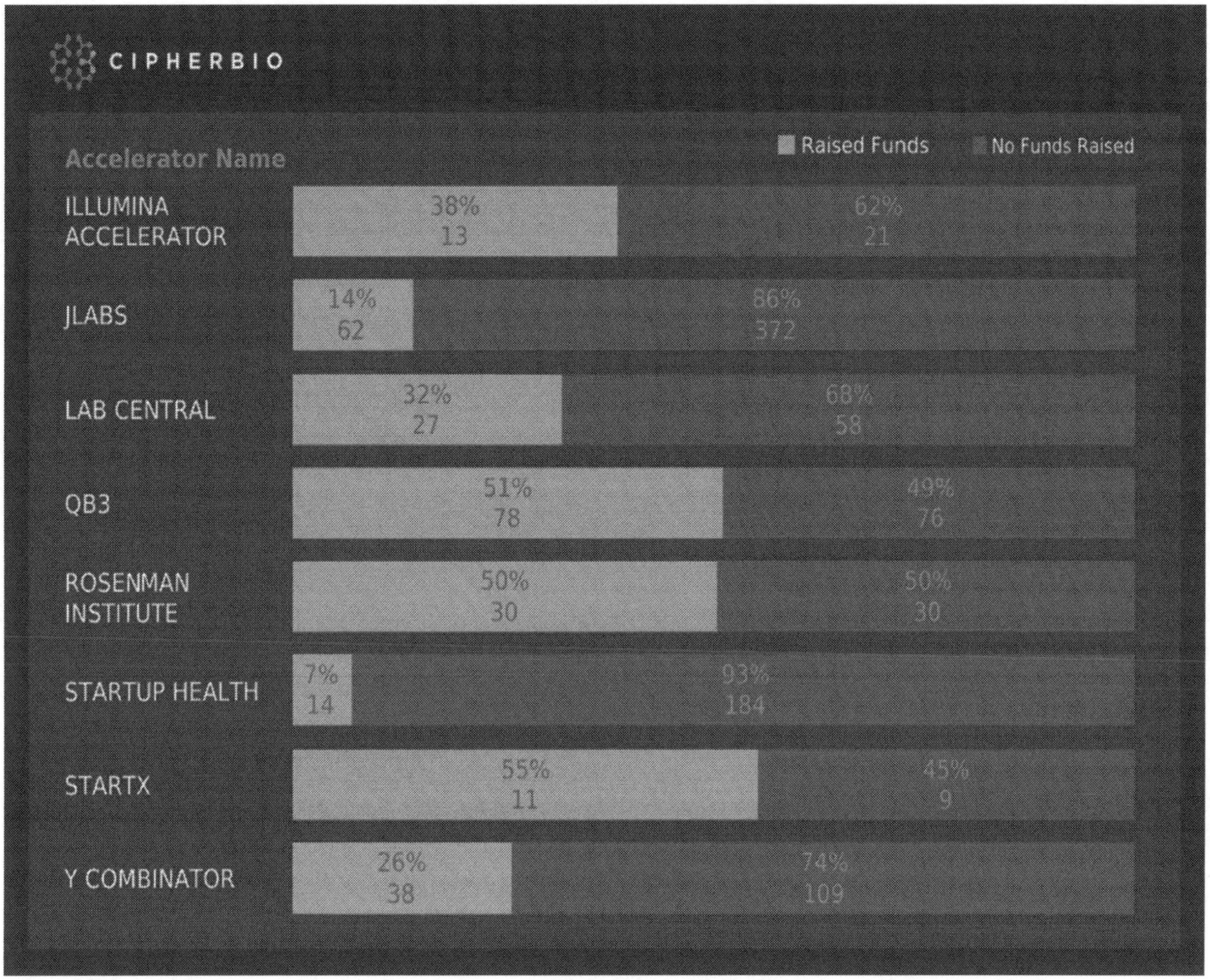

Accelerator or Incubator? What to Look for in a Biotech Startup Program

Early-stage biotech companies and scientists interested in commercialization need great accelerator programs, not more biotech incubators.

Biotech companies and scientists who start out on the road to commercialization may need an accelerator to bring out the entrepreneurial spirit. The incubator and accelerator models are conflated all the time in biotech, much to the fury of anybody who truly understands the terms.

What's a bio-accelerator?

Much like any other business accelerator, a bio-accelerator is a biotech-focused program that should be designed to almost force early startups to generate real early momentum. This three- to four-month bootcamp in which you are pushed to sharpen your business plan ultimately leads to a 'demo day,' often classed as a display of the progress that has been made.

However, it's easy to confuse an accelerator with an incubator: understandings of the terms can change completely in some European countries, (Belgium and Holland, specifically), where the biotech industry has accepted the notion that incubation happens first. As a result, incubators in these regions typically comprise laboratory facilities for small early-stage companies, while a bio-accelerator consists of the next stage up in terms of a facility to harbor often rapidly growing staff numbers. For the purpose of this discussion, it's best to ignore this use of the term.

Bio-incubator versus bio-accelerator: same thing?

We have a standard reply to this question at Rebel Bio, and it usually ends in a sigh: bio-incubators and bio-accelerators are just somewhere to put your lab.

Obviously, that's not bad thing if you need it and can afford it. However, by any standard the name bio-incubator is a misnomer.

Lots of entrepreneurs don't like business incubators for a whole set of reasons. While bio-incubators don't deserve to all be painted with the same brush, the bottom line for what constitutes success for a biotech incubator is occupancy. They get the rent paid and in return they will make sure a company doesn't have to worry about the gas (nitrogen or carbon dioxide in this case) being shut off.

If the incubator is good, it will provide some core lab facilities, although many don't.

Perhaps what is most surprising is that most don't really cater for very early pre-funded startups, and they certainly haven't embraced lean startup culture. More to the point, most newly formed biotech companies can't afford an incubator.

The accelerator program offered at an incubator or more likely to competing biotech incubator spaces that have bloomed over the last decade, some incubators have started offering their own accelerator courses and sometimes mentorship to companies. While their motives might be largely wholesome, there is a danger here that such an organization is a siren on the rocks for young, often naive startups, lulling them into a sense that they are actually progressing and behaving like entrepreneurs when they are not.

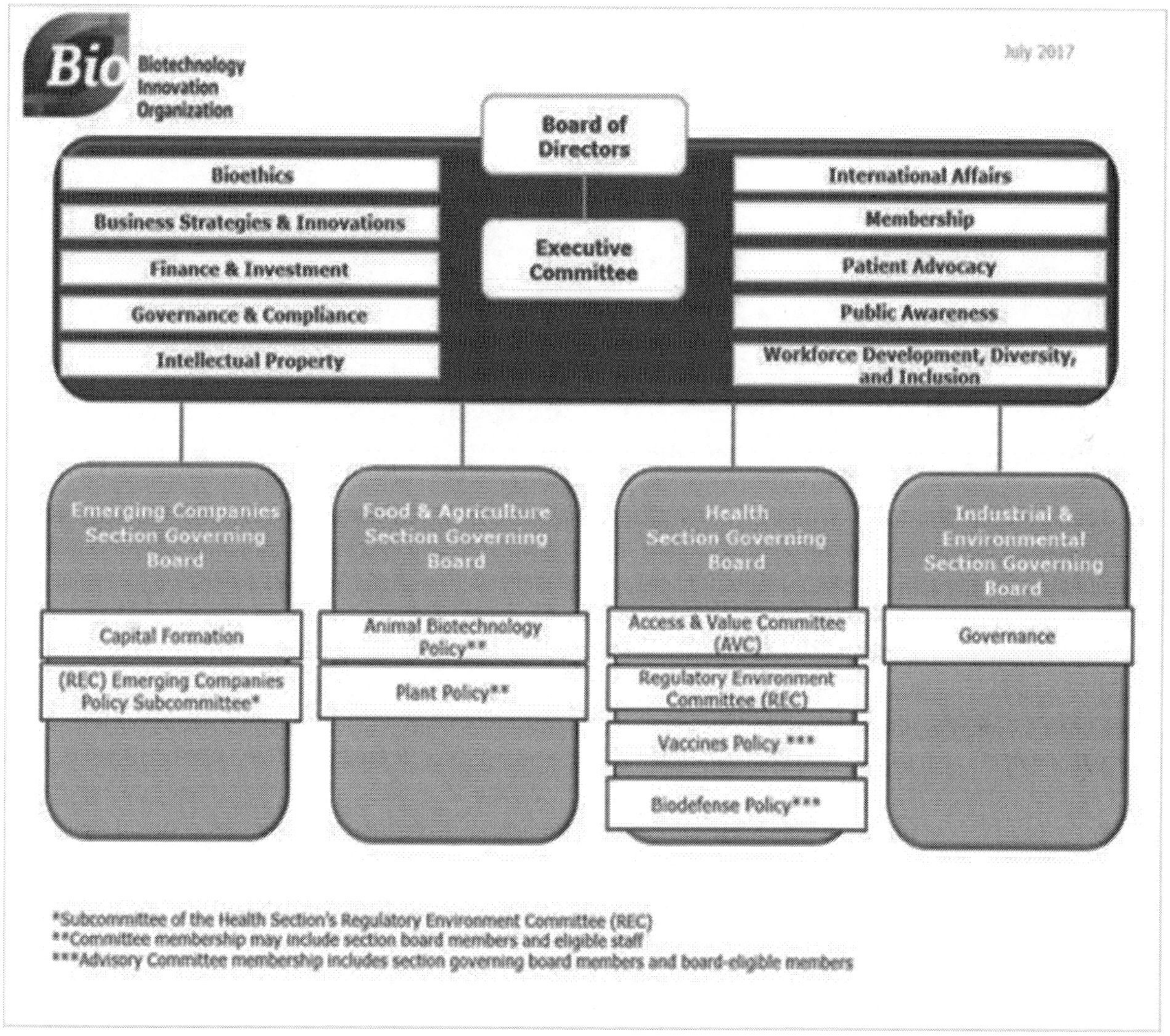

Creating a Board of Directors: Key Considerations for Startup Companies

One of the most important decisions that a startup entrepreneur can make is creating a board of directors that will assist the entrepreneur in growing and governing the business. A company's board of directors is tasked with overseeing and advising management, making key decisions about the company's business strategies, and representing the interests of the company and its stockholders.

Initial Considerations

When forming a board of directors, the startup entrepreneur should first consider the size, structure and skillsets of the proposed member(s). While it might be fairly intuitive that the board should consist of an odd number of directors (so as to avoid a voting tie) and a small enough number to avoid inefficiencies (so as to facilitate coordination of meetings and make feasible action by consent), one should also consider the extent to which the board composition will reflect the ownership interests of the company and whether the board should include an independent director from the outset. While it is customary for a startup company's board seats to be given initially to investors, an independent director with expertise in the company's industry area may provide helpful, disinterested advice as well as the necessary "tie-breaking" vote where consent of a majority is required to take action.

Business Considerations

Board members can provide valuable advice to startup entrepreneurs and help the entrepreneur avoid costly common mistakes. Board members can also fill in any gaps that a startup company has in certain areas of expertise, such as sales and marketing or finance until the company is financially able to fill those roles with fulltime employees. In addition to the skills and background of each individual director, the combined skill set of the board as a whole should be considered when directors are brought into a company. As a group, the board should possess a balance of business and financial expertise, technical knowledge of the industry area(s) relevant to the company, directorship experience on other boards, and ability to devote sufficient time to the affairs of the company.

Legal Requirements

State Law

Most companies are incorporated in Delaware, whose applicable statutory provisions give broad authority to directors in their oversight of a company's operations and do not delineate specific qualifications that a director must have.

Delaware law is also silent as to board composition and independence requirements of directors.

Thus, pointing to Delaware as the example, the main considerations under state law are a director's abilities to fulfill his or her duties and obligations to the company, which include the duty of care (making informed decisions on behalf of the company and acting in good faith) and the duty of loyalty (acting in the best interests of the stockholders and the company, avoiding self-dealing, and disclosing any potential conflicts of interest). In the case of startup companies, the latter consideration may prove the most relevant, as investors in the company may wear several hats.

Long-term Considerations

If and when a company considers going public, it should be mindful of corporate governance rules put forth by the various stock exchanges, including the New York Stock Exchange (NYSE), Nasdaq and the American Stock Exchange.

The exchange rules are largely aimed at establishing director independence and creating boards with a majority of independent directors. The exchange rules lay out tests for determining independence, including those related to compensation arrangements and other material relationships between a director and the company. NYSE and Nasdaq both require listed companies to have a majority of independent directors and further lay out independence requirements with respect to various committees of the board, including the audit, compensation and nominating and governance committees.

Other Factors

When putting together (and growing) the board of directors, a company should also consider intangible factors such as diversity and the assembly of a group of directors that will collectively offer a variety of perspectives and opinions on company decisions while maintaining a culture of open communication.

[1] *See* Delaware General Corporation Law, 8 Del. C. § 141(a).

General Counsel: The Strategic Legal Counsel

The General Counsel ("GC") of today is a nimble executive, an issue-spotting and strategic intellectual who sees beyond silos and can speak to company-wide initiatives with a broad problem-solving perspective. GCs are a key member of the ever-burdened executive team, charged with the duty of providing operational and strategic leadership in a constantly changing environment. Effective GCs understand their organization's business and identify pitfalls and the regulatory landscape governing the organization.

The GC's command of regulatory and business considerations assists with the organization's success and smooths the transition into new services or business models.

Furthermore, the GC as an advisor is well appreciated by CEOs, CFOs, and COOs, who see the GC as a sounding board to safely "beta test" ideas, identify risks, and assess strategic changes that could have wide-ranging legal or business implications.

I have witnessed the importance of the GC advisor in my years advising in-house and in my current role, serving as an "outside fractional" GC for my clients who are not yet in a position to hire a full-time, seasoned GC. In-house legal teams are required to stay abreast of regulatory updates and are expected to answer complex legal questions on short notice.

However, in practice, it can be difficult for an in-house team to be an expert in everything or to have experience with some of the more complex transformations facing its company. This advisory role is critical to emerging companies and can also provide key support to overly leveraged or entry-level in-house legal teams. Outside GC advisors can help support and provide strategic advice to the entire leadership team, effectively adding another executive to manage the workload without the expense of a full-time GC/CLO.

The accessible GC (whether in-house or an outside advisor) is key to a company's forward momentum. The importance of open and frequent communication between the C-suite and the GC, especially in health care and other highly regulated industries, cannot be overstated. Whether by contract or regulation, the business rules of engagement change frequently and can drastically alter the operational framework of an organization.

Inclusion of the GC at the early stages of decisions concerning market growth, business innovation, employment, and board communication will lead to an informed leadership team that takes the right path the first time. As a result, the GC's strategic guidance should be considered a necessary component of a strong leadership team.

Corporate equity review Dividing the Pie

You're starting a new company. Congratulations! Before preparing for your product launch or talking to customers, however, you need to agree upon the allocation and terms for the equity, or ownership, of the company among you and your co-founders.

This is one of the toughest decisions you'll have as a founder, but it's also one of the most important to get right from the get-go.

Dilution

When founders launch a start-up, they own the entire thing. But it's inevitable that your shares will be diluted as the company grows in order to attract employees and investors, and there are very few examples of successful founders owning 100% of their companies at the time of a sale or IPO.

When you raise Series A funding, you'll issue additional shares of stock that will go to your investors, and you can expect those investors to take anywhere from 25% to 50% of the company. In later funding rounds, they may take a smaller percentage, though depending on the terms you negotiate, it can still be as much as in your Series A. Each time, your shares will be diluted accordingly.

You'll also need to leave a pot of equity for future employees, particularly early-stage ones. In general, when you're setting up equity at the beginning, it's a good idea to leave between 10% to 20% in the pie for employees. If you plan on raising funding at some point, your investors will require you to have this—and if it's already in place, you won't have to dilute your shares further to make room for it.

As with most things, there are philosophical differences in the approach to founder equity. One camp believes that founder equity should never be evenly split because it can result in stalemates, which can kill a company fast.

- ☐ **Whose idea was it?** Unless someone is contributing patented technology, this shouldn't be a big factor—Instead, the founders who execute on the idea deserve more equity.

- ☐ **Full-time versus part-time**: If one co-founder is quitting her job to dedicate herself full-time to the company and the other is working part-time, the part-time founder deserves less equity because she's both taking on less risk and providing less value and time commitment to the company. Typically, this person should get less than half of the equity that a full-time founder is getting.

- ☐ **Salary:** It's not uncommon in the early days of a start-up for founders to work for a reduced salary or forego it altogether. But, foregone salary should not be "paid" in the form of equity, for a couple of reasons. It's nearly impossible to determine the right amount of equity for foregone salary, and this practice can raise a host of difficult tax, withholding, and accounting issues. The same advice goes if one founder contributes equipment, working space, or other tangible things—pay for those with convertible debt or series seed preferred.

- ☐ **Capital Contributions**: One co-founder may be in a position to make a significant capital contribution to the company, and you might think she could just get additional founder shares in return. But, it's typically better to allocate founder equity based upon each person's actual level of work contribution (called "sweat equity") and treat financial contributions from a founder the same way you would that of a seed investor—by issuing convertible debt or series seed preferred stock.
- ☐ **Future Roles**: Consider each co-founder's expected role in the company based on her level of skill, capability, and the company's needs. For example, if the company requires significant technology innovation and one founder is a world-class VP of engineering, she may deserve more equity. Just remember that the needs of your company, and perhaps the roles of the founders, will change significantly over time—don't skew the equity split too much over a single contribution or skill.
- ☐ **Future Employees**: Similarly, it's important to think about founder equity stakes relative to the employees that get brought on afterward.
- ☐ If a founder ends up as director of product marketing with a huge equity stake, that will make it challenging to hire other senior executives with smaller option grants. The allocation of equity should take into account both past and future contributions to the company.
- ☐ **Control**: Founder equity should not be allocated based upon how the company should be controlled or managed—you should have a separate agreement that specifies how important decisions get made. It's also crucial to have rights of first refusal (an agreement stating that if a founder wants to sell her shares, she must first offer them to the company), so you don't end up with a partner you didn't bargain for.

Vesting

No matter how you divide the founder equity, those shares should be subject to vesting restrictions, so that until the shares are "vested," the founder does not fully own them. This is important because it prevents a co-founder from leaving after only a few months, and yet retaining a huge part of the company. The last thing you (or an investor) will want is for someone to hold a lot of equity and no longer be contributing to your success.

Under a typical vesting schedule for employees, shares vest over a four-year period, with 25% vesting at the end of the first year (called a "one-year cliff"), which ensures employees stay around for a year before owning any of the company. The remaining shares vest thereafter on a monthly or quarterly basis.

For founders, some shares are typically vested up front (in our experience, 20% to 25%, though it can go as high as 33.3%) Founders also often have provisions that accelerate vesting in the event of a change of control (i.e., an acquisition) or a termination without cause.

Mission Statement: Write a mission statement

BEST Biotech Example

To explore the cellular and molecular mechanisms underlying the development of all breast cancers and seek new therapeutic strategies for the treatment of those diseases. To develop new, emerging technologies, biomedical devices and biologics, establish laboratories, worldwide partnerships and humanitarian missions.

5 Ways to Avoid Legal Problems With Volunteers

Volunteers are great and even essential to your non-profit biopharma company. But, if things go wrong with a volunteer, it can spell bad news for your organization.

For instance, what if a volunteer has an accident while serving with you? What if the volunteer breaks the law or hurts someone else? Your organization could be liable.

Here are five ways to make it less likely that you'll run into problems with your volunteers. Some of these may seem onerous but take the time to do them right and protect both your organization and your volunteers.

Develop volunteer policies and procedures

Consult with an attorney or volunteer specialist to make sure these are adequate. Policies should spell out volunteer duties and address issues such as discrimination, harassment, and other possibly illegal behavior.

By explicitly banning bad behavior, your organization may be protected from liability. Be sure also to include protections for the volunteer from abuse by the organization and its staff.

Write job descriptions for all volunteer positions

Be explicit about expectations for the volunteer and what he or she can and cannot do.

Spell out any possible risk to the volunteer and ask for a signed release from liability. A thorough and concise job description may help protect the organization from liability should the volunteer go beyond what he or she is allowed to do.

Here are some things to include in job descriptions:

- your nonprofit's purpose
- required training for this position
- the duties expected of the volunteer
- the time needed to do the task
- the location where the volunteer will perform the work

Require each volunteer to fill out an application

Most of the time, it pays to require an application. However, sometimes with group projects that involve a "cattle call" for volunteers, you can simply have the volunteers fill out a waiver that releases the organization from liability.

The complexity of the application will depend on the position. If the volunteer is working with vulnerable people such as children or the elderly, the bar should be higher. For menial tasks with little risk to anyone, a shorter application would be suitable. Be careful to have different applications for different jobs. There's no sense in discouraging some volunteers with a long form if it is not necessary.

Here are some things to include in an application, where appropriate:

- Personal information such as address, phone number, email address, person to contact in the case of illness or accident, driver's license, proof of personal insurance, etc.
- Qualifications, when necessary to the job, such as special skills, or educational attainment.

- References who can attest to the applicant's good character or work ethic. References might be from a community member, another nonprofit where the applicant has volunteered, or an employer.
- Written permission to do a background check, essential if the volunteers will be working with children or other at-risk populations
- Waiver of confidentiality so you can gather the information you need and share it appropriately.

Conduct proper screening

Be careful here. Screening is especially important for volunteers who may be in contact with vulnerable people, or who have to drive while doing their volunteer work or engage in other kinds of dangerous work.

However, 31 percent of nonprofits do not perform volunteer screenings according to one study.

Nonprofits often think they can police their volunteers themselves and neglect to perform proper background checks. But that can leave the organization open to liability. Think of screening as part of your safety procedures and risk management.

Screening should always be respectful and protect the privacy of volunteers as much as possible. Get written consent for screening before proceeding. Also, screen from time to time as a precaution.

Screening can be as simple as a personal interview, or can include:

- criminal background checks
- driving records and licenses
- confirmation of insurance
- screening for health conditions or asking for proof of certain vaccinations
- verifying credentials such as a teaching certificate or special skills assessments

Provide excellent training and management

Never just turn a volunteer loose without adequate training. Volunteers appreciate being trained, so they know what to do and when. Train in groups or one on one. Develop written materials that the volunteer can take with them, and train on their specific tasks. Assign the volunteer to a staff person for oversight.

Training can include:

- your organization's code of conduct
- how to act when representing the organization
- how to identify and report abuse
- how to maintain the confidentiality of the organization and the people it serves
    - what you specifically expect from the volunteer
    - how to report any problems
    - who is in charge and how to reach them

Finally, be willing to dismiss a volunteer should they violate any of the rules, are difficult to get along with, are unreliable, or are abusive in any way. Develop a written procedure for staff if they must let a volunteer go.

Always inform the volunteer why you're letting them go, and then document the dismissal, just as you would with a paid staff member. Having a procedure, following it, and recording the action will help you should the volunteer decide to lodge a complaint with your top management or otherwise try to get back at you.

Don't forget to have policies for your staff that cover how they are to treat volunteers. Describe what harassment is and how to avoid it. Set up a grievance procedure that volunteers can use to report any abuse.

Volunteers want to do good and are appreciative when an organization is prepared to work with them. They want good policies in place and to have proper training and management. Keeping volunteers around requires not only gratitude on your part but also an organized approach that is protective of both volunteers and your nonprofit.

Chapter 7

How to Raise $50 Million Dollars in the Next 12 Months, Launching a Mini-IPO, selling to Non-Accredited Investors!

TITLE IV—SMALL COMPANY CAPITAL FORMATION

SEC. 401. AUTHORITY TO EXEMPT CERTAIN SECURITIES.

		New Reg A+	
	Old Reg A	Tier 1	Tier 2
Maximum Offering	$5 million	$20 million	$50 million
Investor Types	Only qualified/ accredited investors	Accredited and nonaccredited	Accredited and nonaccredited
Investment Limits	None	None	For nonaccredited investors, 10% of the greater of annual income or net worth
Financial Disclosures and Other Filing Requirements	Accountant-reviewed financials	Accountant-reviewed financials; exit report on Form 1-Z	Audited financials; ongoing reporting of annual reports (Form 1-K), semiannual reports (Form 1-SA), and current event reports (Form 1-U) via EDGAR
Preemption of State "Blue Sky" Laws	No; registration and state review required in every state where securities are offered	No; SEC & state review is coordinated, may utilize NASAA Coordinated Review	Yes; only SEC review is required

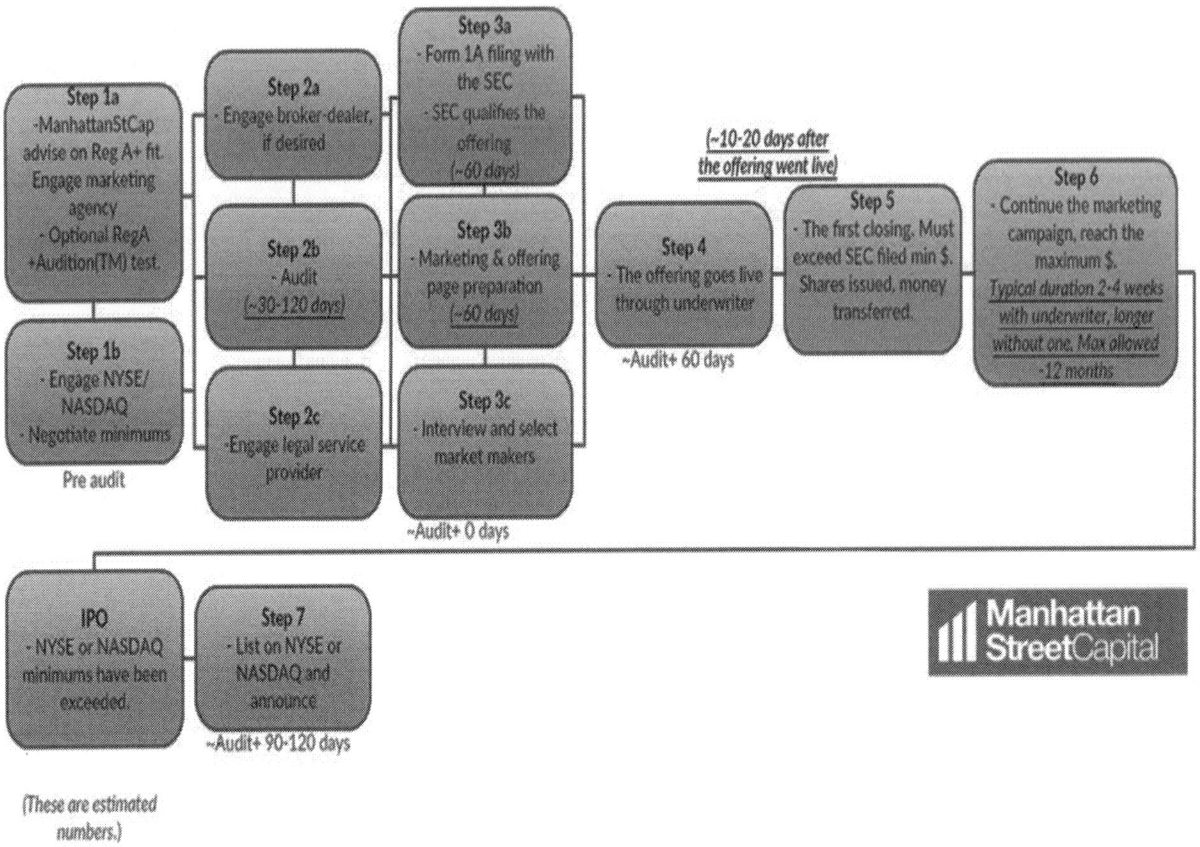
Step 1a
-ManhattanStCap advise on Reg A+ fit. Engage marketing agency
- Optional RegA +Audition(TM) test.
Step 1b
- Engage NYSE/ NASDAQ
- Negotiate minimums
Pre audit
Step 2a
- Engage broker-dealer, if desired
Step 2b
- Audit
(~30-120 days)
Step 2c
-Engage legal service provider
Step 3a
- Form 1A filing with the SEC
- SEC qualifies the offering
(~60 days)
Step 3b
- Marketing & offering page preparation
(~60 days)
Step 3c
- Interview and select market makers
~Audit+ 0 days
Step 4
- The offering goes live through underwriter
~Audit+ 60 days
(~10-20 days after the offering went live)
Step 5
- The first closing. Must exceed SEC filed min $. Shares issued, money transferred.
Step 6
- Continue the marketing campaign, reach the maximum $.
Typical duration 2-4 weeks with underwriter, longer without one. Max allowed ~12 months
IPO
- NYSE or NASDAQ minimums have been exceeded.
Step 7
- List on NYSE or NASDAQ and announce
~Audit+ 90-120 days
Manhattan StreetCapital
(These are estimated numbers.)

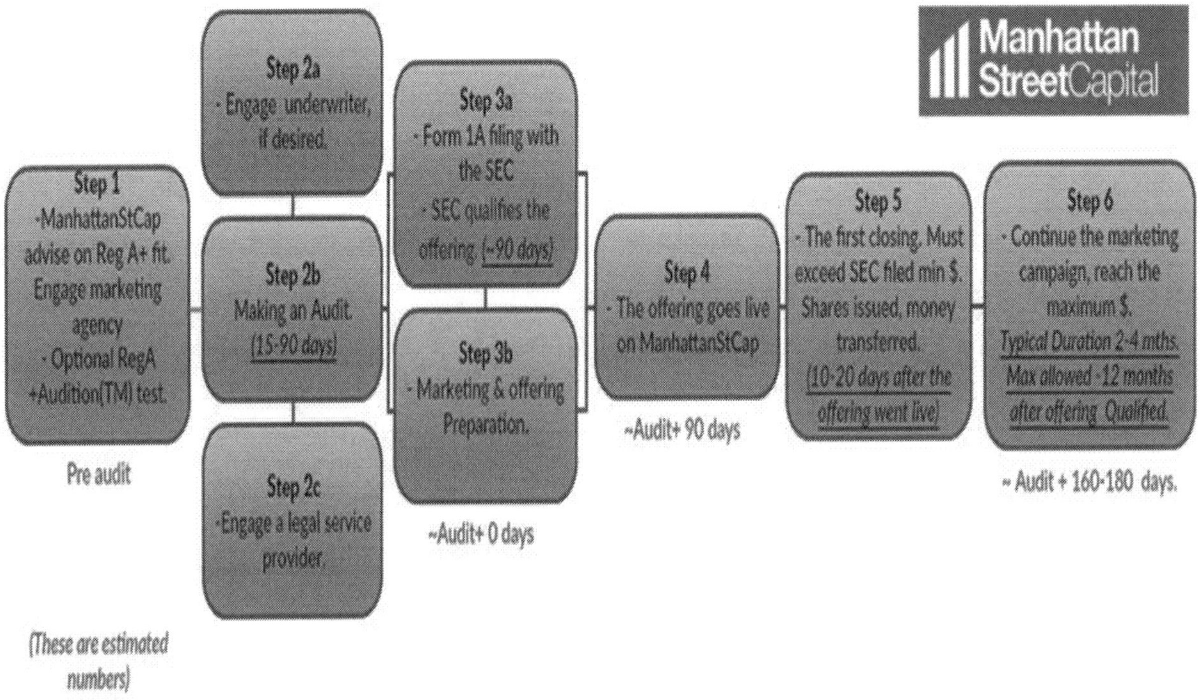
Manhattan StreetCapital
Step 1
-ManhattanStCap advise on Reg A+ fit. Engage marketing agency
- Optional RegA +Audition(TM) test.
Pre audit
Step 2a
- Engage underwriter, if desired.
Step 2b
Making an Audit.
(15-90 days)
Step 2c
-Engage a legal service provider.
Step 3a
- Form 1A filing with the SEC
- SEC qualifies the offering. (~90 days)
Step 3b
- Marketing & offering Preparation.
~Audit+ 0 days
Step 4
- The offering goes live on ManhattanStCap
~Audit+ 90 days
Step 5
- The first closing. Must exceed SEC filed min $. Shares issued, money transferred.
(10-20 days after the offering went live)
Step 6
- Continue the marketing campaign, reach the maximum $.
Typical Duration 2-4 mths. Max allowed ~12 months after offering Qualified.
~ Audit + 160-180 days.
(These are estimated numbers)

IV. Regulation A Compared to Regulation D

Event	REGULATION A	REGULATION D
Transferability	The shares are freely transferrable	Subject to finding appropriate securities exemptions
Reporting Company Rules	You can go over the 2,000 limitation and avoid becoming a reporting company as long as you do not exceed certain thresholds	If you only sell to accredited investors, you will probably have fewer investors and less likelihood of exceeding the 2,000 limitation
FINRA	FINRA views a Regulation A offering similar to a public offering; as a result, broker-dealers have to meet all the public requirements	You have to submit a copy of the Regulation D offering to FINRA, but no approval requirements

72

What to include in your life sciences company fundraising pitch deck

The actual pitch deck you use when pitching investors probably won't matter quite as much as the delivery of your fundraising pitch.

Still, creating that deck is a critical part of the process. It doesn't just give you an opportunity to put together data points into something easy to digest. It gives you a chance to structure your thoughts and your presentation ahead of time. For life sciences, this might be a little trickier. You can find a lot of tech startup pitch decks online, but your business might have some additional challenges on top of that. There will be a lot of overlap in the basics, and you still want to cover all your bases.

Here are some things you should consider either including in your pitch deck, or preparing as part of the presentation. Your life sciences company overview

■ **What does your product, and your company, actually do.**

Talk about the physical (or digital) thing that shows up in the hands of your customer. What does it do for them? How do they interact with it? What's unique about it compared to other products in the market? Even if it's a piece of software, it still ends up on someone's screen.

■ **Identify the pain points**. Put the investors in the shoes of a customer and help explain why they need a product like yours.

■ **Identify your customer**. This may sound straightforward, but you want to be as detailed as possible. Are you starting with a narrow customer base, or creating a broad product that can touch many different demographics? What are the needs of that customer? What do they look like? How do you think about customers beyond the obvious ones?

■ **Talk about some additional benefits your product generates**.

If you collect data, what does that data allow you to do? Can it help you expand into new markets? Does it just help improve the product? Could the data itself turn into a second line of business?

■ **Talk about your mission**.

The mission statement and the vision statement might actually be two different things. Think about what it is you are dedicated to doing, but also what you want to achieve ten years from now. Talk about how you're going to attain that mission. You can touch on the origin story to help explain the point.

■ **Lay out barriers to entry and how you will overcome them**.

You have to show why you'll be able to get past larger incumbents and why you are uniquely positioned to do that. You'll also need to cover any additional risks you might run into along the way.

■ **Lay out key advantages and IP**.

If you're working in the life sciences field, there's a good chance intellectual property's going to be a piece of the puzzle.

Talk about patents you own, how you got them, and how important they are to your business. How much of a competitive advantage do they offer, and how much of an asset are they?

Your business model and operations

- **Dig into the mechanics**.

Lay out your core technology and what makes it superior to others on the market. Show early feedback on prototypes if you have them. If you're more mature, show some results: studies, evidence of how effective it is, and research that backs up your claims.

- **The value proposition**.

You want to show how you're going to actually create value. This may differ between early-stage and later-stage companies.

- **Early-stage**:

Have a deep competitive market analysis to provide some reference points. List out recent exits, M&A, funding rounds, earnings releases, and as much data as you can collect that provides some directional accuracy for your future value.

- **Later-stage**:

You'll still want to do the same as above, but you've probably reached the point where you are listing out more of your raw metrics. Show the ways you're on a path to profitability.

- **Pathway through regulation**.

Talk about how long it will take to get your product to the market, and what hurdles you'll have to get through. Include any regulatory routes you have to take, and how long it will take to get approved — as well as any curveballs that might come up.

- **Dig into the metrics**.

If you have them in front of you, lay them out as clearly as you can. There's a whole laundry list of things you can dig into, but if you want to show how much your growth costs, these are a good place to start:

■ **Customer acquisition cost (CAC):**

How are you acquiring customers, and how much does it cost to acquire a customer?

■ **Lifetime Value (LTV):**

How much revenue are you generating from that customer you acquired. ■ Churn: How do you define the rate at which customers are leaving, and what is that rate?

■ **Licensing**:

If you license your technology, talk about the terms and any revenue or fees.

■ **Projections**:

You'll want to lay out (reasonable) projections for your revenue for the next few years or so to show you're on a solid path to growth.

■ **Walk through your costs and key requiremen**ts.

This is especially important if you're a life sciences company, because you have to show you are able to keep your operational costs under control — which will likely be a lot higher than your typical startup investors are evaluating.

■ **Supply chain**:

If you're producing anything physical, or you need a regular supply of equipment, do you have the correct vendors in place? Walk through some of the large-volume supplies you need to manage and how you'll keep your costs down — for both your operations and for your customers.

■ **Partnerships**:

You've probably decided to cooperate with a few companies that are producing a kind of win-win situation. This can take a lot of forms, such as relationships with suppliers or vendors that you can amplify to a broader audience.

Your life sciences team

■ **Lay out who's on your team**.

Include their backgrounds, and why those backgrounds are important. If someone has a Ph. D. in biology, you'll probably want to highlight that. Show the characteristics of your team that will highlight why you're uniquely suited to this problem.

- **Talk about advisors and board members.**

Collecting a solid group of advisors and board members, much like employees, shows you can get smart people excited about the idea. High-profile board members and advisors can be a stamp of approval and show you've identified your holes in expertise.

- **Identify who's missing.**

Investors are going to spot holes in your expertise and want to know that you're thinking about how to fill those holes. Touch on recruiting and how big you want your team to grow.

Again, these are just a few things that can show up on a slideshow.

(Watch the CardioMatrex tm slide show in Addendum supra)

It might have some very detailed infographics and information, but it's not a replacement for enthusiasm and passion. Investors are making a huge bet on you, just like you are taking a huge risk starting the company.

As you're putting together all this information, think to yourself how you'll structure the conversation and the questions investors might ask. You have to show you believe in the mission enough yourself that you're willing to carry it out — and sometimes that's not easy. Being a great presenter isn't a skill that comes naturally to a lot of people, and it takes practice. It's a difficult and sometimes annoying part of the whole starting-a-company-from-scratch process, but the more prepared you are, the easier it will be.

Tips for preparing for your life sciences fundraising pitch

To convince investors to hand over a big check after a meeting, you just need to be crystal clear on the value you're creating. Here are some things to think about going into the meeting.

Pitching for early-stage life sciences funding

When you're walking into a meeting, there are four key things you need to hit: your strengths, your weaknesses, the opportunity, and the threats to your opportunity.

Make your vision clear. Like any founder, you need to show that you have a clear mission and vision for how you'll get there. Having a great idea isn't good enough. You need to show you have conviction and you'll be able to execute on it. Lay out your ten-year plan on how you'll get there.

Show you can get people on board. As a CEO or top executive, a lot of your time is probably going to be spent recruiting. You'll have to convince smart people to take a huge risk and join your company. You'll also have to retain them. Talking about your existing team and how you'll sell that vision to others shows you'll be able to put together the right group to execute.

Show you have partner support. Starting a company, regardless of industry, is always easier when you aren't doing it in a vacuum. If your products are very technical or require complex supply chains, it helps to show that you either have those supply chains lined up or locked down. Partners also show that you're being thoughtful about distribution. If you don't have partners, talk about how you're going to get them.

Identify your customer. You could dive into the technicalities here, talking about the lifetime value of your customers and the cost it would take to acquire them. But you also have to show you understand their pain points and their needs. More importantly, you have to show why they aren't being served right now. They might not realize it's a pain point, or maybe it's prohibitively difficult. That you can serve this customer is what makes your company a real business.

Provide points of reference. You should talk about the market value you're attacking, but also how you've derived that market value. Dig into acquisitions in the space, overall product consumption, or the size of the potential customer base.

Pitching for later-stage life sciences funding

It's easy to try to give the same pitch that got you funding in your seed and Series A funding rounds. It was successful, after all. But as you start to mature, you theoretically get less risky and investors are going to be looking for more of a guaranteed return. That means you'll have to show traction and growth, which means providing some concrete points. You have to show you're well on your way to the mission you set out when you raised your first round of funding.

As you get into later-stage pitching, a lot of your competitive advantage will probably start to fall under your protected assets, like intellectual property. As you start to prove out the value of your market, at bare minimum you can make the case that you have a minimum value based off your intellectual property. That shouldn't be the foundation of your pitch, to be sure, but it does give you a nice competitive advantage.

Talk about your customers. As you start to mature, you need to show that you're demonstrating product-market fit. The best way to do that, regardless of industry, is to show that you have customers that are either lined up or already paying for your products.

Show the IP you've gathered. A lot of complex technology becomes commoditized over time — just look at how quickly machine learning is now widely available in a lot of applications. You should show that you're being thoughtful about how you defend your position and warding off other companies that might want to unseat you.

Demonstrate real revenue. There are a lot of industries that take a while to start generating revenue. The chips industry, for example, takes a long time before your product even enters the market. The faster you can show you're generating revenue, the better — as it means you understand the urgency of getting a product to market.

Have a Plan B. You might not make it through trials or get approval for your products. Your experiments might come up with a completely different result for some reason. You might even end up running up against an incumbent you didn't anticipate. Ensure that you show you've thought about all that and demonstrate alternatives.

Other important things to include in life sciences fundraising

A good rule of thumb is to think about the SWOT analysis: strengths, weaknesses, opportunities, and threats.

You want to be able to talk through all of those very clearly. There may be regulatory hurdles or massive players that could derail your mission — and you have to have the ability to overcome that. You might have some holes in your expertise, but you have to show you can fill them.

Do your research on the investor you're pitching.

They may have invested in some companies that have followed a similar storyline as yours, or have a similar team. Try to identify patterns if you can and find the firms that's the best fit. You might need help with finding customers or talent, and some firms are better at some things than others.

As always, ask questions. You're auditioning for funding as much as they are auditioning to be your investor. You want to know if they're able to help you in the same way they are analyzing you as an investment opportunity. Plus, it gives you an opportunity to provide some clarity on points you may have missed or want to revisit.

Most important, you need to show that the market actually needs your product. That's the difference between running a real company and just a science experiment in a lab. Explain why no one has owned the market, what's getting in the way, and how you're going to overcome that.

At the end of the day, remember what it is you're about to do: present your mission and vision and ask for a ton of money.

The latter part is probably something that comes very naturally if you believe in what you're working on. The former is all about preparation and practice, and you should still take the time to do a good job. Neither you nor potential investors want to waste their time and a little bit of preparation goes a long way.

Matthew Lynley

Strategies of Legendary Value Investors

Andrew Beattie

TABLE OF CONTENTS

Value investing is a strategy where investors actively look to add stocks they believe have been undervalued by the market, and/or trade for less than their intrinsic values. Like any type of investing, value investing varies in execution with each person. There are, however, some general principles that are shared by all value investors.

These principles have been spelled out by famed investors like Peter Lynch, Kenneth Fisher, Warren Buffett, Bill Miller and others. By reading through financial statements, they seek out mispriced stocks and look to capitalize on a possible reversion to the mean.

We will look at some of the more well-known value investing principles.

Buy Businesses, Not Stocks

If there is one thing that all value investors can agree on, it's that investors should buy businesses, not stocks. This means ignoring trends in stock prices and other market noise. Instead, investors should look at the fundamentals of the company that the stock represents. Investors can make money following trending stocks, but it involves a lot more activity than value investing.

Searching for good businesses selling at a good price based on probable future performance requires a larger time commitment for research, but the payoffs include less time spent buying and selling, as well as fewer commission payments.

Love the Business You Buy Into

You wouldn't pick a spouse based solely on his or her shoes, and you shouldn't pick a stock based on cursory research. You have to love the business you are buying, and that means being passionate about knowing everything about that company. You need to strip the attractive covering from a company's financials and get down to the naked truth. Many companies look far better when you judge them beyond the basic price to earnings (P/E), price to book (P/B) and earnings per share (EPS) ratios and look into the quality of the numbers that make up those figures.

If you keep your standards high and make sure the company's financials look as good naked as they do dressed up, you're much more likely to keep it in your portfolio for a long time. If things change, you'll notice it early. If you like the business you buy, paying attention to its ongoing trials and successes becomes more of a hobby than a chore.

Invest in Companies You Understand

If you don't understand what a company does or how, then you probably shouldn't be buying shares. Critics of value investing like to focus on this main limitation. You are stuck looking for businesses that you can easily understand because you have to be able to make an educated guess about the future earnings of the business. The more complex a business is, the more uncertain your projections will likely be. This moves the emphasis from "educated" to "guess."

You can buy businesses you like but don't completely understand, but you have to factor in uncertainty as added risk.

Any time a value investor has to factor in more risk, they have to look for a larger margin of safety – that is, more of a discount from the calculated true value of the company.

There can be no margin of safety if the company is already trading at many multiples of its earnings, which is a strong sign that however exciting and new the idea is, the business is not a value play. Simple businesses also have an advantage, as it's harder for incompetent management to hurt the company.

Find Well-Managed Companies

Management can make a huge difference in a company. Good management adds value beyond a company's hard assets. Bad management can destroy even the most solid financials. There have been investors who have based their entire investing strategies on finding managers that are honest and able.

Warren Buffett advises that investors should look for three qualities of good management: integrity, intelligence, and energy. He adds that "if they don't have the first, the other two will kill you."

You can get a sense of management's honesty through reading several years' worth of financials. How well did they deliver on past promises? If they failed, did they take responsibility, or gloss it over?

Value investors want managers who act like owners. The best managers ignore the market value of the company and focus on growing the business, thus creating long-term shareholder value. Managers who act like employees often focus on short-term earnings in order to secure a bonus or other performance perk, sometimes to the long-term detriment of the company. Again, there are many ways to judge this, but the size and reporting of compensation is often a dead giveaway. If you're thinking like an owner, then you pay yourself a reasonable wage and depend on gains in your stock holdings for a bonus. At the very least, you want a company that expenses its stock options.

Don't Stress Over Diversification

One of the areas where value investing runs contrary to commonly accepted investing principles is on diversification. There are long stretches where a value investor will be idle.

This is because of the exacting standards of value investing as well as overall market forces. Towards the end of a bull market, everything gets expensive, even the dogs. So, a value investor may have to sit on the sidelines waiting for the inevitable correction.

Time — an important factor in compounding — is lost while waiting to invest. So, when you do find undervalued stocks, you should buy as much as you can. Be warned, this will lead to a portfolio that is high-risk according to traditional measures like beta. Investors are encouraged to avoid concentrating on only a few stocks, but value investors generally feel that they can only keep proper track of a few stocks at a time.

One obvious exception is Peter Lynch, who kept almost all of his funds in stocks at all times. Lynch broke stocks into categories and then cycled his funds through companies in each category. He also spent upwards of 12 hours every day checking and rechecking the many stocks held by his fund. However, as an individual value investor with a different day job, it's better to go with a few stocks for which you've done the homework and feel good about holding long term.

Your Best Investment Is Your Guide

Anytime you have more investment capital, your aim for investing should not be diversity, but finding an investment that is better than the ones you already own. If the opportunities don't beat what you already have in your portfolio, you may as well buy more of the companies you know and love, or simply wait for better times.

During idle times, a value investor can identify the stocks he or she wants and the price at which they'll be worth buying. By keeping a wish list like this, you'll be able to make decisions quickly in a correction.

Ignore the Market 99% of the Time

The market only matters when you enter or exit a position — the rest of the time, it should be ignored. If you approach buying stocks like buying a business, you'll want to hold onto them as long as the fundamentals are strong.

During the time you hold an investment, there will be spots where you could sell for a large profit and others where you're holding an unrealized loss. This is the nature of market volatility.

The reasons for selling a stock are numerous, but a value investor should be as slow to sell as he or she is to buy. When you sell an investment, you expose your portfolio to capital gains and usually have to sell a loser to balance it out. Both of these sales come with transaction costs that make the loss deeper and the gain smaller. By holding investments with unrealized gains for a long time, you forestall capital gains on your portfolio. The longer you avoid capital gains and transaction costs, the more you benefit from compounding.

The Bottom Line

Value investing is a strange mix of common sense and contrarian thinking. While most investors can agree that a detailed examination of a company is important, the idea of sitting out a bull market goes against the grain. It's undeniable that funds held constantly in the market have outperformed cash held outside the market that is waiting for a downturn to end. This is a fact, but a deceiving one. The data is derived from following the performance of market measures like the S&P 500 Index over a number of years. This is where passive investing and value investing get confused.

In both types of investing, the investor avoids unnecessary trading and has a long-term holding period. The difference is that passive investing relies on average returns from an index fund or other diversified instrument. A value investor seeks out above-average companies and invests in them. Therefore, the probable range of return for value investing is much higher.

In other words, if you want the average performance of the market, you're better off buying an index fund right now and piling money into it over time. If you want to outperform the market, however, you need a concentrated portfolio of outstanding companies. When you find them, the superior compounding will make up for the time you spent waiting in a cash position. Value investing demands a lot of discipline on the part of the investor, but in return offers a large potential payoff.

The 4 Basic Elements of Stock Value

TABLE OF CONTENTS

Investing has a set of four basic elements that investors use to break down a stock's value. In this article, we will look at four commonly used ratios and what they can tell you about a stock. Financial ratios are powerful tools to help summarize financial statements and the health of a company or enterprise.

KEY TAKEAWAYS

Financial statements can be used by analysts and investors to compute financial ratios that indicate the health or value of a company and its shares.

P/E, P/B, PEG and dividend yiclds arc four commonly used metrics that can help break down a stock's value and outlook.

Any single ratio is too narrowly focused to stand alone, so combining these and other financial ratios gives a more complete picture.

The Price-To-Book Ratio (P/B)

Made for glass-half-empty people, the price-to-book (P/B) ratio represents the value of the company if it is torn up and sold today. This is useful to know because many companies in mature industries falter in terms of growth, but can still be a good value based on their assets. The book value usually includes equipment, buildings, land and anything else that can be sold, including stock holdings and bonds.

With purely financial firms, the book value can fluctuate with the market as these stocks tend to have a portfolio of assets that goes up and down in value. Industrial companies tend to have a book value based more on physical assets, which depreciate year over year according to accounting rules.

In either case, a low P/B ratio can protect you – but only if it's accurate. This means an investor has to look deeper into the actual assets making up the ratio.

Price-To-Earnings Ratio (P/E)

The price to earnings (P/E) ratio is possibly the most scrutinized of all the ratios. If sudden increases in a stock's price are the sizzle, then the P/E ratio is the steak. A stock can go up in value without significant earnings increases, but the P/E ratio is what decides if it can stay up. Without earnings to back up the price, a stock will eventually fall back down. An important point to note is that one should only compare P/E ratios among companies in similar industries and markets.

The reason for this is simple: A P/E ratio can be thought of as how long a stock will take to pay back your investment if there is no change in the business. A stock trading at $20 per share with earnings of $2 per share has a P/E ratio of 10, which is sometimes seen as meaning that you'll make your money back in 10 years if nothing changes.

The reason stocks tend to have high P/E ratios is that investors try to predict which stocks will enjoy progressively larger earnings. An investor may buy a stock with a P/E ratio of 30 if he or she thinks it will double its earnings every year (shortening the payoff period significantly). If this fails to happen, the stock will fall back down to a more reasonable P/E ratio. If the stock does manage to double earnings, then it will likely continue to trade at a high P/E ratio.

The PEG Ratio

Because the P/E ratio isn't enough in and of itself, many investors use the price to earnings growth (PEG) ratio. Instead of merely looking at the price and earnings, the PEG ratio incorporates the historical growth rate of the company's earnings. This ratio also tells you how company A's stock stacks up against company B's stock.

The PEG ratio is calculated by taking the P/E ratio of a company and dividing it by the year-over-year growth rate of its earnings. The lower the value of your PEG ratio, the better the deal you're getting for the stock's future estimated earnings.

By comparing two stocks using the PEG, you can see how much you're paying for growth in each case. A PEG of 1 means you're breaking even if growth continues as it has in the past. A PEG of 2 means you're paying twice as much for projected growth when compared to a stock with a PEG of 1. This is speculative because there is no guarantee that growth will continue as it has in the past.

The P/E ratio is a snapshot of where a company is and the PEG ratio is a graph plotting where it has been. Armed with this information, an investor has to decide whether it is likely to continue in that direction

Dividend Yield

It's always nice to have a back-up when a stock's growth falters. This is why dividend-paying stocks are attractive to many investors – even when prices drop, you get a paycheck. The dividend yield shows how much of a payday you're getting for your money. By dividing the stock's annual dividend by the stock's price, you get a percentage.

You can think of that percentage as the interest on your money, with the additional chance at growth through the appreciation of the stock.

Although simple on paper, there are some things to watch for with the dividend yield. Inconsistent dividends or suspended payments in the past mean that the dividend yield can't be counted on. Like water, dividends can ebb and flow, so knowing which way the tide is going – like whether dividend payments have increased year over year – is essential to making the decision to buy.

Dividends also vary by industry, with utilities and some banks typically paying a lot whereas tech firms, which often invest almost all their earnings back into the company to fuel growth, paying very little or no dividends.

The Bottom Line

P/E, P/B, PEG and dividend yields are too narrowly focused to stand alone as a single measure of a stock. By combining these methods of valuation, you can get a better view of a stock's worth. Any one of these can be influenced by creative accounting – as can more complex ratios like cash flow.

As you add more tools to your valuation methods, discrepancies get easier to spot. These four main ratios may be overshadowed by thousands of customized metrics, but they will always be useful stepping stones for finding out whether a stock is worth buying.

How to Finance a Biotech Startup: 5 Options to Pursue Funding

Meredith Turits

The Best Financing Options for Biotech Startups

Right now seems like a great time to be at the helm of a biotech startup. There's more money going into U.S. companies from venture capitalists than ever. A record high, in fact: CB Insights reported that in Q2 2018, investors poured $23 billion into startups.[1]

And things are particularly bright for biotech startups, which pulled in $2.8 billion in funding in the first two months of 2018 alone.[2] So, if you're an entrepreneur figuring out how to finance a biotech startup, is going the VC route always the best bet?

Not always, no. It takes quite a lot to be able to secure funding from a venture fund—but especially in a demanding space like biotech. Even though biotech is a hot field, financing a biotech startup is nuanced and involved. You'll also need to make a decision on what kind of financing to seek depending on the stage of your company's development.

We'll go over a few options for how to finance a biotech startup and offer a few things to consider about your company's positioning before you start seeking out capital. Even if you're sure you're going to raise at some point, you'll still want to review all of your options. You don't want to leave free money on the table, that's for sure.

The Unique Challenges of Biotech Companies

If you're in charge of your own profit and loss (income statement), we don't have to tell you that biological technology is an expensive business. Like, very expensive.

Unlike a consumer products company making, say, edible food dyes, or even a software company developing a new communication platform for dentists, proof of concept and prototyping costs are sky-high in biotech.

To even just perform initial R&D, you need to own or have access to industrial machinery, labs, chemicals—whatever it is that you're looking to do and specialize in. And, additionally, you have to pay a premium for highly experienced and trained team members.

So, for anyone looking to hand you cash—whether it's an investor looking for equity or a small business lender looking for an interest payment—you're going to go through a great deal of due diligence. Because, bottom line is that you're going to need a lot of capital to even get things off the ground. And much of the value of your company will be in intangible assets (aka your intellectual property), which are difficult to value.

But, If You Can Pull It Off, Biotech Has a Huge Upside

As you might imagine, though, biotech is incredibly well positioned to make an impact not only financially, but socially, too.

Successful biotech companies are leveraging modern technology that's changing as quickly as we can learn it to create breakthroughs in medical treatments and therapies, drug testing and development, genomics, biofuels, and so much more.

Many companies that have successfully secured biotech funding not only secure financing from multiple sources but also generate returns for those involved. In their article about financing life sciences companies for Nature Biotechnology in July 2011, authors Bruce L. Booth and Bijan Salehizadeh write, "To make a baseball analogy, life sciences has a higher batting average but lower home-run percentage than technology."

Options for Financing Your Biotech Startup

You have a few different financing options you can pursue as a biotech startup. As you're researching how to finance a biotech startup, once thing you'll find is that you might be able to access lots of different types of funding. And, the larger your circle of connections, the more access you'll have to opportunities.

1. Grants and Public Funding From Government, Corporate, and Research Organizations

You'll be pleased to find out that there's a lot of available grant funding for biotech startups.

This is especially excellent news for earlier-stage companies that are still in R&D phases, and need foundational capital to kickstart their business.

Depending on your specific research trajectory, you might be eligible for grants from government agencies including the U.S. Department of Agriculture, National Science Foundation, Department of Energy, and National Institute of Health. Each grant has different eligibility and submission requirements, plus different awards. Grants are not only highly prestigious but also an amazing growth engine for your business—and you won't have to give up equity or pay back interest.

Similarly, you'll find that many established corporate biotech companies (like Pfizer) or larger nonprofits (Prevent Cancer Foundation) sponsor different size grants for biotech startups at different stages. Many are just for post-graduates or post-docs, but some are for health professionals, too. You just have to dig to find the right one for you.

If you'd like to pursue financing your biotech startup with at least some funding from grants—which we'd certainly recommend at least trying your hand at—understand that it'll involve a lot of research.

Grants are highly competitive, so make sure you're qualified for the grants you're applying for and working hard on your application. It might take time, but even scoring one will make a big difference.

We recommend using Science's biotech grant search tool to begin.

2. University Funds

Many biotech startups originate from research kicked off within universities. (A good example that might surprise you: Major-market drug Lyrica for the treatment of chronic pain and epilepsy was developed at Northwestern University.)[3] If your biotech company is the product of a university innovation or sprung from an academic incubator, you might have some financing options.

Several universities have started or are in the process of developing funding to invest in growth and acceleration of companies with academic ties. You might be able to not only receive financial backing but also tap into valuable university resources by getting involved with these programs. Look into any potential opportunities at your specific university if you think this might apply to you.

3. Private Investments From Biotech Experts

If you're in early stages, you might want to directly seek private investment from experts in the biotech space. Especially if you're trying to raise money before you have a lot of hard data, and you need capital to be able to support R&D, you'll want to approach someone who deeply understands your space. That way, you don't have to spend a lot of time explaining what you're doing and asking for trust. And, if anyone's going to take a risk on a business that's really just an idea, it's going to be someone who intimately knows the hypothesis you're betting on.

This makes sense if you're raising pre-seed money—but also if you're seeking out angel investors, too. Plus, the more people you can have on your side in your space to give your startup the stamp of approval, the better outlook for your capital raises.

4. Venture Capital

Now, it's time to get to venture capital. As you might expect, many biotech startups pursue financing from venture funds.

As we briefly mentioned before, biotech is capital intensive by nature, and the R&D process is prolonged, too. When VCs consider their investments, they need to know that they're investing in a highly promising prospect with a strong potential for return.

They also know they have a big enough piece of the pie that their time and advisory work will be worth the sweat. Often, that means that VCs hold out until biotech startups have some hard data under their belt and are raising larger rounds. Otherwise, the juice won't be worth the squeeze, so to speak.

A little down the line, though, VCs are okay with putting in a large amount of capital and paying a slightly larger price to enter at a higher valuation if they deem an investment an exciting opportunity. That might mean you won't be able to access major VC for biotech startup financing until, perhaps, series A instead of a seed round. But don't get discouraged—keep your head down and get the results you need to secure your funding down the line.

5. Startup Loans

As any kind of startup, it's difficult to go to a lender and apply for traditional small business financing like a term loan or business line of credit. Most lenders require some kind of business financials to evaluate. Usually, that means you'll need to have at least a little time in business and some history of how you behave with your business debt (usually in the form of a business credit score).

Of course, new businesses don't have that.

One kind of business financing you might be eligible for, depending on your time in business, revenues, and what you need the cash for, is equipment financing. As a self-collateralizing loan, equipment financing is easier for many newer businesses to access. If you need to finance the purchase of gear, equipment, machinery, or anything similar (as opposed to general working capital), you can apply to a lender with an equipment quote and very good personal credit. If approved, you can use the money to purchase the equipment you need. The equipment serves as collateral.

Also, as you're thinking about small business startup loans, don't forget that a business credit card can be a powerful tool, too, especially in your most nascent days. A 0% intro APR business credit card can give you a nice buffer with several months (up to 15, in some cases) where you can spend and not accrue interest.

Positioning Your Biotech Startup for Its Best Chance at Scoring Funding

Once you identify the type (or types) of funding you think will be best to finance your biotech startup, make sure you put your best foot forward. It's important to come to any potential investor, grant application, or lender with all of your paperwork together. And, it's important to do it at the right time.

1. Determine your pre-money valuation.

If you're raising venture capital, an important part of your process will be valuing your company.

Your valuation is the measure of your company's worth—and it's important for investors to be on the same page with you in order to feel comfortable with not only putting money in, but also taking equity in exchange. Without a realistic valuation, they're not going to own enough of your company to make an investment worth it.

That's why coming to the correct valuation is essential. You'll want to determine what's called your "pre-money valuation." That's the estimated value of your company before the investment round.

2. Have data.

Unless you have a track record of substantial success with prior exits or with biotech sector development at established companies, you'll need to have data. In fact, hard data is a non-negotiable. Because the nature of biotech means that R&D takes a lot of time, you want to bring as much proof of progress as possible.

Be prepared with hard data about the problems you're solving, distinction from your competitors, and the progress made with the technology you're developing.

3. Be smart about timing.

Like any capital infusion, biotech startup financing is no different in that you want to time your funding right.

What are you going to use this funding for? Small business lenders will want to know—venture capitalists, too. Many grants also have specific directives for what you can and can't do with award money.

That's all to say that you might want to consider timing your financing request with a particular phase of research you want to fund, or a new project you're hoping to pursue. Maybe you need to obtain new equipment or hire new staff to expand. Bottom line: Don't just apply for cash to apply.

4. Build your network.

As you're raising capital to scale, it's vital to continue to make connections with experts in your space. They'll be able to introduce you to brilliant people who can share ideas and connect you to sources of new financing.

And, like we mentioned before, you want to have the endorsement of as many trusted, successful biotech professionals as you possibly can. It will not only legitimize the company you're building but also ultimately help you secure funding in your developmental stages.

5. Did we mention data?

This bears repeating: Be fanatical about collecting, presenting, and organizing data for everything you can.

With Biotech Financing, You Have to Walk Before You Can Run

As a biotech company, the dream is to always get big enough that you IPO—an initial public offering in which you list for trading on an exchange like the NASDAQ. But it's a long road to get there. As it should be: Developing an outstanding biological technology product is very difficult. It requires a lot of research and a lot of failure before the good stuff starts happening.

And, right, it also requires a lot of money.

As you're navigating the biotech startup financing journey, above all, remain patient. Biotech companies need to raise more capital than many other types of companies, and they often need to work even harder to do it. But the rewards can be big, so hang tight and keep plugging away at your passions. Build your network, and gather your data.

There's no better time than right now to be in biotech—but like the best research, the best sources of funding aren't realized overnight.

Article Sources:

1. *CBinsights.com. "Venture Capital Funding Report Q2 2018"*
2. *Forbes.com. "In Two Months, Biotech Startups Raised More Money Than In All Of 2013"*
3. *Northwestern.edu. "Northwestern Research"*

Why Biotechs Should Invest in Good Outsourcing Management of CROs

The relationship between biotechs and their CRO partners has been long in the making. These days, a collaboration with CROs is seen as a standard in the drug development industry. However, the management of drug development partners and providers can be highly challenging for biotechs. This is where outsourcing expertise can make the difference between success and the painful alternative.

In recent years, the growing success of the drug development industry has resulted in impactful changes for contract research organizations (CROs) and biotechs. Through mergers and acquisitions, CROs continue to grow and expand their scope of drug development services.

As large CROs have acquired regional capacity or specialist services, the number of smaller, independent CROs has fallen. On the other hand, smaller CROs are becoming more specialized in specific areas of drug development, such as clinical trial supplies or IT.

Additionally, the industry is seeing a third category of providers emerging. This group focuses on IT platforms that, especially in the current Coronavirus situation, can rapidly adapt and interact with sites.

Lacking resources, biotechs rely heavily on CROs

Richard Scaife, Managing Director at OM360 Outsourcing Consultancy & Chairperson at PCMG

But what does that mean for small biotech companies? In the past, biotechs often lacked the resources to move beyond phase I and usually partnered early with large pharma companies.

However, a combination of scientific advances and the availability of investment funding has fueled the successful growth of the biotech industry into later phase trial management.

"What this has done is to push biotechs into having to manage clinical trials without the resources that large pharma companies take for granted," explained Richard Scaife, Managing Director at OM360 Outsourcing Consultancy and Chairperson at PCMG.

"In-depth, project-level knowledge is essential to manage external suppliers effectively and to meet investor expectations. Smaller, investor-funded biotechs lack internal capacity and capabilities, and subsequently, risk over-reliance on CROs."

Investing in CRO management

Now comes the challenge: The huge budgets and commitment of what can be a biotech's only product, means CRO management should be seen as a high-risk investment. Commonly with a medical science focus, a biotech's management team has limited time and resources to fully manage this risk.

"Managing CRO outsourcing is a complicated task, intensive task," Scaife said. *"Once you have made your selection, there's not enough time or budget to change your mind when projects are underway."*

Outsourcing expertise for CRO management Choosing the right CRO is key

Whether large pharma or small biotech, the essentials of outsourcing are the same. The challenge starts with planning sufficient time to find the most suitable partner. A biotech must decide whether it wants to work with a large, full-service CRO or smaller more specialized CROs.

"There's a tremendous risk in taking the 'easy option' and trusting that a big CRO's extensive global resources and capabilities provide assurance of successful trial conduct.

Are those big CROs really focused on small biotechs? Like with all CROs, it depends on who you get, but also how you intend to work together."

That is not to say that all large CROs are not committed to working with small companies. As with any choice, well defined and developed needs and expectations have to be understood in advance.

Beyond specifications, the cultural fit is equally vital but doesn't come from a written proposal. *"It's called a business relationship for a reason,"* said Scaife.

The consequences of neglecting CRO management

"Signing a contract with a CRO is just the beginning of the relationship, nothing is locked down," Scaife warned. *"If a biotech doesn't have the resource to fully control study planning, pre-study feasibility, set up timelines with a realistic budget forecast, protocol development, and how to work constructively with the CRO, higher costs and longer timelines are a near certainty."*

Good Outsourcing Practice can steer projects in the right direction and plan for success rather than conflict. This can ultimately result in trying to fix the problems by replacing the CRO.

"The worst-case scenario – which I've seen – is a complete fallout with the CRO where another CRO is brought in to the rescue rather than preventing or effectively resolving the issues," Scaife added. *"This costs even more money and becomes far more complicated because you need to manage the interaction between the original CRO and your rescue CRO."*

The long-term consequence of this scenario is a delay in the study. *"Time is the enemy, whether developing a new treatment for commercialization or for acquisition, the longer it takes, the lower the value of the product. Time, cost, and quality are always the three things that can suffer if you don't get your CRO management right."*

A good relationship between CROs and their biotech sponsors is important

To avoid the risk of failure, biotech's should think about whether they have the time and resources to manage and work effectively with the CRO. If not, they should consider whether they can train-up internal workers or recruit experienced staff.

"I've heard the term 'the client from hell', the one CROs dread getting a phone call from because it's such an unpleasant experience," Scaife explained. *"If you are going to succeed as a biotech, you want to have full engagement with the people in*

the CRO. It's always easy to blame somebody else when things don't work out. But it takes two to tango, it really does, and that's where the trust comes into it."

An ultimate biotech goal is successful due diligence

For a biotech, the relationship they have with their CRO partners and other providers is essential in the long term. Scaife explained that, ultimately, every biotech will be subject to due diligence.

"What happens to a biotech in the end? It will take products to commercialization or it will sell the product to a pharma to progress the development. Whatever they do, they will be subject to due diligence."

"Due diligence for either investors or potential acquisitors is incredibly intensive and time-sensitive. Outsourcing-related questions will include, 'Where are your contracts? How did you negotiate these contracts? How did you select those providers?' They need to know everything. At this point, your outsourcing management becomes even more important."

The future of R&D outsourcing management

In the future, Scaife believes the value of good outsourcing practice within procurement frameworks will become increasingly important in the drug development industry. While biotechs only have finite resources and small in-house teams, these principles and practices have a valuable role in helping them effectively manage their CRO partners and other providers.

"Biotechs can tap into that experience, rather than relying on their own experience, which can have a limited perspective. The same rule applies to the increasing number of freelance outsourcing experts as it does to CROs.

They have a broader experience, are usually more senior as well, and are not intimidated by changing companies and working in different environments."

The world is witnessing the big bang of scientific discovery in the medical device sector

- *While historians point to the impressive advances made in the medical sciences during the twentieth century, experts project that the pace of discovery will quadruple in the next twenty-one years.*

- *This ocean of discovery comes at a time when NIH funding for life sciences research is at its highest level, ever. It comes at a time when the baby-boomers will soon create previously unseen demand for health care services and for novel treatment options.*
- *It comes at a time when the world has been flattened, so that companies that conduct research or provide services to the medical device sector can be operated virtually anywhere in the world.*
- *The convergence of discovery, demand and resources in this manner points to obvious opportunities for companies that have learned to leverage medical device research. Whether this*
- *investment is structured as seed-stage capital for new ventures, growth capital for adolescent companies or capital for strategic acquisitions, the ability to recognize the characteristics of a successful medical device venture is the key to success.*

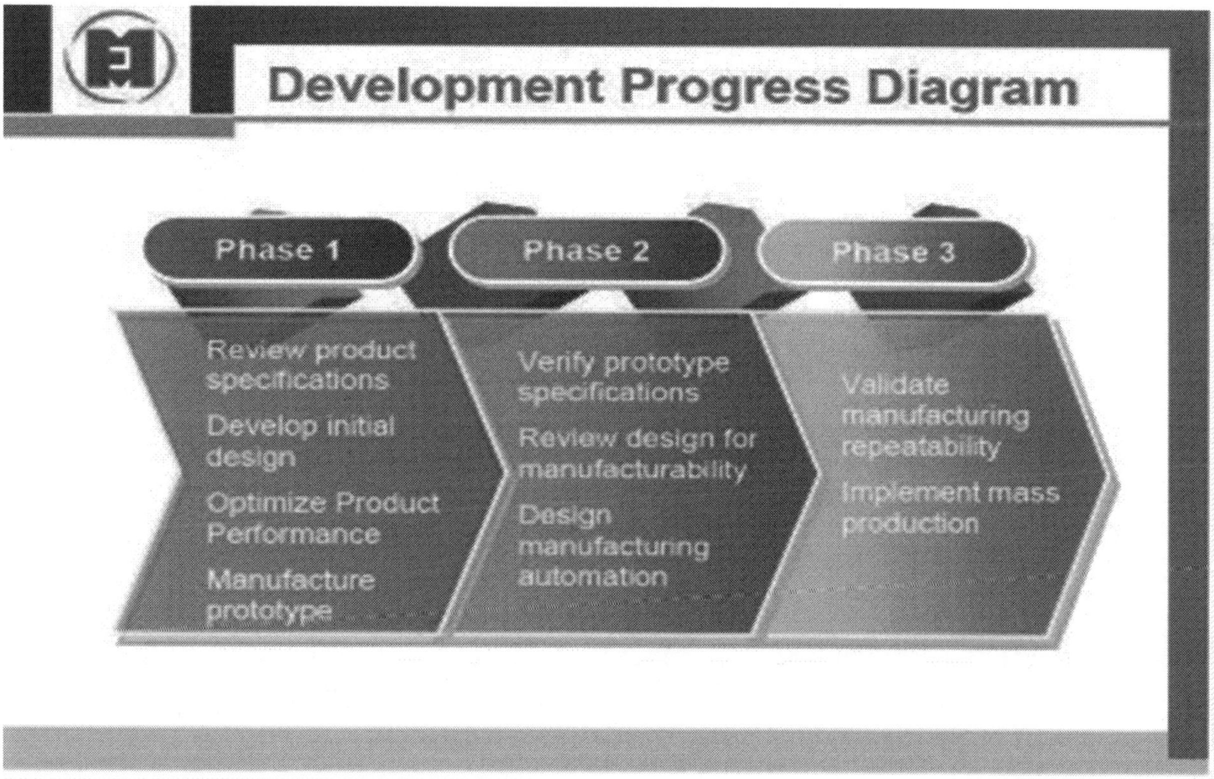

http://www.mdtmag.com/articles/2014/01/workflow-analysis-and-medical-device-development

Workflow Analysis and Medical Device Development

Michelle Jones, Technical Writer

Workflow analysis has been a central part of business improvement for several years now; however, it is still a relatively new concept in medical device engineering. Medical device development is a rapidly growing industry and globalization is increasing competition for smaller manufacturers. Improvements to the product development workflows may be able provide the competitive edge needed to speed up development and be the first to reach the market with new devices.

The development and manufacturing of new medical devices starts with the physicians and medical professionals. A new device must provide improvements beyond cost savings in the manufacturing process, so a workflow analysis must be integrated into the decision-making process and early development stages, as well as in the manufacturing.

The key to a smooth development process is for the physicians involved to have the opportunity to create a very clear and objective set of requirements.

A successful piece of medical equipment depends largely on how much value it adds to a medical professional's work, how affordable it is and how easy it is to operate. Ease of operation and usefulness should be at the heart of all medical devices.

Therefore, the first step in implementing a workflow analysis is to ensure that there is a common language between the physicians involved and the developing engineers. A robust, methodological approach that is managed by a well-designed workflow can reduce the development time and the development cycles substantially. This first step should include developing a list of specifications for the new device, which is then categorized and described in detail. At this point simplified solutions for document management are very useful for all involved.

Because medical devices are precision instruments that are guided by the skilled hand of a physician or medical profession, it is very difficult for an engineer to develop a feeling for the tool they are designing. A skilled physician finds this very difficult to explain and the result is that newly developed medical devices often do not fully meet the initial expected design. This results in numerous development cycles until the physician is happy with the new prototype.

The next stage of the process is manufacturing. During manufacturing automation flexibility can also help to improve the process.

Automation Flexibility

An efficient and modern workflow requires automation; however, traditional workflow automation tends to be a simple linear path with fixed points where there is a pass or fail. This model works well in business and manufacturing but it lacks the dynamic flexibility that is required in development and testing.

The solution is workflow software, which provides automation but allows an element of flexibility in the process.

Automation has been used in automotive, pharmaceuticals, consumer and electronics industries for years, but the use of robotics in medical device manufacturing has been slower on the uptake.

Traditional automation has been too expensive for niche medical device manufacturers to implement. Flexible automation is providing a new opportunity for manufacturers to meet commercial pressures to automate production. Automation flexibility allows different products to be produced on the same system, and allows changes to a product specification to be implemented without the need to rebuild the production line.

Medical device manufacturers often focus on the research and design of a new product and overlook the requirements of the actual manufacturing process. A device needs not only to be perfect for the physician, but it needs to be designed in such a way that it can be manufactured in a cost-efficient way.

Automated manufacturing provides benefits to medical device production beyond the initial construction. The nature of medical devices means that they need to be constructed in an extremely clean environment. There can be no risk of cross contamination of devices from humans during production. Using robots in the construction and packaging of devices eliminates almost all risk of contamination.

Other benefits to automating medical manufacturing include improved product quality by eliminating human error; improving worker safety; increased speed of production; reduction in training and staff cover, and faster time to market.

While one of the biggest advantages of flexible systems is the increase in profitability once installed and to reduction in risk, they also allow for the continuous improvement of product development. With flexible automation mature products can be quickly optimized if it is realized that the product does not perfectly suit a physician's needs. Likewise, the production of the device can also be optimized.

Automation also provides huge cost savings in testing. One example is that of testing balloon catheters.

An automated test can be completed in 30 seconds while a human tester will take around two minutes. This represents a cost reduction of around $43,000 a year in the final stages of manufacturing.

As research, development, manufacturing and testing all become more competitive, automation is starting to play a vital role in allowing companies to compete in a global market.

The Bayh-Dole Revolution

- The political groundwork for the medical device boom was laid in 1980 when the Bayh-Dole Act was passed. Prior to the Bayh-Dole Act, partnerships between academia and private medical device companies were severely constrained. Any new product developed with government-funded research belonged to the government. For obvious reasons, the government was not in the best position to exploit and commercialize new inventions. The Bayh-Dole Act represented a sea change in federal policy on the private exploitation of government-funded research. The policy, restated, was simple: allowing commercial interests to exploit devices funded with U.S. tax dollars was the best and the fastest way to achieve medical advancement and give the government the highest return on its research investment.

- The Bayh-Dole Act allows research institutions to patent and retain ownership of inventions they create using federal grant monies, but there are strings. For starters, the academic institution must enter into a funding agreement with a federal agency.

- The funding agreement requires the institution to disclose to the agency new inventions derived from the research paid for by a particular grant. But the institution can elect to retain ownership of the invention by notifying the agency as well.

- In order to retain ownership, the institution must give the United States a non-exclusive license to use the invention (although the United States rarely makes use of these licenses). The institution is allowed to license the invention to a company owned by a variety of private interests, including researchers, private equity firms and device manufacturers. The private company can exploit the licensed technology for commercial gain but may not sit on the technology. If the company does not move forward with reasonable diligence, the federal agency that made the research grant can exercise its "march-in rights" and reclaim ownership of the technology. The Bayh-Dole Act also places restrictions on the manufacturing of products developed from federally funded research, requiring them to be manufactured exclusively in the United States.
- **The Three Stages of a Successful Medical Device Venture**
- Assume that researchers at an institution have made a promising invention that has resulted in patentable technologies. The institution and its researchers now license the technology to a newly formed medical device company. The period immediately
- following the license is the venture phase. If the company can develop the relationships it needs to survive, it moves to the second stage, the growth stage. If successful at testing its products, the company then moves to the third stage, the commercialization stage.
- A mature medical device venture has the critical mass to fully commercialize a proven technology or position itself to be acquired by a larger entity that could even more effectively commercialize the technology. A technology licensed from a research institution only has value if it is fully commercialized, meaning that a venture's success depends on whether it can successfully reach maturity by navigating through the venture and growth stages. To get through these stages it is essential to have a clear understanding of what the venture's likely structure and business goals will be at each stage.

- Phase 1—The Venture Stage
- Medical device ventures that spin-out of research institutions all have the same goals at the venture stage:
- (1) obtain exclusive license rights to commercialize promising, patented technologies; (2) structure proper relationships with research institutions, investors, vendors and device manufacturers; and (3) develop a corporate structure that maximizes their intellectual property and relationships to the greatest possible advantage.
- THE IMPORTANCE OF INTELLECTUAL PROPERTY
- Medical devices derive economic value from their uniqueness. If a venture-stage device company does not take steps to safeguard its intellectual property, others may attempt to exploit the underlying technology. If others are using the technology, the technology loses its uniqueness, and the value of the technology is lost or diminished. Consequently, protecting patents is critical for a company that seeks to develop and commercialize a new medical device.
- If the patents are licensed from an academic institution that was the beneficiary of federal grant monies, the device venture should take great pains to conduct due diligence to ensure that technology was appropriately patented by the institution before the technology is licensed. Too often venture-stage device companies invest significant time and resources into a technology, only to learn that the technology was not appropriately patented by the institution that is licensing it to them. Other times, the technology that is the subject of the venture infringes on others' patent claims. In either event, it is better to determine whether there is a problem with the underlying intellectual property at the outset, rather than after the company has been set up and employees have been hired. If this is not done at the outset, troubling intellectual property questions will almost certainly come to light when investors bring in sophisticated due diligence teams to examine the venture's intellectual property prior to making an investment.
- STRUCTURING EFFECTIVE RELATIONSHIPS

- Venture-stage medical device companies often emerge from research institutions that use federal research funds to spark invention. The Bayh-Dole Act incentivizes the institution to attempt to develop new technologies and to share license fees with the researchers/inventors who developed the technologies. The most common means of doing this is to license a new patented technology to a venture-stage device company that is owned in part by the researchers/inventors. The research institution can participate in the venture by taking an ownership stake in the company, a license fee for the technology or both.
- The institution derives economic benefit from the license fees it receives from the venture, as well as the prestige associated with having its name associated with cutting-edge research. The more recognition it receives for such research, the easier it will be to attract additional private and public research funding for other projects.
- Another critical part of a successful venture-stage device company is a group of researchers/inventors who are eager to take their research out of the laboratory and into a commercial setting. Although many researcher/inventors will be eager to see the subject of their work taken into a setting in which they could derive economic benefit from it, many companies fail at the venture stage because they do not have the necessary mass of researchers.
- This most often occurs when there are multiple groups of researchers/inventors at an institution whose work contributes to a new patented technology. One group may be eager to take the technology into a translational setting, while others may be more comfortable remaining in the laboratory working on pre-clinical research. In many cases, academic or personal rivalries act as barriers to full participation in the venture. In other cases, researchers either lack the will or acumen to participate in a venture driven by profit motives rather than academic values. When the start-up company begins to operate without one of the critical researchers or research group's participation, difficulties will arise when the company begins to leverage the research that the missing researchers contributed. When investing in a venture stage company, it is important not only to ensure that the technology is sound but also to

ensure that all of the critical researchers/inventors are committed to working with the venture to take the technology to the next stage.

- After the venture-stage company has secured the appropriate intellectual property and the participation of the key researchers/inventors, the company has the building blocks of a successful medical device company, but building blocks are not enough.
- A January 2004 report issued by the Food and Drug Administration (FDA) and the Association of American Medical Colleges estimated the cost of bringing a new drug or medical device to market to be $800 million. As the venture-stage device company grows, so will its need for funding.
- Private investors' participation in the venture is required. This investment can come from a variety of sources. In some cases, device manufacturers will invest directly in the venture, taking a direct ownership position. More often, however, these companies shy away from venture-stage companies, preferring instead to participate in more developed companies whose devices have been taken through FDA testing. Most venture-stage device companies will receive funding from venture capital groups or angel investors. These groups will tend to cluster their investment in companies that focus on specialized and discrete areas (e.g., nanotechnologies, orthopedics, stents). Devices aimed at treating diseases with broad commercial appeal (e.g., cardiac stents) are much more likely to receive funding than those which are aimed at rare diseases.

Biotech vs. Pharmaceuticals: What's the Difference?

Biotechnology and pharmaceutical companies both produce medicines, but the medicines made by biotechnology companies are derived from living organisms while those made by pharmaceutical companies generally have a chemical basis.

The coining of the term biopharma further complicates matters.[1] The term describes companies that are using both biotechnology and chemical sources in their medical research and development (R&D) efforts.

Biotechnology

Common products such as beer and wine, laundry detergent, and anything made of plastic are all biotechnology products. Humans have employed biotechnology since ancient times to breed animals and improve their crops.

However, in the modern financial world, biotechnology companies comprise an industry sector collectively known as the biotech. They research, develop, and produce a wide variety of commercial products, though most of them focus on medical or agricultural applications.

Biotechnology firms use the processes of living organisms as they manufacture products or solve problems. The identification and sourcing of DNA have helped the industry make great leaps. Companies in this sector have developed pest-resistant crops, created biofuels like ethanol, and developed gene cloning.

There also have been big product introductions in biopharma drugs.

Pharmaceuticals

As an industry, pharmaceutical companies research, develop, and market medicines made primarily from artificial sources.

Some modern pharmaceutical companies have a long history, such as Bayer AG, the German company whose founder trademarked aspirin in 1899.[7] As of 2019, the world's top pharmaceutical company was Johnson & Johnson, followed by Novartis and Merck.[8]

The Businesses of Biotech and Pharmaceuticals

Purely from the investor's perspective, biotech and pharmaceuticals are very different propositions. An analyst will look at the amount a firm spends on research and development (R&D) as a percentage of sales to compare one company to another.

Biotechnology companies generally have very high operating costs as they are involved in research, development, and testing that takes years to complete.[9] The result could be a historic breakthrough or utter failure. Investors in their stocks are along for the ride, up or down.

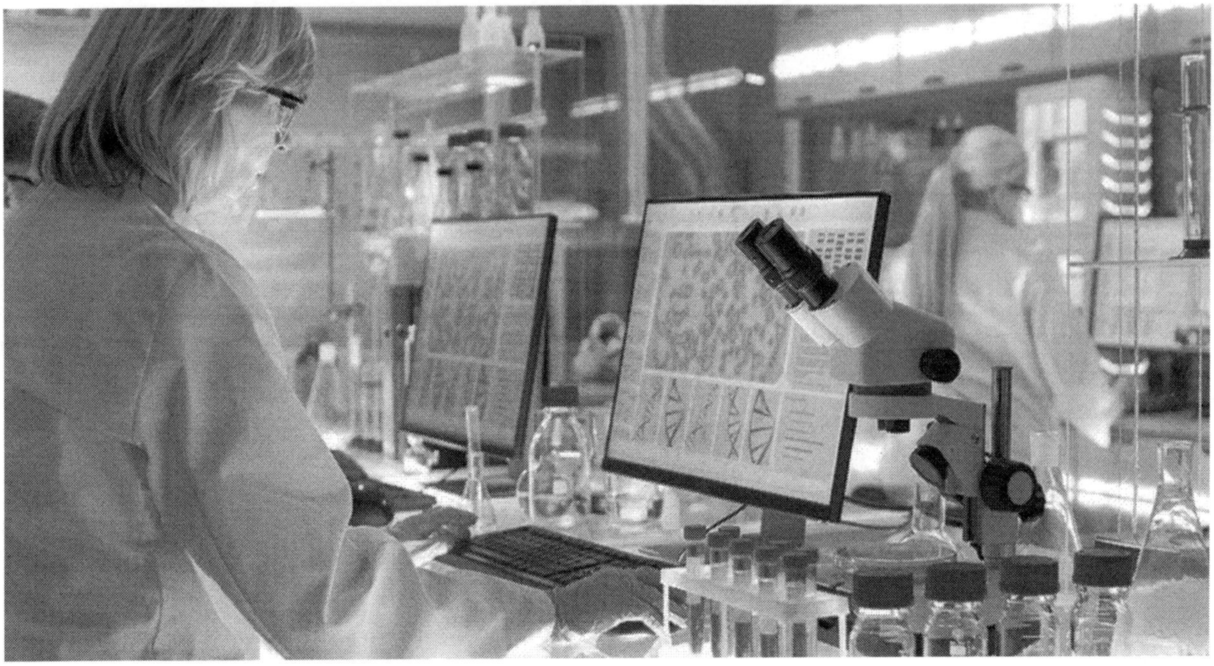

https://www.forbes.com/sites/forbestechcouncil/2019/05/29/the-future-of-pharma-the-role-of-biotech-companies/#2f2b22316bb3

The Future of Pharma: The Role Of Biotech Companies

Naheed Kurji

President & CEO at Cyclica

Despite the growth of the world's population and the increasing demand for drugs, the pharmaceutical industry has traditionally not innovated at the same pace. According to the *BBC*, Dr. Kees de Joncheere from the World Health Organization stated, "The system [pharmaceutical industry] has served us well in terms of developing good new medicines, but in the past 10–20 years there has been very little breakthrough in innovation." From 2006-2015, the average number of approved new molecular entities (NME) and new biologic license application (BLA) filings by the FDA was approximately 32, and research (via the *Washington Post*) indicates that 78% of patents approved by the FDA correspond to medications already in the market.

Over the past couple of years, we have seen a shift. In 2017 and 2018, the number of approved NMEs and BLAs increased to 46 and 59 respectively, compared to 45 in 2015. In 2018, 19 of the 59 novel approved drugs were considered first-in-class, 34 received orphan designation for treating rare diseases, and 24 received fast-track designation as they are intended for serious conditions with unmet medical needs. While this is encouraging, it is important to note that a 2019 IQVIA Institute report found that 64% of FDA-approved drugs in 2018 (via *Fierce Biotech*) originated from emerging biopharma companies.

Looking forward, I predict that it will become increasingly important for the industry to continue to develop breakthrough treatments that offer greater benefits beyond incremental improvements and discover novel treatments for unmet medical needs, including rare and orphan diseases. As the president and CEO of a biotech company, I believe that much of the innovation of these new breakthrough treatments will be spearheaded by emerging biotech companies.

(While some make distinctions between biotech and biopharma, biotech in this context refers to companies that are not considered large pharmaceutical companies, irrespective of their modality.) As a result, the industry will likely experience disintegration, a new balance of power among stakeholders and a greater focus on personalized medicines.

Industry Transformation And Disintegration

With the advancements in technology provided by biotech companies and others, pharma may experience an industry-wide disintegration.

Large pharma companies, traditionally responsible for all aspects of the drug discovery pipeline, will continue to outsource these processes to smaller, disruptive companies with simple and affordable alternatives. As Clayton Christensen in *The Innovator's Prescription* explains, this disintegration will allow large pharma companies to curb investments from less profitable activities within their business and refocus efforts to result in greater profits and productivity. In a recent article published by Endpoints News (registration required), the authors suggest growing competition and decreased return on investment of R&D as key reasons for the cutting-back of non-core business processes.

Often this disintegration involves outsourcing aspects of the pharmaceutical supply chain to specialist companies like contract research organizations (CROs), as well as contract development and manufacturing organizations (CDMOs). I've also seen large pharma look to small biotech companies for in-licensing drugs. According to the IQVIA Institute report, emerging biopharma companies "patented almost two-thirds of new drugs launched in 2018," although large pharma stills plays an important role. Overall, from discovery to clinical trials, it seems disintegration is well underway in pharma.

A New Balance Of Power

The disintegration of the drug discovery, development and distribution pipeline could result in a new balance of power in the industry and provide entrants with an opportunity to succeed in an industry previously saturated with substantial barriers to entry.

There continues to be a growing number of early stage, well-funded biotech companies -- and companies focused on artificial intelligence for drug discovery and development -- rapidly emerging on the global stage, such as Nimbus Therapeutics, Puma Biotech, Blueprint Medicines and Recursion Pharmaceuticals. As the CEO of one of these companies, I've seen investors, both traditional and corporate, flocking. We are seeing big moves in the M&A space; according to *The New York Times* (paywall), the value of deals for both biotech and pharmaceutical companies reportedly approaching $146 billion within the first two months of 2019 in the U.S. -- more than what was announced in all of 2018, 2017, or 2018.

The *New York Times* article noted that "acquisitions of American biotech companies are surging, and so are the prices that buyers are willing to pay." As a result, large pharma companies may look to hold onto their position by overpaying for high-potential biotech companies, which could provide a great opportunity to other new entrants.

An Emphasis On Prevention And Precision

In my experience, pharma has traditionally been attracted to large, profitable markets and developing drugs that are of "blockbuster status" -- usually at the expense of smaller markets with less reimbursement, and less opportunity to drive return on investment.

It is hard to imagine a shift focused on prevention given the industry's appetite for large markets.

However, with the catalytic effect of entirely new therapies, advances in technology and the consumerization of health, I expect more targeted drugs that will prevent disease and address the needs of specific groups of patients in other global markets. **With the emergence of preventive medicine and precision medicine (an approach that my company and others, such as Verge Genomics and the Beijing Genomics Institute, use), valuable drugs will arise because of this diagnostic precision.**

According to a recent article in Science Daily, "Sequencing of the human genome and the development of powerful and affordable DNA sequencing technologies has ushered in a new era of precision oncology, in which patients are treated with customized therapies designed to target the specific mutations within their tumor."

The challenges are bigger than ever, but the future of pharma looks promising. Biotech companies could lead the charge in scientific and business model innovation and will be responsible for much of these shifts in pharma. And while consolidation of biotech by large pharma companies is likely to occur, a new class of biotech companies that rival large pharma will emerge. I believe the pharmaceutical industry will reinvent itself and will play a significant role in improving the health of billions of people around the world.

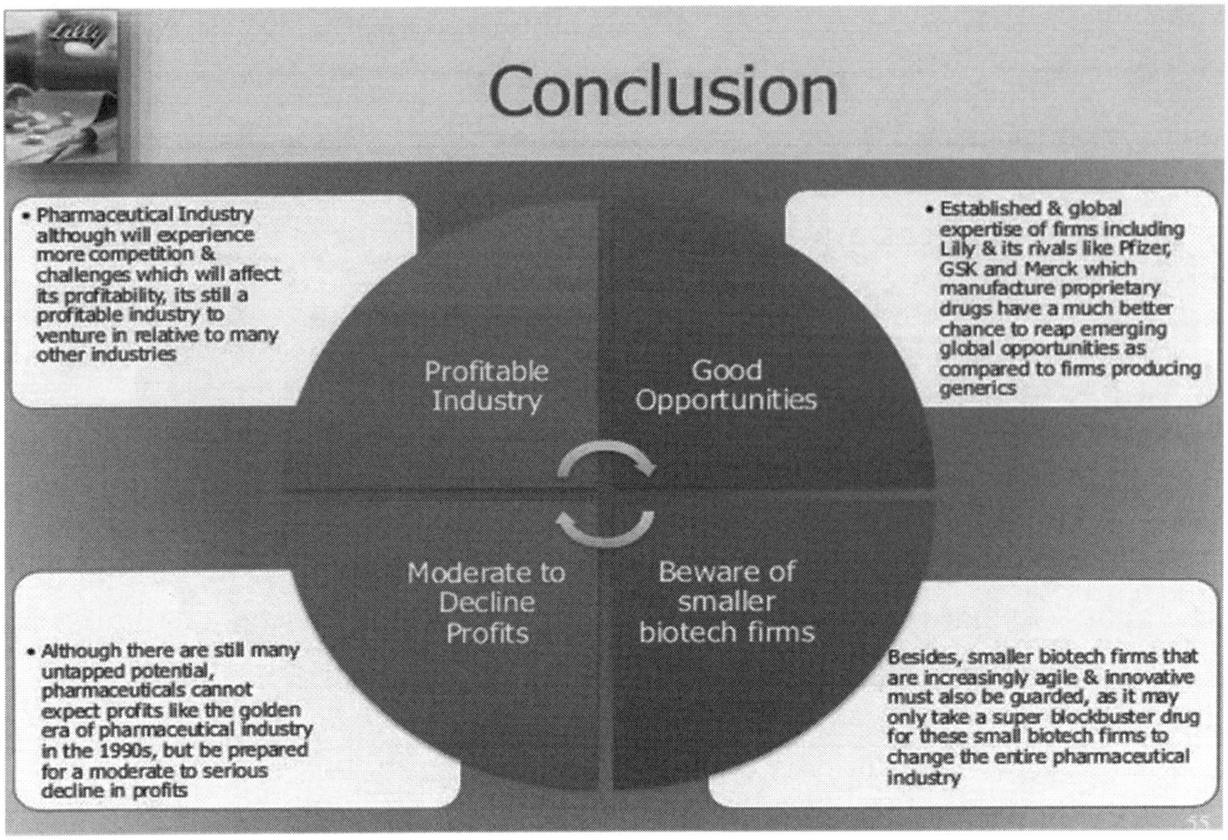

"Beware of Smaller Biotech Firms!?"

The above slide from an Eli Lily PowerPoint presentation clearly warns big pharma of the substantial threat of smaller biotech firms to disrupt the entire pharmaceutical industry!

What do they see on the horizon which will challenge their drug empires?

Will the next unicorn biotech's completely disrupt the pharma empire cartels? Perhaps even someone reading our research books will be a part of the team which will lead these new enterprises!

Biotech Stocks Catch Fire

I think biotech is going to be a focus of the entire world for years," Loncar said. "I think this opened people's eyes to that."

Institutional and individual investors are crowding into targeted biotech stocks — hoping the next innovation in the coronavirus pandemic will pay off big. It's an "amazing time in medicine."

Loncar believes that will likely continue to be the case for years to come. Covid-19 treatment and vaccine news has floated most biotech boats, he says. The market for biotech initial public offerings is among the strongest the industry has seen in years. In addition, follow-on offerings from biotech stocks have already outpaced 2019 numbers.

Biotech stocks are reviving a powerful rally started late last year. In the fourth quarter of 2019, biotechs surged, sending the more than 500 stocks in IBD's Medical-Biomed/Biotech industry group to a collective gain of 32% for the quarter.

Meanwhile, the Nasdaq rose 12%. A strong earnings season and a major run of mergers throughout 2019 bolstered biotech investing.

What are the right ingredients for a blockbuster unicorn IPO?

This year, biotech stocks plunged alongside the broader market as the coronavirus pandemic slammed Wall Street. But after closing at their lowest point this year March 18, the industry group has soared 56%, as of Friday which closely shadowed the Nasdaq's 61% rebound, and clobbered the S&P 500's 48% bounce.

Three more biotechs go public Friday as nothing seems able to slow down the 2020 train.

In a recent interview, Nasdaq's head of healthcare listings Jordan Saxe told Endpoints News the tally was 56 IPOs with a total $11.3 billion raised. With three more biotechs going public Friday, the number is now closer to 60, a number not seen in any of the last four years.

And more are coming, with Galecto filing its S-1 on Thursday. Saxe added that a "conservative" estimate of the final 2020 IPO number will end up between 65 and 70.

020 will stand out in the history of biotech for a variety of reasons, starting with the unprecedented, rapid-fire response to Covid-19. But somewhere in the top 5 there will be a special spotlight on the IPO boom, which has been funneling billions of dollars into drug development and offering some key players a shot at rock star status

Now is the Time to jump in!

These are exciting times for biotechnology, pharmaceuticals, and medical device development, as many innovative biotech companies will be launched by new entrepreneurs. As the rapid pace of innovation accelerates, who knows what incredible medical breakthroughs we will see in the next few years, led by new generations of scientists, lawyers, and entrepreneurs!

Addendum

Reference and study materials:

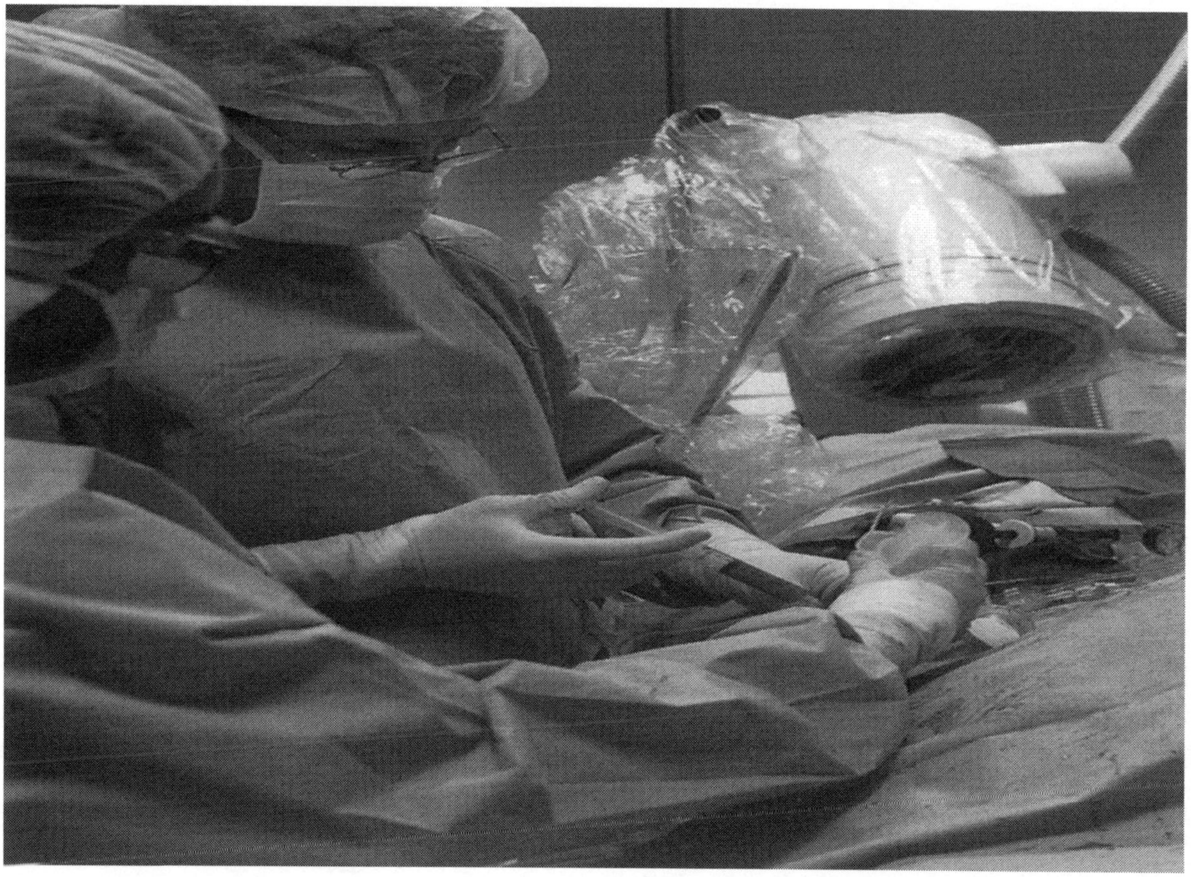

Boy Gets First of Kind Stem Cell Transplant Doctors at Beaumont Hospital in Royal Oak, Mich., led by Dr. Cindy Grines and Dr. William O'Neill, suggested an experimental treatment. The patient, 16-year-old Dimitri Bonnville, had a massive heart attack after being shot in the heart with a nail gun. "This treatment was

Dimitri's only option, aside from a heart transplant," says William O'Neill, M.D., Beaumont's chief of cardiology

An invitation to join the
Quest for the Holy Grail
Of Regenerative Cardiology

" If a cure is not affordable, it is not a solution." Dr Devi Shetty

CardioMatrex ™, is a first-in-class, off the shelf therapeutic combining stem cells and tissue-engineering matrix, to regenerate and or restore dying and diseased hearts in a brief 45-minute procedure similar to an angioplasty.

Join the Quest to develop a new cardio biologic – let's collaborate to finally bring a revolutionary change in the future of interventional cardiology.

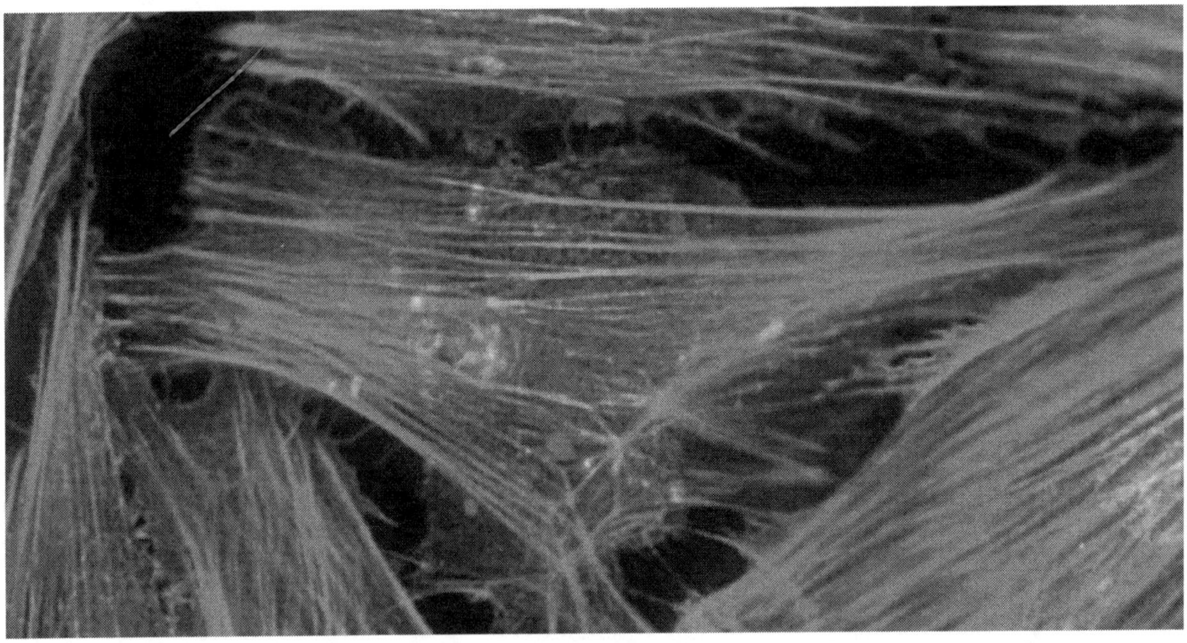

CardioMatrex Tissue Engineering Product

CardioMatrex ™

The Future of Cardio Therapeutics

THE WORLD'S FIRST COMMERCIALLY PRODUCED- COMBINATION BIOLOGICS THERAPEUTIC, FOR ADVANCED HEART DISEASE, COMBINING HUMAN GRADE EXPANDED ADULT STEM CELLS, SUSPENDED WITHIN NANO-MATRIX AND HYDROGELS

CardioMatrex ™, also has the potential to be used prophylactically, to slow or essentially prevent heart disease.

CardioMatrex Tissue Engineering Biologix Corporation, is a virtual biopharmaceutical company, which is now sharing the developmental research acquired over many years in an open-source collaboration.

Billions of Dollars, Euros, British pounds, and Yen have funded 100's of the world's best scientists over the last 20 years, creating a vast body of work, research and clinical studies in the quest to develop an off-the-shelf cardio therapeutic.

The time has arrived to make this illusive dream a reality!

We are seeking students, scientists, lawyers and global leaders looking for a quest, and medical holy grail. We have a real-world company and potentially the greatest new heart biologic drug ever developed, which will change forever the future of interventional cardiology. This company requires new teams of investigators and collaborators, and new corporate officers, directors and impassioned leaders, who will review the vast body of research and begin to see and understand the truly amazing potential of CardioMatrex ™.

However, this will not be easy or inexpensive. Biologics drug production labs are notoriously expensive to build for commercial levels of production. Also, the FDA has only approved a hand full of stem cell-based products in the last decade because stem cell-based biologics are held to the very highest standards ever imposed on any drug manufacturer. There is also tremendous resistance from many stakeholders, including hospitals, medical providers, and pharmaceutical companies, as interventional heart procedures are the most lucrative income of most hospitals, and if those expensive heart operations suddenly vanished because someone discovered a magical cure, many of these hospitals would not have any profit margin and would have to close like so many have already.

American interventional cardiologists are the highest paid physicians in the world. Why would they want to change the current paradigm?

Please try to imagine, a simple 45-minute, non-surgical catheter procedure similar to an angioplasty, performed under local anesthesia; CardioMatrex ™, would revolutionize the practice of cardiology!

So, we had to look at the whole world to determine which country had the highest levels of heart disease, and would have the political and medical professionals which would align with this special, holy grail medical mission.

Mission Statement

To explore the cellular and molecular mechanisms underlying the development of heart disease and seek new therapeutic strategies for the treatment of those diseases. To develop new, emerging technologies, biomedical devices and biologics, establish laboratories, worldwide partnerships and humanitarian missions.

The Quest for the cardiovascular holy grail: myocardial regeneration

The CardioMatrex mission is to bring advanced new drugs to the world for a fraction of their US costs.

Our first global mission is to bring our cardio therapeutics to India.

More than 2 million Indians need, but cannot afford, heart surgery!

India's no.1 killer: Heart disease

Largest-ever study of deaths shows heart ailments have replaced communicable diseases as the biggest killer in rural & urban India.

Now researchers say India, a country with more than one billion people, will likely account for 60 per cent of heart disease patients worldwide.

The heart disease mutation carried by 60 million!

Indian scientists express this genetic risk as an odds ratio; where 1.2 would be a small effect and 2.0 a large one. For the MYBPC3 mutation, *the odds ratio is almost off-scale, a staggering 7.0.!*

Carriers usually show few symptoms until middle age, but after that age most are symptomatic and suffer from a range of effects, at worst sudden cardiac death. The mutation almost guarantees the development of the disease and Indians suffer heart attacks at an earlier age, often without prior symptoms or warning.

CardioMatrex's proprietary technology expands populations of cord blood stem cells to create a therapeutic dose to treat such patients. The expanded CD133 cells are combined with various tissue engineering jells, such as self-assembling nano-peptides; hydrogels, collagen, or nano matrix to create a completely restorative therapeutic. To produce 500 doses of Cardio-Matrex per day,($180 million dollars/ year @ $1000 dollars/dose) requires cord blood banks to assure a continuous uninterrupted supply of genetically screened and HLA tested strategic reserves. Note: upon M&A or other Exit Strategy, in a short 5 years; these cord blood banks reserves are valued at between $400-$600 million dollars combined. How exactly? Please review medical and financial data attached.

CardioMatrex is a tissue engineering product, capable of the regenerating aged and diseased heart tissues. Available for critically ill patients, this humanitarian lifesaving biologic, represents a quantum leap ahead of all competitors.

Cardio-Matrex Tissue Engineering Biologix Inc.

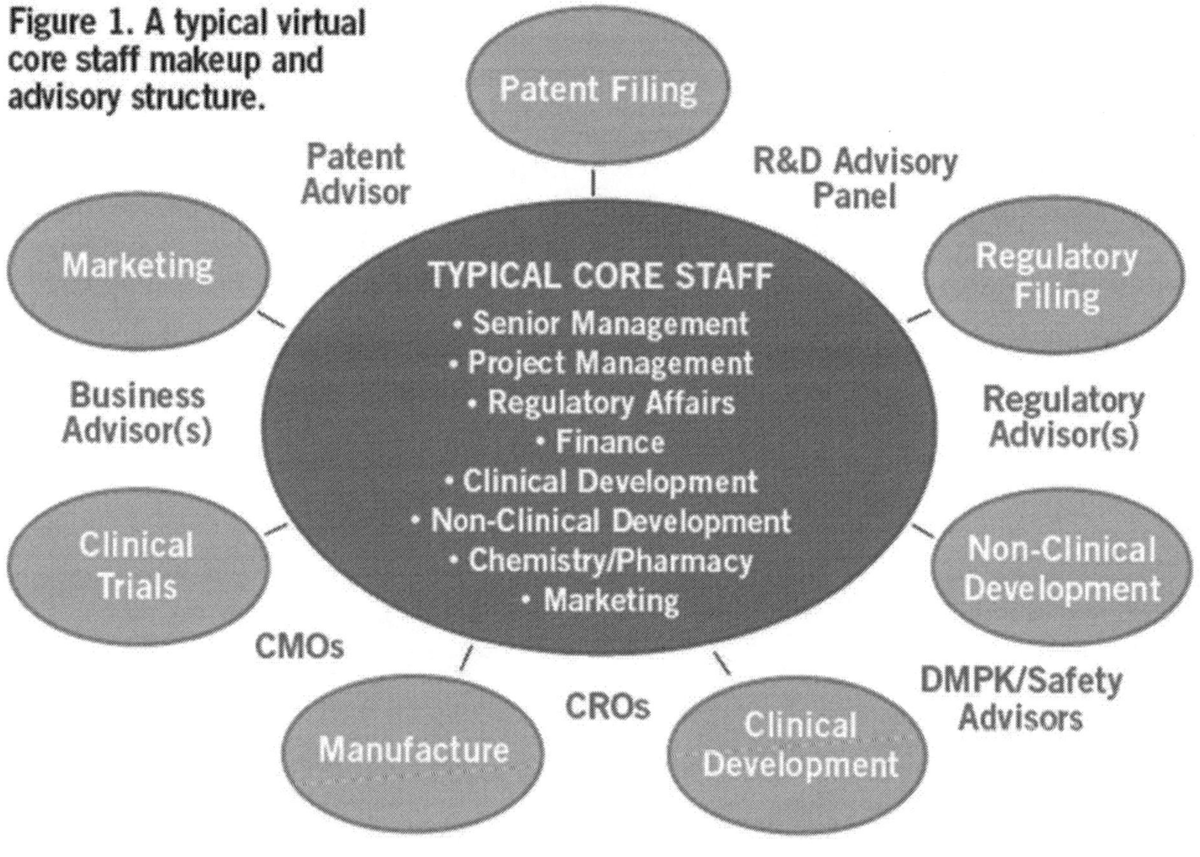

Regulatory strategy.

By treating thousands of patients in phase III trials, under a humanitarian regulatory exemption, leading to approvals for the new drugs in India, CardioMatrex Inc, is collecting enormous amounts of "real world" data, over the first 5 years, which the FDA now recognizes as 'fast track' to approvals back in the states.

Let's be clear; CardioMatrex or another biosimilar is the future of interventional cardiology. This is actually a world class opportunity. It's time to seize the moment!

In Arthurian romance the mystical, magical quest of the Grail is a popular story that has its roots in medieval times, though its seeds may be from much earlier. It uses allegories to blend together pagan motifs, Christian tradition and political and social concerns of the day into a story of spiritual evolution for the main protagonists who must remain true to the quest.

The quest was not really to find a material object but to complete a series of tests and lessons to achieve a state of spiritual perfection, and perhaps that is why its popularity remains as undiminished now as it was in earlier times.

The long-sought Holy Grail for heart attack patients has been a method to regenerate healthy new tissue, but the basic building blocks required to remodel an injured heart have remained elusive—until now.

Repair of the damaged cardiac tissue has been considered the holy grail of cardiac medicine driving researchers for years. Myocardial damage in an adult heart leads to widespread cardiomyocyte loss without active replacement of the dead cardiac tissue, ultimately resulting in formation of scar at the site of injury. Current therapies are designed only to limit the extent of scar formation and are unable to offer restoration of lost cardiac tissue, leading to a progressive decline in cardiac function. As a consequence, cardiac diseases continue to rise and are a significant cause of morbidity and mortality around the world.

The last 10 years have witnessed the dawn of stem cell therapy for cardiac repair with promising true cellular replacement and restoration of cardiac tissue damaged due to pathological injury. Multiple stem cell types derived from bone marrow, heart, adipose tissue, and cortical bone have been tested in small and large animal models of myocardial damage. Different populations of cardiac stem cells have been reported to date and, importantly, all of them have been shown to differentiate into three cardiac cell types, i.e., myocytes, endothelial cells, and smooth muscle cells, contribute towards neovascularization, and significantly improve function after myocardial damage.

Heart disease remains the number 1 killer

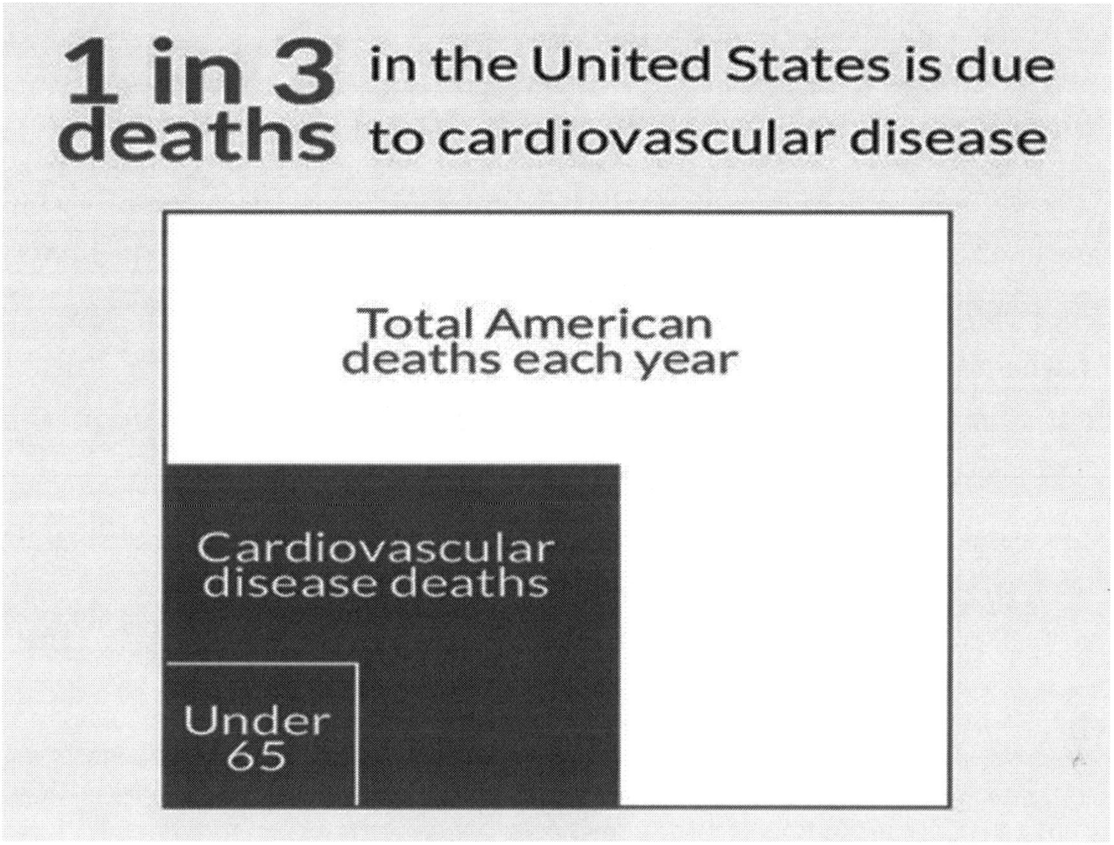

The world's biggest killer is **ischemic heart disease**, responsible for 16% of the world's total deaths

https://millionhearts.hhs.gov/learn-prevent/cost-consequences.html

Costs & Consequences

Heart disease and stroke can be fatal, but they can also lead to serious illness, disability, and lower quality of life. Suffering a stroke may lead to significant disability, such as paralysis, speech difficulties, and emotional problems. Following a heart attack, individuals frequently suffer fatigue and depression, and they may find it more difficult to engage in physical activities.

Key Facts

Together, heart disease and stroke are among the most widespread and costly health problems facing the nation today. On a personal level, families who experience heart disease or stroke have to deal with not only medical bills but also lost wages and the real potential of a decreased standard of living.

- Approximately 1.5 million heart attacks and strokes occur every year in the United States.
- More than 800,000 people in the United States die from cardiovascular disease each year—that's 1 in every 3 deaths, and about 160,000 of them occur in people under age 65.
- Heart disease kills roughly the same number of people in the United States each year as cancer, lower respiratory diseases (including pneumonia), and accidents combined.
- Heart disease and stroke cost the nation an estimated $316.6 billion in health care costs and lost productivity in 2015.
- ABOUT 1 IN 6 HEALTHCARE DOLLARS IS SPENT ON HEART DISEASE!

Lifetime Costs of Medical Care After Heart Failure

Heart failure (HF) is a global pandemic affecting at least 26 million people worldwide and is increasing in prevalence. HF health expenditures are considerable and will increase dramatically with an ageing population. Despite the significant advances in therapies and prevention, mortality and morbidity are still high and quality of life poor. The prevalence, incidence, mortality and morbidity rates reported show geographic variations, depending on the different aetiologias and clinical characteristics observed among patients with HF.

Currently every year in US there are still 915,000 new cases of HF.

Cardiovascular services remain among the top clinical areas of healthcare expenditures nationally and, at the same time, are consistently among the top financially performing services within hospitals.[2]

Hospitalization for acute myocardial infarction (MI) remains 1 of the top 5 most expensive principal diagnoses in the United States.[1] One of the largest cost components of a hospitalization for MI is coronary revascularization, mostly with percutaneous coronary intervention (PCI).

More than 23 million adults worldwide have heart failure [1]. Although survival after heart failure diagnosis has improved over time, mortality from heart failure remains high. Approximately 50% of people diagnosed with heart failure will die within 5 years [2]. Many of these patients will progress to advanced heart failure (AHF, known as 'stage D'), which is characterized by symptoms at rest despite maximal medical therapy [3]. These patients are considered refractory, and upon reaching this stage both patient and physician are faced with difficult ethical decisions. Consideration of advanced therapies such as left ventricular assist devices (LVADs) or transplant, involvement of palliative care, transition to hospice care, and end-of-life issues such as advance directives and implantable cardioverter-defibrillator (ICD) deactivation need to be addressed.

Implantable cardioverter defibrillators and cardiac resynchronization therapy

Primary prevention of sudden cardiac death in patients with systolic heart failure has rapidly become the most common indication for ICD implantation. Multiple trials have shown a clear mortality benefit in patients with cardiomyopathy and ventricular arrhythmia [21,22]. The mortality benefit may come at a price; although an older study showed that ICDs do not seem to affect patients' quality of life [23], newer studies have challenged this notion. One recent study reported more than 10-fold higher levels of phobic anxiety among patients with ICDs, especially among those who had received shocks [24•]. A large meta-analysis of over 5000 ICD patients reported an 11–28% incidence of depressive disorders and 11–26% incidence of anxiety disorder [25].

The concept of 'quality of death' in patients with ICDs is a challenging issue when patients approach end of life from progressive pump failure. Because ICDs perform the same function as external defibrillation, a decision to forego resuscitation should logically lead to deactivation of the ICD.

Indeed, there have been media reports of patients receiving multiple shocks, while families watch helplessly [26]. In a telephone survey of next of kin of patients with ICDs who died of any cause, 8% reported that their family member received a shock from their ICD in the minutes before death. Fewer than one-third of these next of kin reported a discussion about end-of-life management of defibrillators [27

Pfizer gets U.S. approval for $225,000 a year heart drug

Pfizer, which has touted tafamidis as a potential blockbuster product, set a list price of $225,000 a year for the medicine, which would be sold under the brand name Vyndaqel. Vyndaqel currently sells for about $100,000 a year outside the United States as a treatment for FAP. It was approved in Japan for transthyretin amyloid cardiomyopathy in May at a price of around $750,000 a year that was set by a government body, Pfizer said.

Pfizer believes there could be 400,000 to 500,000 patients in developed markets around the world and said the current rate of those diagnosed may be as low as 0.5 percent to 1 percent.

Both Alnylam Pharmaceuticals and Ionis Pharmaceuticals Inc have approved medicines that treat a similar disease called hereditary TTR amyloidosis, also caused by a buildup of transthyretin protein in the body. Those drugs cost around $450,000 a year.

Pfizer has touted tafamidis as one of its "15 in 5" - 15 experimental treatments in development, each with at least $1 billion annual sales potential that the drugmaker hopes to launch over a five-year period.

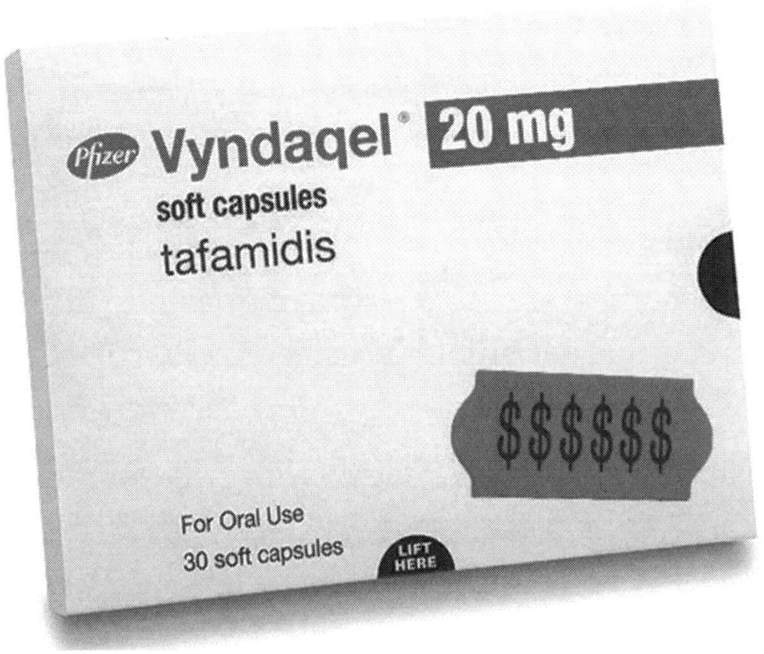

https://www.cardiovascularbusiness.com/topics/healthcare-economics/uss-most-expensive-cv-drug-needs-93-price-cut

Anicka Slachta | *February 14, 2020* | *Economics & Policy*

"It is the most expensive cardiovascular drug ever launched in the U.S., raising concerns about cost-effectiveness, affordability and access," Kazi et al. wrote. "A timely and rigorous cost-effectiveness evaluation would help inform clinical and policy discussions regarding uptake of tafamidis and may influence drug pricing as the drug enters the market."

But, at a price point of $225,000 per year, the medication isn't a feasible option for everyone.

Considering the fact that any savings from fewer CV hospitalizations per patient per year would be offset by patients surviving longer, Kazi and colleagues calculated U.S. healthcare spending would increase by $32.3 billion per year if all eligible patients received tafamidis therapy.

https://www.bloomberg.com/news/articles/2019-11-19/heart-failure-drug-from-pfizer-attracts-new-critics-over-price

Doctors Who Helped Develop Heart Drug Now Balk at $225,000-a-Year Price

The breakthrough pill costs $651 a day, and may be used by far more patients than anticipated.

Dr. Mathew Maurer – new drug Tafamidis – Pfizer

"Drugs don't work if people can't afford to take them"! Analysts are forecasting annual sales to exceed $1 billion in 2024, according to Refinitiv data. The company has been in talks with insurers and is confident the drug will be reimbursed at the $225,000 price, he said.

Reversing Heart Damage:

A Q&A WITH DR. STEVEN HOUSER

Posted March 5, 2020 by Temple Health

Temple cardiovascular researchers are developing new therapies that may soon dramatically change how patients are treated after a heart attack or heart failure. Cardiovascular disease still claims a life about every 90 seconds today.

Steven R. Houser, PhD, is Director of the Cardiovascular Research Center, Senior Associate Dean of Research, and Chair of Physiology at the Lewis Katz School of Medicine at Temple University.

He is also a former President of the American Heart Association.

Dr. Houser is on a mission to reverse heart damage, and his work is funded by over $25 million in research grants. But what drives him is deeply personal. Learn how his team's cell-therapy approach can help hearts heal more normally.

Dr. Houser: The Holy Grail for ischemic heart disease researchers like me is to find a way to replace dead tissue with normal, functioning heart muscle. We're at the forefront of research in this area.

About 10 years ago I set out to look for a cell that could grow new muscle and blood vessels for the heart. We tested many cell types and found a cortical bone stem cell with properties that appear to enhance the repair of the heart after a heart attack. A real bonus is that these cells are easy to obtain and grow in the lab.

The Food and Drug Administration (FDA) has approved numerous stem cell–based treatments for clinical trials. A 2013 report from the Pharmaceutical Research and Manufacturers of America lists 69 cell therapies as having clinical trials under review with the FDA, including 15 in phase 3 trials. The therapeutic categories represented in these trials include cardiovascular disease, skin diseases, cancer and related conditions, digestive disorders, transplantation, genetic disorders, musculoskeletal disorders, and eye conditions, among others.[14]

Still, the earliest stem cell therapies are likely years away. To date, the only stem cell–based treatment approved by the FDA for use in this country is for bone marrow transplantation.[15] As of 2010 (the latest year for which data are available), **more than 17,000 blood cancer patients had had successful stem cell transplants.[16]**

The Regulation of Stem Cells

In February 2014, the U.S. Court of Appeals for the District of Columbia Circuit upheld a 2012 ruling that a patient's stem cells for therapeutic use fall under the aegis of the FDA.[42] The appeals case involved the company Regenerative Sciences, which was using patients' MSCs in its Regenexx procedure to treat orthopedic problems.[43]

The FDA's Center for Biologics Evaluation and Research (CBER) regulates human cells, tissues, and cellular and tissue-based products (HCT/P) intended for implantation, transplantation, infusion, or transfer into a human recipient, including hematopoietic stem cells.

The Regenexx case highlights an ongoing debate about whether autologous MSCs are biological drugs subject to FDA approval or simply human cellular and tissue products. Some medical centers collect, concentrate, and reinject MSCs into a patient to treat osteoarthritis but do not add other agents to the injection. The FDA contends that any process that includes culturing, expansion, and added growth factors or antibiotics requires regulation because the process constitutes significant manipulation. Regenerexx has countered that the process does not involve the development of a new drug, which could be given to a number of patients, but rather a patient's own MSCs, which affects just that one patient.

To date, no U.S. companies have received FDA approval for any autologous MSC therapy, although a study is ongoing to assess the feasibility and safety of autologous MSCs for osteoarthritis.[45] One of the major risks with MSCs is that they could potentially lead to cancer or differentiation into bone or cartilage.[46]

mesoblast

https://www.mesoblast.com/product-candidates/cardiovascular-diseases/congestive-heart-failure

Innovative technology platform enables scalable manufacturing

Mesoblast's novel allogeneic product candidates are based on rare (approximately 1:100,000 in bone marrow) mesenchymal lineage cells that respond to tissue damage, secreting mediators that promote tissue repair and modulate immune responses.

Mesenchymal lineage cells are collected from the bone marrow of healthy adult donors and proprietary processes are utilized to expand them to a uniform, well characterized, and highly reproducible cell population. This enables manufacturing at industrial scale for commercial purposes. Another key feature of Mesoblast's cells is they can be administered to patients without the need for donor–recipient matching or recipient immune suppression.

Proprietary media formulations, advances in development of 3D bioreactor technology and automation are intended to deliver step-changes improvement in product yield.

Australia's Mesoblast, with a market value of about $500 million, is attempting to alter advanced heart failure, a leading cause of hospitalizations and deaths and an enormous cost burden.

They are among the farthest along in the stem cell industry at a time when Wall Street investors have focused on potentially big payoffs from immune-system based cancer therapies and rare disease treatments.

FDA Approves New York Blood Center's HEMACORD™ for Stem Cell Transplantation

3 http://www.prnewswire.com/news-releases/fda-approves-new-york-blood-centers-hemacord-for-stem-cell-transplantation-133646483.html

First FDA-Licensed Stem Cell Product

NEW YORK, The Food and Drug Administration has licensed HEMACORD™ (Hematopoietic Progenitor Cells-Cord, HPC-C) for allogeneic hematopoietic (blood-forming) stem cell transplantation, the first such approval of a stem cell product in the world.

According to the Food and Drug Administration's notification to New York Blood Center (NYBC), HEMACORD™ is "indicated for use in unrelated donor hematopoietic progenitor cell transplantation procedures... in patients with disorders affecting the hematopoietic system that are inherited, acquired, or result from myeloablative treatment." Such conditions could include patients with hematologic malignancies, primary immunodeficiency diseases, bone marrow failure, and beta-thalassemia. HEMACORD™ is indicated for use with children.

"We are thrilled to be the first public cord blood bank with an FDA-licensed product for transplantation," said Christopher D. Hillyer, MD, President and CEO of New York Blood Center (NYBC). Since 1996, NYBC's National Cord Blood Program (NCBP) at the Howard P. Milstein National Cord Blood Center has provided cord blood units for transplantation under an Investigational New Drug (IND) exemption from the FDA. The mission of the NCBP is to facilitate access to cord blood as a treatment option for patients, notably those from diverse ethnic backgrounds.

To obtain FDA licensure of HEMACORD™, all collection and manufacturing conditions of the cord blood units met FDA standards for product potency, purity and efficacy, and patient safety. NCBP's Biologics License Application (BLA) included extensive documentation of the systems and controls used, and the validations performed to ensure compliance with FDA standards in all steps of manufacturing (collections, processing, testing, typing, cryopreservation, storage, distribution and shipping) cord blood units for clinical use. Further, it included the safety data from the transplantation of more than 4,000 cord blood grafts. In advance of the BLA submission, NCBP moved its entire manufacturing and storage resources to a state-of-the-art facility in Long Island City, New York.

"The application process has been a rigorous and educational one for all of us at the National Cord Blood Program," said Pablo Rubinstein, MD, NYBC Vice President and Program Director of NCBP. "We have always understood that providing high quality cord blood units for clinical use requires thorough scientific and technical definitions of methods, detailed analysis of results, and hard work. Achieving systematic compliance with FDA Good Manufacturing Practices and Good Tissue Practices offers further assurance of the consistency, potency, purity, safety and efficacy of NCBP cord blood units."

About National Cord Blood Program (NCBP): Launched in 1992, New York Blood Center's (NYBC) National Cord Blood Program (www.ncbp.us) at the Howard P. Milstein National Cord Blood Center, was the first established umbilical cord blood bank to collect, process, test and store cord blood units and make them available for transplantation to patients in need of hematopoietic stem cell transplantation. The NCBP has provided more than 4,200 cord blood units for transplantation worldwide since its inception. NCBP is a public cord blood bank and accepts requests from Transplant Centers and Registries all over the world. Cord blood units can be accessed and searched directly through NCBP's WebSearch (https://tc.placentalblood.org/). Cord blood units can also be accessed through Bone Marrow Donors Worldwide (BMDW), the National Marrow Donor Program, or by calling 718-752-4710 or 866-767-6227.

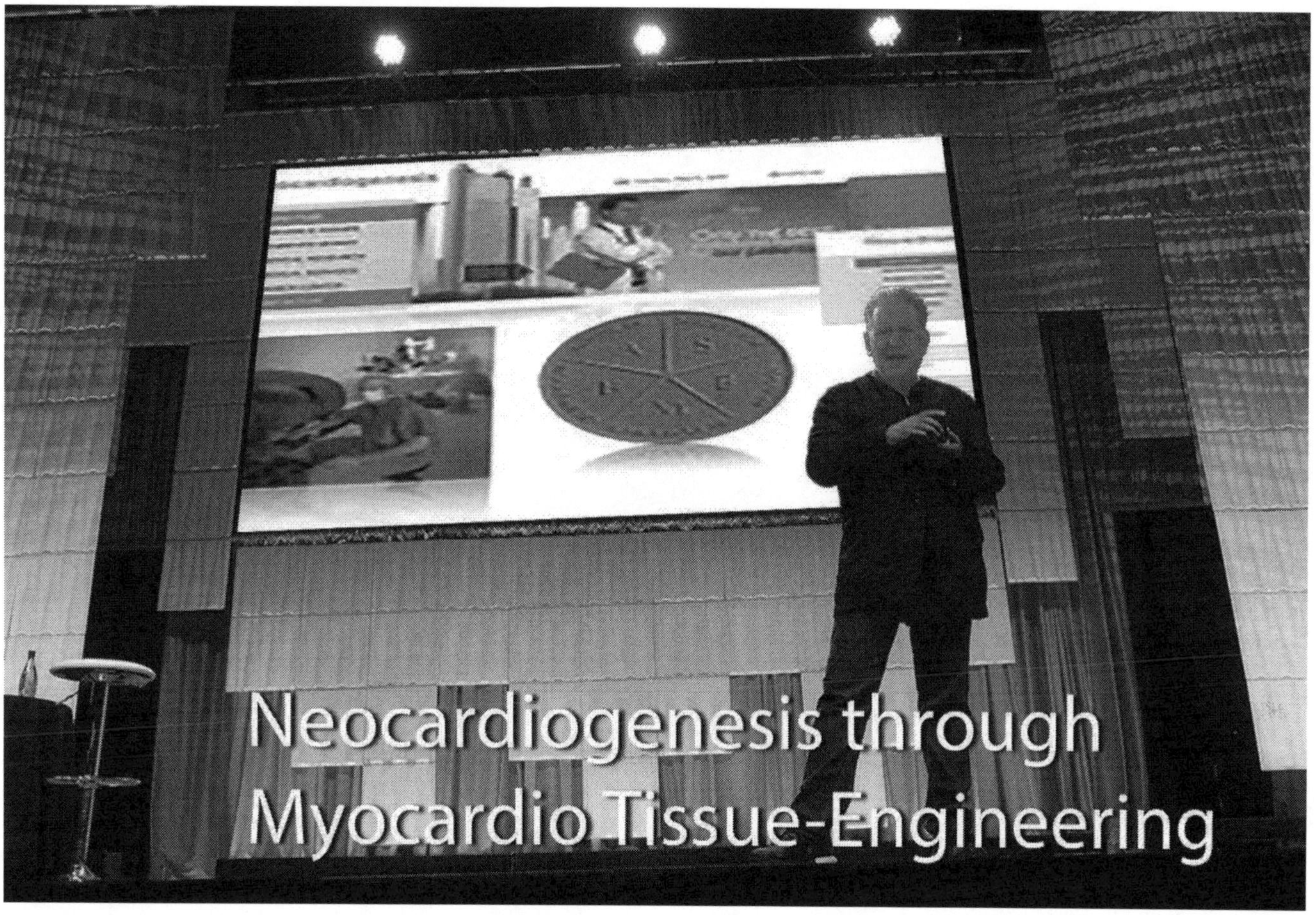

Neocardiogenesis through Myocardial Tissue Engineering (NMTE) ©2011, Keesee WW et al

Classical tissue engineering is based on seeding cells into biodegradable polymer scaffolds or gels, culturing and expanding them in bioreactors, and finally implanting the resulting tissue into the recipient organism, where the maturation of the new organ takes place. Capitalizing on this basic concept, tissue engineering has rapidly evolved in the past decade into an integrating discipline in which every organ forms a science of tissue engineering: Each of these sciences are interfacing with different scientific communities, including biotechnology, biopharmaceutical manufacturing, chemical engineering, cell biology, developmental biology, gene therapy, medical sciences, and organic chemistry. With so many "tissue engineers" at work on this globe...managing and covering all specialized methods implemented in current tissue engineering activities is a mission impossible.

Hansjorg Hauser & Martin Fussenegger Methods in Molecular Medicine: Tissue Engineering 2nd Edition 2007.

Introduction

Congestive heart failure is a major medical challenge in developed countries and heart disease is still the number one killer and biggest health crisis of all, with millions of deaths each year globally. No longer does it afflict only the old. More than 64 million Americans suffer from it, but only 25 million are over 65 years or older. The total cost of treating cardiovascular diseases and stroke in the U.S. in 2004 was estimated to reach $368 billion 86. Current therapeutic strategies to treat CHF are limited to surgical transplantation, pharmaceutical therapies, and artificial mechanical support. These treatment options have substantially improved the quality of the care, but there are notable limitations to each approach.22

Heart transplantation has shown to be the most successful treatment option to treat severe CHF. As of March 2000, over 55,000 heart transplants had been performed. A rather small number considering the magnitude of the pathology. Short term survival rates remain high at 81%; however, the widespread usage has been limited by the shortage of donor organs. Each day, it has been reported, 100 patients waiting for transplants actually die. We have seen the factual evidence and know, that new studies (+175 clinical studies and published papers) in regenerative cardiology have demonstrated that direct intramyocardial reinfusion of autologous cell sources, to be safe and have, relatively high percentages 50-80% efficacy for patients, adding years to their life and life to their years, that would not of been possible without it.

Advances in regenerative biology have spurred the development of cellular based therapies at a rate that could not have been imagined even five years ago. Cells from many sources are being purified, cultured, genetically modified, frozen, thawed, and infused to treat a host of diseases.

New pharmaceuticals such as vasodilators, ACE inhibitors, statins, B-blockers, diuretics, inotropes, and antiarrhythmic drugs have reduced mortality of CHF patients, but there has been little improvement in the functional performance of compromised myocardium's. Substantial percentages of patients receiving pharmacological treatments develop more severe congestive heart failure, leading to more invasive treatments. A tiny population of patients, estimated at 300-400 per year, use mechanical circulatory support devices as a bridge after cardiac surgery. Current limitations include infections, device size and weight, thrombogenicity, and electrical power and product wiring defects.

A recent search of the national database for HD, identified more than 250,000 patients had been rejected for a third coronary bypass operation. The very fact that they were rejected for bypass would most likely also mean, that they would of already tried or been excluded from qualifying for balloon angioplasty. These end-stage patients have exhausted all medical options. These are questions that articulate the concerns of those particular patients whose disease was, or is now, becoming far advanced, and have found themselves among the 5 M congestive heart failure patients in our country. These patients pass each day with the conscious and subconscious realization that their magnificent heart, that has served them well, 100,000 times per day, 36 million times per year and 3 billion times in their long lifetime, is now losing its ability to function.

Cardiac aging, myocardial infarction and ischemic cardiomyopathy are characterized by various forms of structural damage that are common to all cardiac diseases. The identification of a pluripotent cardiac stem cell (CSC) requires a new evaluation of possible interventions that can repair the myocardium damaged by age, stress, infarct, or combinations. Advanced age is typically associated with multiple sites of injury, which appear as areas of myocardial loss in various phases of healing, scattered throughout the ventricular wall. Neo-cardio-matrix-engineering (NMTE) may provide viable solutions to the ever-escalating pandemic amounts of heart patients that have no further options.

Bioengineered scaffolds and cardiac repair

A substantial effort in cardiac regeneration research has focused on identifying suitable cell types for replacing lost cardiomyocytes and the proliferation and differentiation capabilities of those cells. The rationale behind this research is that the lack of spontaneous cardiac regeneration after myocardial infraction is due to cardiomyocyte terminal differentiation and inability to proliferate, coupled with inadequate availability of progenitor cells capable of forming new cardiomyocyte. Supplementing the damaged heart with progenitor cells or another source of cardiomyocytes is a logical option following this rationale.

However, the vast majority of cells implanted in the myocardium do not survive, and those that do survive do not fully integrate into the myocardium as functional cardiomyocytes or endothelial cells, failing to couple electrically or mechanically with remaining myocardium. 58

Vincent F.M. Segers, MD & Richard T. Lee, MD

Engineered Heart Tissue

The field of tissue engineered heart tissue is relatively new with the first published journal article appearing in 1997 1. Within the last decade, there have been approximately 60 journal articles and some reviews published in the field. The various strategies in current literature are described as follows.

Utilize polymeric scaffolding material as a support matrix

Incorporating the various types of stem cells within the biodegradable gels

Incorporating various polymeric temperature sensitive surfaces

Eschenhagen, a patriarch of neo-cardio-matrix engineering (NCME), developed a 3-D model of a tissue engineered heart muscle in a collagen matrix. The initial model was refined to generate engineered heart tissue (EHT) by casting a mixture of neonatal cardio myocytes and collagen into plastic molds.

According to Eschenhagen and Zimmermann:

In 1994, our idea to generate 3-dimensional cardiac tissue constructs came from the observation that it is fairly easy to genetically manipulate cultured immature cardiac myocytes in the classic 2-dimesional culture format (and to observe biochemical and molecular consequences) but difficult to obtain reliable information from these cells in terms of contractile function. The experiments quickly yielded success, and cardiac myocytes spontaneously generated a coherently and regularly beating cardiac tissue-like structure (cardiac myocyte-populated matrix CMPM) that developed measurable forces when suspended in organ baths and connected to a force transducer (Eschenhagen et al 1997)1-23-24-34.

The Dynamic Heart

As opposed to static structures of the body, like bones, cartilage, and various relatively uncomplicated organs, the heart is a dynamic organ with a complex mechanical function. The restoration via tissue engineering of the heart poses unique challenges and solutions. The heart is a heterogenesis, complex helical structure with asymmetric and anisotropic features, with spiraling muscle bands, valves, vessels and electrical conduction system. The key mechanism underlying the hearts durable and strong performance is the vortex function of the myocardial muscle spiral during systole (Buckberg et al 2002) 35. Furthermore, the myocardium is a highly anisotropic structure, that is, the orientation of muscle fibers may be varying from site to site, as do the vascular density and the contractile pattern. With high metabolic output demands the heart is angiotropic and densely vascularized.

Recent studies have reported on the use of various types of scaffolds and the combinational use of divergent stem/progenitor cells in seeding and expansion in 3-D bioreactors.

In addition, two fundamental types of bioengineered heart valves are being produced: decellularized xenogenic valves and recellularized valves with the recipients own cells. Also, bioartificial blood vessels are being produced with collagens and cells from previously harvested endothelial cells from the patient's own autologous fibroblasts.

Also, quite notably, the recent discoveries that demonstrate the use/function of designer self-assembling peptide nanofiber scaffolds for 3-D dimensional cultures will be used in many promising new medical applications, such as spinal cord injuries, as well as the rapidly expanding field of neo-cardio-matrix-engineering (NCME).

It is certainly not hard to imagine, a direct transendocardial re-infusion of an expanded autologous stem cell cocktail in a slurry of self-assembling nano-peptides. WW Keesee Trust

Healthy tissue can be considered comprising three dynamic components.

(i) cells (ii) the extra-cellular matrix or natural scaffold and (iii) other elements such as growth factors that signal to the cells. *Although non conclusive, the evidence strongly suggests that successful cardiac regeneration may, not be, enabled by injection of one cell type alone*. Newly formed cells require an extracellular environment providing growth factors, nutrients, mechanical support, and physiological integration.58

Creation of Cardiac Tissue

The most elemental approach in the creation of cardiac tissue has been to control the microenvironment of the proposed cells designated for later infusion *in vitro*, growing in 3-dimensional scaffolds. These scaffolds can be constructed in different sizes and shapes and display functional and morphological properties of differentiated cardiac muscle *in vitro. (*Eschenhagen) 1 Spontaneous contractions start a few days after construction, and applying cyclical stretch in order to mechanically condition the matrix can improve functional and mechanical properties. These three-dimensional blocks of tissue can be used for clinical studies and for in vitro drug testing. Many attempts at engineering myocardium have used collagen or matrigel as a scaffold and neonatal cardiomyocytes as a cell source.

Methodology for Cardioid Formation

The method for cardioids formation has been described in detail (Baar K, Birla, R, et al) 19-26. Cardioids are formed from the spontaneous delamination of a confluent monolayer of neonatal cardiac myocytes. The cardioid model has several unique characteristics that make it an attractive model for cardiac muscle. Cardioid formation is dependent on the self-organization of individual cardiac cells into a 3-dimensional tissue construct. This process eliminates the need for synthetic scaffolding material in the contractile region of the tissue construct, and allows cardioids to exhibit uninhibited repetitive contractions.

Secondly, during cardioid formation, extracellular matrix (ECM) components are generated by cardiac fibroblasts that are plated with the cardiac myocytes.

Thirdly, the entire process is spontaneous and allows for the generation of new cells to dictate the new 3-D environment. The 3-D organization of cardioids is not dictated by the geometry of pre-fabricated polymeric scaffolds.

According to R.K. Birla, Section of Cardiac Surgery/University of Michigan.

The cell monolayer initiates spontaneous contractions and the entire cell monolayer beats as a continuum during the entire culture period. Here we have described an in vitro method for the formation of contractile 3-D cardiac muscle, which we have termed cardioids. One of the most attractive features is that isolated cardiac cells self-organize to form 3-D cardiac muscle. Cardioids exhibit several physiologically relevant metrics of function. Cardioids can be electrically stimulated to generate active force and can be electrically paced at frequencies of 1-7Hz. In addition, they are responsive to calcium and various cardio-active drugs, and may provide viable cardiac tissue for clinical or research applications.

Dr. Birla's work has been funded by DARPA.19-26

Tissue Engineering With Adult Stem Cells

Dr. Anthony Atala MD

Investigators around the world, including our institution, have been working towards the development of several cell types, tissues and organs for clinical application. The predominant cell type for tissue engineering applications today is the predetermined progenitor cells, which are present in almost every tissue. Our institute has successfully engineered multiple tissues for organ reconstruction using specific progenitor cells, including urinary bladder (Atala, 2001), uterus (Duel et al, 1996), vagina (De Filippo et al, 2003), and penile tissue (Falke et al, 2003).

The first tissue engineered hollow organ successfully transplanted into patients was the urinary bladder, a composite tissue, engineered to form smooth muscle cells and urothelial cells (Atala et al., 2006). 59-60-61-62-63

Former Harvard University surgeon and medical researcher, currently at Wake Forest University, Anthony Atala expresses it as follows:

"I have one goal...to cure the patient. They said 10 years ago, that human organs could not be built." One of the new generations of physician-scientists, Atala created the *FIRST HUMAN ORGAN*, a bladder, using tissue engineering. Other organs followed and he was able to form uteruses, vaginas, and large blood vessels.

Believe it or not, Atalas' group has constructed a fully functioning RABBIT PENIS. Apparently, randy rabbits with newly engineered members chase their female counterparts around the cage, barely four weeks after surgery.

Atala continues, "Why is it that surgeon's think that if a piece of your heart gives out, you have to change the whole heart? You don't! Our organs have tremendous reserves. When someone comes to a doctor with heart pain or kidney trouble, you don't need much repair to get back to a normal lifestyle. And a stem cell patch may be the best approach."

When asked about whether making customized organs and tissues patient-by-patient will be cost effective, Atala replies:

"You can't argue with autologous, and it's the best way to go, regardless of the cost. Immunosuppressant drugs are nasty things. I think that people who suggest that we can control rejection with better HLA matches haven't spent much time at the bedside of someone on prednisone. There are too many genes that make us different, and more are discovered every year."

"I don't believe that we'll solve immune rejection in my lifetime or perhaps ever..." 81.

When compared to embryonic stem cells, adult stem cells have many similarities. They can differentiate into all three germ layers, that express common markers, and they preserve telomere length. However, the adult stem cells demonstrate considerable advantages. They easily differentiate into specific cell lineages; they do not form teratomas if injected in vivo; they do not need feeder layers to grow; and they do not require the sacrifice of human embryos for their isolation. Adult stem cells are negative for tissue-specific markers and can be positive for embryonic cell antigens (Peterson et al., 1999). These cells are able to differentiate into committed cells of other tissues, a feature defined as plasticity. This would allow for engineering of composite tissues composed of multiple cells types using one single source of adult stem cells. The preferred cells to use are autologous cells, in which a biopsy of tissue is obtained from the host, the cells are dissociated and expand in culture, and the expanded cells are implanted into the same host. (Atala, 2001, 2005). Therefore, use of adult stem cells opens a new avenue for cellular therapy and for the engineering of tissues and organs.

Great clinical and scientific interest in the use of adult stem cells for cardiac tissue engineering has emerged over the last decade. In addition, as we reported infra, more than 175 clinical studies and papers have been published for various cellular therapies for heart disease, mainly on the quest for the holy grail of stem cell cardio-biology. A German group (Strauer et al., 2001)65 reported the first human application of adult stem cells for the treatment of myocardial infraction. Mononuclear bone marrow cells of the patient were prepared, and 6 days after infraction, 12 million cells were injected in the infract-related artery. At 10 weeks after the stem cell transplantation, the transmural infract area had been reduced from 24.6-to-15.7% of left ventricle circumference, whereas ejection fraction, cardiac index, and stroke volume had increased 20-30%. More research in a randomized setting and more clinical studies are critically needed now.

Atala claims to be able to build a hollow organ in just five weeks: four weeks to expand the cells and one week to seed and build the "construct", the three-dimensional structure of the organ.

Major advances have been achieved in engineering of tissues within the past decade. However, like every new evolving field, regenerative medicine and tissue engineering are expensive. Several of the clinical trials involving bioengineered products have been placed on hold because of the costs involved with the specific technology. As with any therapy, the cost that the medical health care system can allow for a specific technology is limited, therefore, the costs of bioengineered products have to be reduced for them to have an impact clinically.

Tissue engineering and Regenerative Medicine: Methods in Enzymology

Vol. 420 Stem Cell Tools and Other Experimental Protocols 2009

The Role of Endothelial Cells in Cardiac Regeneration and Tissue Engineering

The structural complexity of the myocardium goes far beyond the mere viability of cardiomyocytes. Other cell types like endothelial cells have important roles in both the embryonic and adult heart. In the normal myocardium, every cardiomyocyte is surrounded by a network of capillaries and cardiomyocytes interact directly with adjacent endothelial cells. Cardiomyocytes depend on endothelial cells not only for blood supply but also for paracrine signals and growth factors that control contractility and promote cardiomyocyte organization and survival. 7

The most obvious role of endothelial cells in cardiac regeneration and tissue engineering in general is oxygen and nutrient supplied by vascularization of the newly formed tissue. Therefore, the ability to support vascularization is one of the most important roles and requirements of tissue engineering scaffolds. 8

This concept applies also to injectable scaffolds. Cell survival will depend upon recruitment of endothelial cells and newly growing functional vessels, within these matrix scaffolds. Some materials support vascularization better than others.

Self-assembling peptides are short peptides that can form a solid scaffold within the myocardium after injection. In many materials including collagen gels and alginate gels, cultured endothelial cells undergo apoptosis, while endothelial apoptosis in self-assembling peptides in the heart is less prominent. Segers 58 showed that, after injection of self-assembling peptides in the heart, endothelial cells are recruited and form functional vessels within 4 weeks, as opposed to few endothelial cells that are recruited in basement membrane material called Matrigel. (Graham et al 2002)

The endocardial endothelium plays an important role in cardiac development. Endothelial cells can also regulate myocardial performance (Hoshijima et al 2005). Cardiomyocytes also depend upon endothelial cells not only for blood supply but also for paracrine signals and growth factors that control contractility and promote cardiomyocyte organization and survival. Physiological observations of secreting endothelin I and angiotensin conversions suggest that vascularization is essential for physiological performance.

According to Segers et al, in fact, engineered heart tissue (EHT) develops a two-fold higher contractile force if generated from an unpurified cell population than that generated from a pure cardiomyocyte fraction (Wang et al 2006). 58

It has been shown that co-culturing endothelial cells with cardiomyocytes promotes cell survival (Narmoneva et al) 40. And Hsieh et al showed that PDGF-BB is a *CRUTIAL FACTOR* in the signaling of endothelial and cardiomyocytes that are beneficial in injectable scaffolds because of decreased apoptosis and increased cardiac function after MI.

Endothelial cells form typical networks of vascular connections with capillary-like tubes cultured in 3-D dimensional scaffolds, whereas cardiomyocytes cultured alone form small islands of dying cells. Most interesting, when both cells are cultured together, the endothelial cells form tubular structures and the cardiomyocytes attach to these vascular tubes. (Narmoneva et al) 40 This data shows that endothelial cells promote the assembly of cardiomyocytes on the capillary endothelial tubes by their direct physical interaction with the cardiomyocytes.

This suggests that endothelial cells as well as various cells included in the cellular spectrum of homogeneous bone marrow, and other noncardiomyocytes must be considered in strategies for cardiac regeneration. For instance, cardiac fibroblasts, another important cell population, both quantitatively and qualitatively, but are regarded suspiciously because of the consequences of excessive fibrous; contribute and have functional roles in the myocardium, such as passive mechanical properties, and organization of the collagenous matrix, and may be essential in the future considerations of neo-cardio-matrix engineering (NCME).

Myocardial Restoration and Tissue Engineering

According to Theo Kofidis et al, the following caveats and requirements arise for the myocardial restoration using bioartificial, cell-enriched tissues: 9-10

1. Is the production of natural and efficient heart muscle possible with the currently available tools? If so, what type of cell and what kind of bioartificial matrix is better suited for the production of bioartificial heart tissue?
2. The engineered tissue graft should exhibit strong viability and stability for a sustained myocardial replacement.
3. The inoculated cells should preferably bear differentiation potential to cardiomyocytes or other contractile elements.
4. The engineered tissue should be conservable in a viable and functional state to be implanted into the diseased heart muscle at a later time point and in the frame of an elective and well-controlled procedure.
5. The myocardial tissue construct should encompass vessel and neuronal networks to allow for perfusion and signal conduction.
6. The bioartificial matrix, which forms the framework for cellular seeding, has to exhibit adequate porosity and biodegradability to facilitate cell engraftment

and infiltration, without losing integrity in a given time span following implantation in vivo.

Aspects of Cardiac Electrical Stimulation

Recently Cannizzaro, 12 have shown that electrical stimulation directs neonatal cardiomyocytes to assemble into native-like tissue *in vitro*, and by employing this 'biomimetic' approach, discusses how electrical field stimulation can influence cell behavior. The utility of engineered cardiac grafts depends on cell survival, integration, functionality, and electrical coupling.

Native heart tissue has low-resistance pathways for electrical signal propagation due to the presence of gap junctions and high cell density. Individual cells are packed tightly together and held in place by tight junctions, such that the myocardium acts like a synctium.

To induce synchronous contractions of the cultured cardiac constructs, electrical signals are applied and designed to mimic the orchestrating and synchronous native electrical contractions of the heart.

Bioreactor electrical characteristics

Stimulation efficiency is determined by the ability to attain the desired physiological responses with minimal damage to the surrounding tissue. For each application, electrical stimulation conditions should be optimized by not only choosing appropriate electrode geometry but also studying electrode material properties and the charge-transfer characteristics at the electrode-electrolyte interface. Electrodes must be biocompatible to avoid toxic shock or immune responses in the adjacent tissue or medium, and they should efficiently transfer charge from the electrode material where it is carried by free electrons to the medium where it is carried by free ions.13

In a microelectrode array (MEA) study on cardiomyocyte activity, Giovangrandi et al 14 clearly showed how cardiomyocyte beat closely follows imposed temperature profiles; as beat rate increases the temperature increases and also conversely as the temperature increases the hearts beat rate increases.

Electrical field stimulation apparatus is available commercially or custom-designed hardware with computer controller may be custom made, which will require additional software and circuit design expertise. 44-45

In addition, more advanced bioreactors that integrate electrical stimulation with medium perfusion are needed to engineer tissue of sufficient thickness for clinical applications.39

Tissue engineering using human embryonic stem cells

The possibility of using stem cells for tissue engineering has greatly encouraged scientists to design new platforms in the fields of regenerative and reconstructive medicine. Among cell types suggested as a cell source for tissue engineering (TE), human embryonic stem cells (hESC's) are one of the most promising. Isolated from the inner mass of preimplantation stage blastocysts, they possess the ability to differentiate into practically all adult cell types. In addition, their unlimited self-renewal capacity enables the generation of sufficient amounts of cells for cell based TE applications.

Several important challenges need to be addressed, such as isolation of the desired cell type and gaining control over its differentiation and proliferation. As for having the ultimate cell source to accomplish these goals, human embryonic stem cells (hESCs) hold great promise. Ever sense they were identified by Thomson et al, they have shown /exhibited capacity to differentiate into cells representing all three embryonic germ layers (Itskovitz-Eldor et al 2000), including neurons (Reubinoff et al., 2001), and endothelial cells (Levenberg et al.,2002), and have an almost unlimited self-renewal capacity. Never the less, they also possess critical limitations because undifferentiated hESC's have the inherent capacity to form tumors *in vitro*.

HESCs are the most potent stem cells available for TE, and controlling their differentiation is a notable challenge. In general, hESCs can be induced to differentiate once removed from the MEF feeders and introduced with bioactive signals. This is done either directly or through the formation of embryonic bodies (EB's). EB's are small clumps of hESC colonies grown in suspension, which form three-dimensional (3-D) spheroid bodies representing a differentiation model with the widest possible spectrum of cell types. Differentiating cells within the EB requires the interaction of paracrine effects of the 3 embryonic germ layers, in developing 3-D micro- environments that reproduce *in vivo* native structures as faithfully as possible. Although direct differentiation is possible, most differentiation systems rely on EB formations.

The next challenge is the isolation of the desired cell type. Methods for isolating specific cell types include either positively selecting the desired cells or negatively removing the undesired cells. Defining the target cell population is crucial when using these strategies and planning the next stages and appropriate time points for seeding cells into scaffolds and transplanting them into animal models.

Lavik and Langer, 2004, used TE scaffolds designed to provide cells with a solid 3-D matrix.

Scaling up a bioprocess

Large-scale production of functional tissues requires bioprocesses that are scalable, tightly controlled, and easily managed. Each step of the hESC-based systems should be scaled up in a regulated and systematic fashion. Perhaps the most challenging process is to control the formation and cultivation of EBs. Eb's remain the preferable approach in many differentiation protocols. Made of a small aggregate of hESC's grown in suspension, EB's are independently growing and differentiating units. In addition, cells within the EBs at times, respond differently and at times unpredictably to bioactive cues, stimuli, and growth factors. The desired target cell population has been either somatic cell types or progenitor cells, although some laboratories followed protocols for mesenchymal linage. Shahar Cohen, Lucy Leshanski, and Joseph Itskovitz-Eldor

Engineering cardiac tissue from embryonic stem cells

Cardiac tissue engineering is an emerging field that holds great promise for developing revolutionary treatments for heart disease. A large number of patients who are not candidates for transplants and other interventions may benefit from smaller structures of muscles, valves, or vessels. Cardiac tissue engineering may not only provide advanced surgical implants in these patients, but the development of these cells *in vitro*, provides a substantially improved method for testing new drugs and therapeutic agents, and will dramatically enhance our understanding of cardiac cell biology. Li et al., 1999, 2000, and Sakai et al, have grown small 3-dimensional cardiac grafts and implanted them in host myocardia.

Two important critical observations from this work were. The survival of the grafted material, in the right ventricular outflow tract, and the apparent vascularization of the implants. In conclusion, engineered heart tissue prevented further dialation, induced systolic wall thickening of infarcted myocardial segments, and improved fractional area shortening of infarcted hearts compared with controls. (Xi-Min Guo et al 2006)70

Based on these methods, Guo et al, created cardiac tissue using cardiomyocytes derived from mouse embryonic stem cells (mESCs). In this study, a step-by-step strategy was used to derive cardiomyocytes as described infra, to produce embryoid bodies in large scale ramp up, in their bioreactors, inducing cardiac differentiation of ESCs, and enriching the cardiomyocytes in Percoll density gradients.

The cells were then mixed with liquid collagen to construct heart tissue and subsequently stretched mechanically*, in vitro*, which ultimately proved to be a reasonably fair copy, of structurally and functional native heart constructs.

In their innovative study, neonatal rat cardiomyocyte sheets detached from PIPAPm-grafted surfaces were overlaid to construct cardiac grafts. Layered cell sheets began to pulse simultaneously, and morphological communications by connexin43 were established between the layered sheets. *In vivo*, layered cardiomyocyte sheets were then transplanted into subcutaneous tissues of the animals. Three weeks after transplantation, electromyograms detected spontaneous beating in the transplanted tissues. Histological studies, in addition, showed, characteristic structures of heart tissue and of multiple neo -vascularizations within the contractile tissue.

Long term survival of pulsatile cardiac grafts was confirmed for up to 12 weeks. Miyahara et al., 2006, 71 cultured adipose tissue-derived mesenchymal stem cells using temperature-responsive culture dishes. Four weeks after coronary ligation, the monolayered mesenchymal were transplanted into scarred myocardium. After transplantation, the engrafted sheet gradually grew to form a thick stratum that included newly formed vessels, undifferentiated cells, and a few cardiomyocytes, and triggered angiogenesis. Unlike fibroblast cell sheeting, the monolayer mesenchymal cells reversed wall thinning, in the infract areas, of the rats. In brief, cell sheet engineering, using temperature responsive cell cultures has been very effective in fabricating electrically bioactively pulsating, cardiac grafts in both *in vitro* and *in vivo* models. This technology should have an enormous potential for constructing functional cardiac engineered tissue for clinical tissue repair. Liquid collagen and cell sheeting has proven so far to be the best strategy for engineering cardiac tissue (Guo et al 2006).70

Tissue engineering with mesenchymal stem cells (MSCs)

One of the most researched stem cells for therapies involving diseased and damaged tissue, the mesenchymal stem cell, is certainly most promising. Mesenchymal stem cells are named for the mesenchyme during embryonic development or the embryonic mesodermal, and can differentiate into all types of connective tissue phenotypes , such as bone marrow stromal, bone, cartilage , skeletal muscle, dense fibrous tissues such as tendons, and ligaments and interstitial tissue and adipose tissues. MSC's are capable of self-replication, and able to differentiate successfully into multiple cell lineages that resemble myoblasts, osteoblasts, fibroblasts, adipocytes, chrondrocytes , and have key markers of endothelial, cardiomyocytes, and neural like cells. MSC's have been used successfully alone in stem cell therapies and may be seeded into matrix for tissue engineering applications. Mesenchymal cells reside in various stem cell niches in the body and are believed to be an excellent choice for tissue engineering and regeneration of diminished organs like the heart.

MSCs -how do I love thee-let me count the ways...

MSC's demonstrated therapeutic capacity has captured the imagination of the cellular biologist/medical regenerative communities, and many new biomedical companies have been created recently based on the potential efficacy of MSC related products, and therapies.

Recently bone marrow-derived cells have been shown to differentiate into non-mesenchymal cell lineages, such as cardiac, neural, renal, (Alhadlaq and Mao, 2004) 72-73

Why are MSC's perceived to be superior to autologous tissue grafts in the generation of human tissue and organs? Autologous tissue grafts represent the the current "gold standard" for the reconstruction of defects resulting from trauma, chronic diseases, congenital anomalies, and tumor resection.

However, autologous tissue grafting is based on the concept that a diseased or damaged tissue must be replaced by like tissue that is healthy. Thus, the key drawback of autologous tissue grafting is donor site trauma and morbidity. Also, spare healthy tissue is scarce because of biological design during evolution. In contrast,

MSC-based therapeutic approaches may circumvent the key deficiencies associated with autologous grafting procedures. Second, MSC's can differentiate into multiple cell lineages thus providing the possibility that a common cell source can heal many tissues. Finally, MSC's or MSC-derived cells can be seeded in biocompatible scaffolds, which can be shaped into anatomical structure that is to be replaced by MSCs. The construct is then surgically implanted to heal the defect. 72-73

Nicholas Marion and Jeremy Mao

Mesenchymal Stem Cells and Tissue Engineering

As we know, MSC's can be autologous and eliminate the issues of immunorejection and alien pathogens or they may prove to be very immuno- friendly as an allogenic; generically available as a jar of spaghetti sauce on your refrigerator shelf.

This aside, the ability of MSC's to revolutionize bone and joint replacement is not only possible but a reality, as the FDA has approved the first autologous cellular-based product which has been used on thousands of patients. In addition, the EMEA, and CAT, Committee for Advanced Therapies, as of late 2009-early 2010, has established a special regulatory pipeline and a possible epediated approval process for the entire EU, with a call for companies with similar and related osteo-cellular products to get a pre-submission review and eventually certified by CAT.

For example, the general life span of a surgically successful total joint replacement is 8-10 years, which is as far too short of a duration, and creates further questions about what are the options for the patients, after the replaced joints wear out? Current hip replacement therapy involves the sawing off the patient's upper and lower leg bone, cutting off the native ball joint and attaching a steel ball joint. Many patients never fully recover and most live with constant pain. Compare this to a tiny sponge-like-matrix, seeded with the patient's own cells; a tiny incision at the hip, and the little sponge is placed in the deteriorating hip bone, and the incision is closed. The hip repairs itself and there are no adverse side-effects.

Recently Mao et al, as well as others, reported an entirely new articular condyle with both cartilage and bone layers from a single population of MSCs. Clusters of MSCs initiate joint osteogenesis, which leads to apparently superior outcomes, and may prove to be the long-term solution. (Archer et al., 2003; Dowthwaite et al., 2003).

Isolation and expansion

Friedenstein et al, 75 back in the 70's observed, that when bone-marrow was isolated and cultured, there were subsets of various cells, and fibroblast-like cells capable of multiple doublings and differentiations; and they developed protocols for the isolation and expansion of these newly discovered cells. From that time our understanding of MSCs has advanced tremendously. Numerous studies on the fibroblast-like-cells have reported upon the potential of differentiations and expansion. The protocol by centrifugation in a density gradient to separate bone marrow-derived mononucleated cells from plasma and red blood cells is still widely used today. Enrichment techniques using positive selection of cell surface markers have been used and flow cytometry has been an additional enrichment tool (Marion et al., 2005; Lee et al., 2004)74. However, others point out that there still is no reliable phenotype to allow prospective isolation of purified MSCs by FACS analysis. As a consequence, the isolation of more specific antibodies must be a priority in ongoing and future research. Having isolated cells from the aspirate of human bone marrow, how does an investigator verify the 'stem nature' of the cells?

According to Lennon and Caplan, 80-87 the *in vivo* ceramic cube assay, is the standard for identifying MSCs. The *in vivo* ceramic cube assay system is complemented by the use of a number of in vitro assays, each of which is specific for different differentiated cells. Although no cell surface marker unique to MSCs have been identified to date, an extensive extension profile of cytokines and their receptors, adhesion and extracellular matrix, shared by these cells has been described.

The CD34, which has been extensively researched, and cited in 7000 published studies, can be used as specific markers for hematopoietic stem cells. Once the enriched bone marrow sample is placed atop the Percoll or Ficoll gradient and centrifuged, the dense cells and the antibody units are drawn to the bottom, leaving the desired cells on the top of the gradient (Marion et al., 2005) 74. The enriched layer will contain a high concentration of MSCs, which can be plated and then expanded. Although the hematopoietic stem cell marker CD34 is not expressed by *ex vivo* culture expanded mesenchymal stem cells, it is possible to directly isolate early MSCs from fresh bone marrow on the basis of CD34 expression, 124 but oddly enough, not after culture, as the CD34 antigen is rapidly lost.

According to Lennon et al, perhaps the most important parameter in MSC technology, is the selection of the proper lot of fetal bovine serum (FBS), and in their experience, is not a good idea to merely purchase serum 'off the shelf', without testing it, and additionally discovered that, a batch of serum from one species will probably not support proliferation of MSCs from another.

Human MSCs (hMSCs) demonstrate initial lag during the beginnings of expansion, but is subsequently followed by rapid expansion doublings of 12-24 hours. Further the estimated number of hMSCs, in a 2 ml of bone marrow aspirate is between 12.5 and 35.5 billion (Spees et al., 2004)76. In addition, the multipotency of hMSCs, is further retained up to 23 population doublings (Banfi et al., 2000)77. No changes in the morphology of the MSCs are observed until after 38 doublings (Bruder et al., 1997)78. Immortalized MSC cell lines have been developed (Osyczka et al., 2002), and although not usable for clinical studies, are valuable as experimental tools.

Isolation protocol

Human bone marrow-derived MSCs

1. Ficoll-Paque-room temperature (e.g. Stem Cells Inc.,Vancover,BC)
2. Bone marrow sample-room temperature (e.G. AllCells, LLC, Berkeley, Ca.)
3. 10 ml marrow +5ml DPBS +125 U/ml heparin (total vol., 15ml).

4. Basal culture media (89%) DMEM-low glucose, 10% fetal bovine serum (FBS),1% antibiotics.
5. RosetteSep MSC enrichment cocktail (Stem Cells Inc.)
6. 100 ml PBS with 2% FBS and 1mM EDTA.
7. Transfer the bone marrow sample to a 50-ml conical tube. Add 750u1 RosetteSep(50 u1/1 ml of bone marrow, 50u1 x 15 ml=750 u1)
8. Incubate for 20 minutes at room temperature.
9. Add 15 ml of PBS 2% FBS 1 mM EDTA solution to bone marrow. Total volume is 30 ml.
10. Add 15 ml Ficoll-Paque to two new 50-ml conical tubes.
11. Layer bone marrow solution gently on top of the Ficoll-Paque in each tube. Do not allow marrow to mix with the Ficoll-Paque.
12. Centrifuge for 25 min at 300g with brake off at room temperature.
13. Remove enriched cells from the Ficoll-Paque interface.
14. Wash enriched cells with PBS-FBS-EDTA solution in a 50ml tube and centrifuge at 1000rpm for 10 min, with brake off.
15. Plate cells approximately 0.5-1 million total per petri dish with basal culture media.(now referred to as primary cultures or passage 0 (P0),)
16. Change medium every 2 days. Remove nonadherent cells during medium changes. Some of the adherent colonies are of mesenchymal linage

Additionally, it was discovered that MSCs could be induced to overcome their mesenchymal-ness, and differentiate after a relatively simple treatment of fully defined media, into cells with neuronal characteristics within 5 hours of induction 89 109; surprisingly, this differentiation was reversible. After incubation of the cells in neuronal induction medium for up to 24 hours and reculturing of the cells in standard growth medium, cells readapted to an MSC-like phenotype. Additionally, several groups have shown that BM-derived MSCs are able to differentiate into functional cardiomyocytes, both in vitro and in vivo 9-93- 94-117-118-119

Expanding human MSCs

Plating and initial seeding MSCs: Optimally, plate the cells in Dexter's original medium (DOM).

Dexters Original Medium for stromal cells/MSC (DOM)

a. 350 ml Iscove's modified Dulbecco's medium (IMDM)

b. 75ml heat-inactivated (HI)horse serum

c. 75 ml HI fetak calf serum

d. 5 ml L-glutamine (200 mM stock)

e. 2.5 ml Pen/Strep (stock=10,000 U/ml penicillin and 10,000 ug/ml streptomycin)

f. 500 ul 2-ME (10-1 M stock)

g. 500 ul hydrocortisone (10-3 M stock)

Following the initial seeding the MSCs are allowed to adhere to the flasks overnight. The next morning, non-adherent cells can be gently flushed from the flasks and replated in a second flask, in the same medium. The initial flask is refed with fresh medium for MSC expansion without differentiation. DOM is the richest medium for MSC expansion.

Genetic Engineering of Mesenchymal Stem Cells 2006

Osteogenic differentiation

As bone marrow is a rich source of many subsets of cells including MSCs, it is certainly not surprising that osteogenic differentiation was the first identified lineage of MSC s. According to Marion et al, several well-explored cocktails have been shown to induce MSCs to differentiate into osteoblasts. Among others, ascorbic acid, the bioactive component of AsAP as an osteogenic supplement. The osteogenic differentiation of MSCs is verified by several osteogenic matrix molecules, and ultimately by the regeneration of bone in vivo. Tissue engineered bone must have the appropriate structural characteristics that approximate natural bone. Total joint replacement is one of the many examples of MSC therapies whose proof of concept has been verified (Rahaman and Mao 2005)72-73.

Recent studies by Caplan and Dennis (2006)80, suggest that new aspects of the MSCs , mainly tropic effects, that secret a variety of cytokines that function by both paracrine and autocrine pathways, create interactions between the synthesized MSCs , enhancing our understanding of these fundamental pathways and advancing practical approaches in MSC-based tissue engineering.

New clinical studies in the area of cardiac infract, stroke regeneration, and joint restoration will provide preliminary data, testing the tropic effects of MSCs. Although bone marrow is the most customarily available source of MSCs, they may also be isolated from adipose tissue, fresh or banked human umbilical cord blood, placental tissue, and human teeth (Mao, 2005)72. MSCs will certainly play an important role in future tissue engineering advances.

Genetic engineering of MSCs

MSCs are relatively easy to expand in culture and can be transduced with exogenous genes without the need for additional cytokines and conversely appear to have several advantages over the use of HSCs in gene therapy. Additionally, transduction of MSCs does not seem to impair their ability to home to several organs, 146-147, nor does it appear to affect their ability for self-renewal. The in vivo use of genetically engineered MSCs in animal models is the first steps in this development. In a number of studies of gene transfer into MSCs, it was demonstrated that human stromal cells could be efficiently transduced with exogenous genes employing a variety of vectors, without a marked effect on their inherent stem cell characteristics. 149-150-151-152 In addition, it was shown that the transfer of genes into human MSCs by the use of retroviral vectors resulted in long term in vitro and in vivo expression of GFP 153-154-155. Subsequently, transduction protocols have been developed to reach transduction percentages of 80-90%. 151

Several strategies under investigation using MSCs therapeutically are ongoing. MSCs can be transplanted into poorly healing bone fractures, and also into damaged heart muscle, where they can actively participate or support reparation processes. 162-163-164

Gene therapy can be employed for the correction of osteogenesis imperfta, or brittle bone disease; by transplantation of autologous MSCs containing a wild-type gene for type I collagen 83-165-166. Long term cultured stromal bone marrow cells, with more than 20 passages, retrovirally transduced with LacZ and neoR genes were shown to form bone and to express exogenous genes after transplantation into femurs.114 In addition to many notable examples, it also seems feasible to use engineered MSCs as a delivery vehicle of genes for the treatment of both hemophilia A and B, as well as other genetic diseases.

Adenoviral-mediated infections have the advantage over the use of retroviruses sense they do not require cell divisions for gene insertion and have a low toxicity. Multiple copies of the intended gene can be inserted into the genome of the target cell. However, the down side appears to be that these copies transferred to the MSCs cannot be controlled and are very unpredictable.

Cryopreservation of hMSCs

Bruder et al, 78 reportedly cryopreserved in liquid nitrogen, a portion of cells at the end of primary culture, and then thawed the batch. These cells were then taken through the same protocol of extensive subcultivation as the unfrozen, same-batch of cells. Cryopreservation was not found to have an adverse effect on further cell expansion. Thawed hMScs are similar in morphology to those that have never been frozen and then thawed. They may have elongated, slender processes or may be somewhat more compact one day after seeding, however after an adjustment to the medium, become identical to the fresh-unfrozen cells.

Tissue Engineering of Heart Valves

Heart valve replacement represents the most common surgical therapy for end-stage valvular heart disease. The major drawback of all contemporary heart valve replacements, which they all have in common, is their lack of growth, repair and remodeling capabilities. To overcome these limitations, the emerging field of tissue engineering is currently focused on the *in vitro* generation of functional, living heart valve replacements.

Currently available heart valve prostheses for the treatment of advanced heart disease represent non-living foreign material and therefore are inherently different from the tissue they replace. Thus, they are associated with substantial morbidity and mortality with regard to increased risks of thromboembolism, increased rates of infections, immunological reactions, and assorted mechanical failures. In the future of in vitro heart valve engineering and replacement, we will see living autologous replacements with the capacity of regeneration and reparation (R&R). 46-47-48-50

State-of-the-art heart valves replacements exhibits disadvantages such as mechanical failure, structural deterioration, and the need for permanent anticoagulation. Allogenic homo grafts are reported to be more efficient in their long-term performance but are also not free of morphological changes, such as dilations, regurgitation, or structural failure (Staab et al 1999)54.

Therefore, scientists and surgeons have shifted their interest in generating a valve, which can be engineered and costumed to the patient's needs in vitro and which can be implanted into the host and grow with him. It should require little or no anticoagulant and exhibit enough mechanical stability to withstand the hemodynamic load at the outflow tract. There are currently two main approaches to tissue engineered heart valves.

Regeneration and repopulation

Regeneration is based upon implantation of a biologic or otherwise absorbable matrix with advantageous biodegradation characteristics. Repopulation involves implantation of a decellularized animal valve. After a cleaning process from the native animal cells, leaving only native connective tissue matrix left for implantation, which is implanted with the patient's cells and align along the valve surface to form an endothelial layer. Both methods have advantages and also disadvantages, both in the manufacturing and *in vivo* level. Other recent approaches involve seeding scaffolds with endothelial cells, endothelial progenitors, and mesenchymal stem cells.

Rieder et al, have demonstrated that the lowest level of immune system reaction was with decellurized human tissues. The cellularized porcine valves triggered a much stronger macrophage response. Thus, they favor the human allograft, not xenografts, as a basis of their decellularized technology for tissue engineering heart valves.

Another alternate approach, involves polylactic acid which is reabsorbable in synthetic scaffolds. The dominant material is polyglycolic (PLA/PGA), initially used for skin substitutes, which is FDA approved. Vacanti et al, of Harvard's Children's Hospital utilized a more compliant polyhydroxyalkanoate scaffold. Another material that allows for cell seeding and cell matrix is HA, which have been modified into hydrogels (Masters et al).53

Several groups have demonstrated the feasibility of creating living cardiovascular structures by cell seeding on synthetic polymers, collagen, as well as xenogenic, previously mentioned scaffolds.

Advancement milestones have been achieved, which comprise the successful replacement of a single pulmonary valve leaflet by an autologous tissue engineered leaflet. Hoerstrup et al 48, and Sutherland et al, followed this work with an *in vitro* completely autologous trileaflet heart valves based on ovine and human stromal cells.

The process *of in vitro* engineering of heart valves requires the harvest of autologous cells. After isolation, cells are expanded *in vitro*, 49 until a sufficient number of cells for tissue engineering are obtained. Cells are seeded onto the biodegradable heart valve scaffolds. Bioreactors are used to guide tissue maturation and formation, applying mechanical stimulation to the growing tissue, which have shown to result in an improved and implantable heart valve.3

Alternative human cell sources

Several alternative human cell sources have been investigated for their use in heart valve replacement engineering. Among the most promising are the vascular-derived cells, bone marrow-derived cells, and umbilical cord-derived cells. The obtained mixed-cell population consisting of myofibroblasts and endothelial cells is sorted by fluorescence-activated cell sorting (FACS), and the pure cell populations are cultivated and used for seeding and fabrication.

Additional thoughts

Heart valve scaffolds can be produced on several matrices including synthetic and biological. Several synthetic biodegradable polymers, such as polyglactin

1, polyglycolic acid (PGA) 5, polylactid acid (PLA), as well as PHA, have been investigated. Another approach for fabricating complete, trileaflet heart valves is the use of PGA coated with poly-4-hydroxybutyrate (P4HB). This biologically derived and rapidly absorbable copolymer is strong and pliable. Owing to its thermoplasticity, in can be molded into almost any shape, and complete degradation has been observed within 8 weeks after implantation (Hoerstrup et al).

Different types of bioreactors have been developed for this process such as pulsatile flow reactors, and diastolic pulse duplicators (Mol et al 2005), and as we noted infra, new and better bioreactors need to be designed and engineered50-39.

Tissue engineering of vascular grafts

Atherosclerotic vascular disease is the primary cause of morbidity and mortality in the U.S. Treatment of cardiovascular disease leads to more than 1.8 million surgical procedures annually that require arterial prostheses, including both coronary and peripheral vascular grafts (American Heart Lung Association, 2002)22-85. Typically autologous vein or, less frequently, artery is employed in surgical revascularization procedures. In the coronary system, the saphenous vein and internal mammary artery are the most commonly selected. The internal mammary offers the highest long term graft patency rates, with saphenous vein grafts being more prone to progressive intimal hyperplasia and accelerated atherosclerotic change. Individual patients often require multiple coronary artery bypasses, and the more preferable saphenous vein or internal mammary grafts are insufficient or unsuitable because of intrinsic vessel disease or prior use in revascularization (Eagle et al) 55

Alternatives for graft material include autologous venous or arterial sources and cryopreserved nonautologous saphenous vein or umbilical vein; however, both options have inferior patency rates. Although synthetic grafts have been relatively successful in the replacement of larger-diameter vessels, i.e., 6-10mm, they are rarely used for coronary bypass surgery, because they routinely thrombose early after implantation (Nerem and Seliktar).57 These limitations in quality and quantity of ideal graftable materials have led to a situation, in which approximately 100,000 patients per year, which require imminent revascularization, are rejected each year.22

These patients face a slow tedious death of palliative medical therapy and often suffer myocardial infractions (MI) and /or endure limb amputations as blood flow becomes progressively restricted.

Thus the critical need to develop small-diameter, less than 6 mm vascular grafts has prompted many investigators to develop tissue based vascular replacements that more closely mimic native vascular tissue.

L'Heureaux et al 1998 28-29 described the first entirely autologous vascular grafts. Their approach was to layer continuous sheets of fibroblasts and human umbilical smooth muscle cells around a central mandrel to form tubular vessels. After a 6-13-week culture period, the inner lumen of the tubular construct was seeded with endothelial cells. Although these artificial vessels were able to withstand high pressures, displaying rupture strengths greater than 2000 mmHg, their strength is derived primarily from the adventitial layer rather than the medial layer, which carries the majority of the load in a native artery (Nerem and Selikar)57. These vessels suffered a 50% thrombosis rate after one week, in transplantation procedures into canines.

Niklason et al, 1999, 2001,27-31-32 developed a technique for engineering arteries from explanted autologous vascular cells that are cultured on highly porous, degradable polyglycolic acid (PGA) scaffolds in specifically designed bioreactors that subject the tubular scaffolds to physiological pulsatile radial distension that mimics the human cardiovascular system. After 8 weeks of culture time, the polymer scaffold has largely degraded and has been replaced by a dense medial layer consisting of smooth muscle cells and collagenous extracellular matrix. Once the lumen has been seeded with endothelial cells, the resulting vascular structure histologically resembles artery and remains patent for up to 4 weeks after implantation in miniature swine. Burst strengths of over 2000 mmHg and good contractile response have been reported, in these engineered vessels.

Fundamental requirements

Specific mechanical requirements for artificial vascular prostheses have been outlined by the American National standards Institute and the Association for the Advancement of Medical Instrumentation (ANSI/AAMI VP20-19994). According to these guidelines, any implantable arterial construct must be able to withstand normal physiological pressures of 80-120 mmHG, have burst strength of at least 1680 mmHg, and suture retention strength of over 273g (Barron et al 2003).37

Niklason's et al, 27-31-32, overall goal is to develop an arterial graft that closely resembles the structure and properties found in native vessels. Arteries are composed of three distinct layers, each of which confers unique functional properties. The inner most layer, the endothelial cell layer functions to prevent spontaneous thrombosis in the vessel, as well as regulate the cell tone of vascular smooth muscle. The medial layer is composed of smooth muscle cells and their secreted extracellular matrix components including elastin, proteoglycans, and collagen. It has been observed that it is the media that contributes to the mechanical strength of the vessel as well as inherent contractibility and relaxation in response to external stimuli. The adventitial layer is composed mostly of fibroblasts as well as extracellular matrix. Within this outer layer also lie the microscopic blood vessels that supply blood to the artery via *vasa vasorum*. The ideal tissue designed blood vessel will certainly mimic this time-tested model. The fabrication of tissue-engineered vessels that appear to reproduce the native arterial structures is not empirical evidence that a clinically equivalent replacement has been achieved. Only *in vivo* implantation clinical studies provide a definitive measurement of biocompatibility, and we await results of these trials.

Much further work is necessary, however Nikason et al, have moved the field several important steps forward in the process of achieving a tissue engineered graft, with the necessary mechanical and physiologically properties. In time, this course of discovery will have enormous impact in the lives of thousands of patients.

Clinical studies are ongoing. Such grafts could be used as bypass grafts or dialysis shunts. Common arguments about the lengthy process of weeks to isolate and expand the endothelial cells of the patient in sufficient numbers required for seeding are rendered moot by the culture of stem cells in new generations of 3-D bioreactor systems, which will expedite vessel preconditioning, mechanical and electrical coupling improvements.

Injectable biomaterials

Cell therapy does not generally allow control of the local cellular environment. However injectable scaffolds can combine advances in materials sciences and progenitor cell biology to modify the cellular microenvironment in vivo. Ideally an injectable myocardial scaffold promotes repair after infarction by providing a matrix in support of neocardiogenesis.

Christman et al 2 showed that, fibrin glue improved myoblast graft retention and survival, reduced infract expansion, and induced neovascularization in the infarcted myocardium. These findings, supported by Ryu et al 2005, 3 showed that the implantation of bone marrow mononuclear cells using injectable fibrin matrix enhanced revascularization in the infarcted myocardium compared to cell implantation without matrix.

Synthetic biomaterials can be designed with a variety of biological features. Some short peptides have the unique properties of self-organization and self assembly (Zhang et al 2005).11 Once injected these materials respond to the physiological environment within the tissue and self-associates in particular patterns to form organized structures. These self-assembling peptides, because of their regular repeats of alternating hydrophilic and hydrophobic amino acids, form stable structures based on protein B-sheets. Scaffold formation occurs within minutes after exposure to physiological salt conditions, a property that greatly enhances the viability of the materials in cardio-matrix assembly.

Cardiac myocytes cultured in these scaffolds exhibit a high degree of special organization and differentiation similar to myocardium, with spontaneous contractions. Upon injection in vivo, these nanofiber microenvironments are spontaneously vascularized (Davis et al 2005).5

Key factors in material selection

The bioscaffold should be able to provide not only physical support for the cells but also the chemical and biological cues needed for functional tissue generation.

Optimal features of materials for cardiac tissue engineering

Innate properties

1. Noncytotoxic
2. Nonimmunogenic
3. Noninfectious
4. Biodegradable with nontoxic products

5. Porosity
6. Mechanical strength/elasticity
7. Injectable

Biological properties

1. Support cell attachment
2. Support cell survival and proliferation
3. Drive migration of progenitors
4. Support development of functional vasculature
5. Support mechanical and electrical integration

Smart properties

1. Shape memory
2. Trigger release of growth factors

(Segers & Lee) 58

Management of the microenvironment by tissue engineering consists of attracting the progenitor cells, enhancing their survival; driving their differentiation and promoting their mechanical and electrical coupling. Biomaterials such as self-assembling peptides form stable hydrogels.

Upon injection to a physiological environment, they form a scaffold of interwoven nano-fibers because of the changes in ionic strength and ph.

Materials with shape memory transform to a present form at a given temperature. Bioactive factors can be incorporated by noncovalent binding to the scaffold. Depending upon the type of reactions between the delivered cells and the scaffold, binding can be weak or strong, with respectively, fast and slow release. Factors can be linked to the scaffold by substrate peptide sequences, and may be released after myocardial infarction (MI).

Natural materials

Drawbacks of natural materials isolated by extraction, e.g., collagen can be overcome by selecting fragments with specific functions instead of using crude materials (Ito et al). Hence, although biological materials can be difficult and expensive to engineer and purify, known properties of natural biomaterials can be used as a template for synthetic materials to circumvent drawbacks associated with natural scaffolds and to select and amplify the desired properties.

Synthetic materials

Synthetic materials can be manufactured on a large scale, and their structure and mechanical properties can be more easily controlled and manipulated than natural materials. To improve cellular adhesion, cell-adhesion motifs may be engineered into biomaterials. A potential drawback of most synthetic materials is their lack of specific cell-recognition signals.

Surface properties of biomaterials affect cell spreading and proliferation and differentiation. For instance, differentiation of mesenchymal stem cells is dependent upon specific coatings of the biomaterials.

Mesenchymal stem cells are sensitive to surface chemistry, and the N-enriched surfaces by means of glow discharge plasma techniques can influence human mesenchymal responses, and potentially affecting differentiation towards osteoblasts. 16

Another important element in the development of bioactive materials is the control of porosity. This property of porosity has not been studied extensively of date, for cardiac tissue engineering17.

Pores smaller than 100nn result in decreased diffusion of oxygen, nutrients, and growth factors, leading to poor survival of implanted cells. Larger pores eg100um, are beneficial for cell migration and proliferation in the scaffold, but pores larger than the size of an endothelial cell are difficult to bridge , and may lead to decreased angiogenesis. 17

A balance of porosity size is an important element which can affect critical aspects such as angiogenesis, migration, remodeling, and scaffold material degradation.

Smart biomaterials

Smart biomaterials have been defined as materials that are responsive to environmental cues, such as ionic strength, temperature, enzymes, pH; that cause or react to responses, including protein release. Besides protein delivery, engineered scaffolds have potential for controlling or improving gene transfer. Synthetic materials, including peptide-based delivery systems, are being developed at several laboratories that include alternatives to using viruses as vectors. Peptide vectors are, because of their exceptional adaptiality, particularly applicable to this approach. (Zhang et al) 11

Combination products and final thoughts

With a combination of specific cells, such as full spectrum, mononuclear bone marrow stem cells, mesenchymal, endothelial, fibroblasts, neural, autologous, allogenic, embryonic and/or others selected for requisite properties; combined with designer self-assembling nano-cardio-matrix scaffolds, and/or other suitable construction modalities, both natural and synthetic in the future will include all of these elements for bionatural engineering efficacy.

Transendocardial (Perin et al) catheter-based combination injectables, forming living-cardio-matrix will eventually circumvent the need for routine invasive surgery, making draconian open-heart surgery as it has been practiced today and through our lifetimes, a historical passing reference and footnote in old medical journals.

Statistical realities:

By 2016, over 2 million Americans are projected to contract end-stage renal disease, with a cost of $1 trillion. In 2009, nearly 80,000 people needed organ transplants, fewer than 24, 000 were performed; and 6000 died waiting. Of those receiving organs, 40% died within the first three years after surgery.2 One in five of our elders 65 and over will require an organ transplant during their remaining years.83- Heart disease and stroke figures top 380 billion dollars per year.

In 2008, over 19 million people or 7.3% of the population, suffered with diabetes, at a cost of $140 billion. Add to this list cancer, Alzheimer's, spinal cord injuries, Parkinson's, MS, etc, behind these sobering facts, patients and their families ask, "Will there be a cure? And will it be in time for us?"

I want things to happen quickly. I certainly want to benefit within my lifetime. I don't want to get out of this wheelchair at 75. I am 51, and am now very healthy, and would like to get out of this chair very soon. I'm not willing to resign myself to being an advocate for research that will only benefit people only after I am gone. I'm not that noble.82

Christopher Reeve (1952-2004), in a 2003 interview

Global Regulatory Considerations:

A recent review of the FDA submission records showed that less than five companies have actually had PMA's (Pre-Market Authorization) approved for various heart valves. Also, as we stated infra, only one company in the USA has actually had any cellular based product approved for osteo-regenesis. Another tissue engineered skin company was approved as a Class II product (2000), which seemed like a break for them in the success of their company, as conventional wisdom tells us that, under new FDA rules, their product could have easily been Class III, and held to much more rigorous regulatory procedures. They are the fortunate ones, as safety and efficacy are well established. Patients routinely do not die from a skin graft. Even with their ten years of FDA approval, they are still struggling for approval in the EU. With over 200,000 prescriptions for engineered skin , they have not one adverse event report in FDA records.

In the US, administration of cellular products for cardiac repair remains investigational, and must be conducted under an Investigational New Drug application (IND), that has been reviewed and allowed to proceed by the Food and Drug Administration (FDA). No cellular-based tissue engineered products or therapies aside from the crude heart valves mentioned infra have been approved for cardiovascular therapies.

International regulatory strategies must be implemented. It is necessary to think about the potential to standardize the format of regulatory submissions that will facilitate access across jurisdictions that are accepted worldwide. As we know, the regulatory procedures in the EU/CAT is a centralized procedure, whereby companies submit one authorization application, to the EMEA and a single evaluation is carried out through the Committee for Medicinal Products for Human Use (CHMP). The EMEA will only be accepting electronic submissions of cCTD as of 2010.

In today's global environment, multi-center international trials are becoming a necessity. Top quality multinational research requires experienced medical and regulatory support: pre-trial assessments of the regulatory environment, familiarity with the timelines, an understanding of the issues surrounding the shipment of products, GCP expertise, mechanisms for safety reporting, and many other details.

The need to develop all required data as early as possible and to meet the various requirements in all markets; a global regulatory strategy needs to be prepared early and updated continuously. Using a best practices approach, companies need to understand pre-clinical and clinical parameters, as well as intellectual property, legal, business, local health care, reimbursement, and other issues for successful global filings.

EMA and the Committee for Advanced Therapies: (CAT)

The EMA is key to a potentially vast and hopefully lucrative alternative to the 'make or break' policies of the FDA, in regards to new exceptional cellular and tissue engineering products, and although similar in many ways are also a uniquely and positive force for SME's (small medium enterprises) as they call 'micro-small-medium-companies which they believe, will come many of the new break-through discoveries.

As of late 2009- early 2010, the CAT, is openly inviting new osteo-regenensis products from these SME's, to be reviewed and hopefully approved in the not-too-distant future.

CAT procedural legal strategy

We discovered that, if new cellular and/tissue engineering products did not have the usual requisite numbers of clinical trials, from Phase I-III, there may be some hope. Investment of many millions of dollars/Euros, for funding of these clinical studies, has certainly been one of the major stumbling hurdles, that will not only bankrupt the tiny companies, but prevent these medical breakthroughs, from ever seeing the light of day.

It is now possible to replace results of pre-clinical and clinical trials by detailed references to published scientific literature, if well established and in use for 10 years. The "well-established medicinal use" rules require of course, patient safety and recognized efficacy. As we apply these rules to the previously mentioned, established FDA approved (1999) Skin Company; we observe that they only have maybe 2 old and very small clinical trials, to show. However, they have, over ten years of actually treating patients, with their products and have virtually no major adverse reports. Also, the amount of scientific literature on tissue engineering over the decade may be used as mitigating the necessity of clinical trials. The general elements are:

1. Extent 2. Geographical basis 3. Monitored pharmacoviglance. 10 years used.

Regulation on Advanced Therapies

This includes somatic cell therapies and tissue engineered products, and compliance must be approved before Dec.30.2011 or Dec.30. 2012, unless exempt.

CAT Implementation of the Regulation

1. Evaluation 2. Classification 3. Certification

Scientific advice and procedure assistance may be requested and pre-submission meetings need to be filed 7 months before submission. At this time the Rapporteur and Co-Rapporteur are assigned. EMEA establishes a 'product team' for each centralized procedure. Applicants are defined as Micro-Small or Medium (SME's) Enterprise.

SUBMISSION OF APPLICATION; BOTH DATE AND DELIVERY OF DOSSIER TO EMEA; PREFERRED SUBMISSION DATES

DOSSIER

1. 1 FULL COPY MODULES 1-5 PLUS
2. ACTIVE SUBSTANCE MASTER FILE, IF ANY
3. ADDITIONAL COPIES OF MODS 1&2
4. ONE e-copy in WORD' MICROSOFT
5. PLUS SUBMIT TO RAPPORTEUR AND CO-RAPPORTEUR IN PARALLEL WITH EMA;
6. OUTTER AND INNER PACKAGING – PRODUCT LABELING
7. PRODUCTS WITH GENETICALLY MODIFIED ORGANISMS NEED COPY OF WRITTEN CONSENT
8. EEA- EUROPEAN ECONOMIC AREA

9. EU-CTD – COMMON TECHINICAL DOCUMENT – 5 MODULES, MOD 1-EU ADMIN AND PRESCRIBING INFO. MOD 2-3-4-5 COMMON TO ALL REGIONS; INCLUDE HIGH LEVEL SUMMARIES – QUALITY, NON-CLINICAL AND CLINICAL DOCS.

VALIDATAION BY EMA; ALL EXPERTS CHECK IT OUT

CHMP- COMMITTEE FOR MEDICINAL PRODUCTS FOR HUMAN USE.

MANAGEMENT OF APPLICATIONS; DETAILS ENTERED INTO EMEA TRACKING SYSTEM;

(SIAMED)

SAMPLES AND SAMPLE ANALYSIS; CHMP MAY ORDER TESTING AND ALSO PROVIDE PREVIOUS VALIDATIONS;

PRE-AUTHORIZATION INSPECTIONS; GMP-GCP-AND GLP;

RAPPORTEUR AND CO-RAPPORTEUR PROVIDE QUESTIONS FOR TEAM;

ACCELERATED ASSESMENT;

NOTICE OF INTENT TO SUBMIT A REQUEST FOR ACCELERATED ASSESSMENT; 'LETTER OF INTENT'; CAN BE SUBMITTED ANYTIME PRIOR TO SUBMISSION OF MARKETING APPLICATION;

DECENTRALIZED PROCEDURES FOR 1 –OR MORE STATES ONLY;

KEY; APPLICATIONS ARTICLE 10A DIRECTIVE 2001/83.EC

POSSIBLE TO REPLACE RESULTS OF PRE-CLINICAL AND CLINICAL DATA

MAJOR PROBLEMS DURING EVALUATION

CELL BANKS

1. DIFFERENT CELL BANKS USED DURING DEVELOPMENT

2. INSUFFICIENT CHARACTERIZATION

3. LACK OF COMPARATIBILITY STUDIES BETWEEN HISTORICAL CELL BANKS AND FINAL MCB.

4. INSUFFICIENT STABILITY DATA FOR FINAL MCB

VIRAL STOCKS

1. SEVERAL VIRAL STOCKS USED DURING DEVELOPMENT

2. THE PROPOSED COMMERCIAL VIRAL STOCK, NOT USED IN THE STUDY
3. INSUFFICIANT CHARACTERIZATION OF PREVIOUS STOCKS
4. LACK OF COMPARABILITY STUDIES BETWEEN STOCKS

CHARACTERIZATION

1. TESTS INSUFFICIENT
2. PROCEDURES NOT VALIDATED

PRODUCTION PROCESS

STABILITY

1. SHELF LIFE

CRITICAL ISSUES OF SAFETY

GIVE RATIONAL APPROACH

PROVIDE JUSTIFICATION WHERE DATA INSUFFICIENT

REQUEST ADVICE EARLY

CAT; MINIMUN GUIDELINES STILL UNDER REVIEW

FOR SME's

ATMP

ALL NEW PRODUCTS TO CAT RECEIVE AN ADVISORY OPINION. THEN RECOMMEDATION IS SENT TO EMEA FOR DECISION. ONCE THE PRODUCTS ARE AUTHORIZED THEN THE 'AGENCY' CARRIES OUT FURTHER EVALUATIONS SAFETY – EFFACASY.

CERTIFICATION PROCEDURE

The certification procedure is one of the new procedures provided for Advanced Therapy Medicinal Products (ATMPs) in the Regulation on Advanced Therapies; (Art.18 of Regulation EC No. 1394/2007) and Commission Regulation (EC) No 668/2009 provides certification procedure. The certification procedure is the scientific evaluation by the CAT of quality and non-clinical data for ATMPs under development by Small and Medium-sized Enterprises (SMEs). After further evaluation, the EMEA will issue a certificate, and a 90-day expedited procedure has been developed.

How to get support from the EMA?

There are a number of opportunities available for interaction with the EMA, which will depend on your product's developmental status and possible strong public need/support for your product/technology.

As we mentioned infra, there is currently an apparent great interest in new bio-engineered products for hip, knees; repair/replace/regenerate. The following offices may be contacted:

SME Office, dedicated assistance for micro, small and medium companies.

EMA office of scientific advice and protocol assistance.

ITF; Innovation Task Force

Within eight weeks of receipt of a request from an applicant, the ITF arranges free-of-charge briefing meetings to facilitate the informal exchange of information and to encourage guidance early in the development process. Also this may involve in-put from EMEA scientific committees and other expert groups as necessary.

Orphan medicinal product designation

Global strategic planning and management

It is necessary to realize that as multi-national corporations and SMEs go, the importance of regulatory affairs; FDA/EMA/CAT law are critically necessary, in the highest levels of global strategic planning and management. Opportunities will arise, in the development of new generations of crucial products/patents/ cellular therapies and tissue engineered biologics, that will substantially alter the course of medicine the way it is practiced today, and hopefully very soon, help the desperate and ill patients that need these therapies and solutions now.

The practice of law has become a global endeavor, requiring a wide range of professionals to collaborate in a fast-paced, pressure-filled environment. The ability to smoothly integrate projects, caseloads and regulatory compliance, can add tremendous value to a bio-legal and regulatory department's level of service. Many corporate counsels are managing rising workloads and reducing outside counsel costs by as much as 30-50 percent through the strategic use of their own staff in combination with project professionals, such as attorneys and paralegals. When assembling a project team, it is important to formulate a plan that includes a staff assignment list, objectives and deadlines. Identify the skills required by the team and whether the expertise is available internally or if outside assistance is necessary. Also consider logistics, such as if the team will handle all activities for the project, or if it will need to coordinate with outside counsel, and what requirements there will be in terms of new technology and equipment.

Regulatory Affairs: biomedical legal team

Many of the same considerations apply to the bio-regulatory teams that create and direct potential new product pathways through a complex maze of regulatory 'agency' procedures, which are not getting easier, and are constantly becoming more complex and rigorous. INDs, PMAs, Humanitarian Use, NDAs, with biologics and biopharmaceuticals; advanced cellular therapies, cell processing facilities (CPFs) and composite tissue engineered products, appear to be held to the very highest level of regulatory compliance in the entire history of the FDA.

Stringent FDA Federal Regulations control much of biomedical manufacturing; here is a brief glimpse into this regulatory field:

The Office of Cellular, Tissue, and Gene Therapies (OCTGT) in the Center for Biologics Evaluations and Research (CBER), and the FDA have review responsibilities for cellular products. The requirement for an IND application is largely predicated upon the perceived risk to the donor and recipient of the cells. Procedures that involve ex-vivo culture of cells and/or their genetic modifications are classified as "more than minimal" manipulation and must be performed under an IND. This requires that the cell products be prepared under Good Manufacturing Practices (cGMP).

Product Manufacturing and Testing:

CGMP are defined as a set of current scientifically sound methods, practices, or principals that are implemented during product development and production to ensure consistent manufacture of safe, pure, and potent products, and are spelled out in Title 21 of the Code of Federal Regulations (CFR) Parts 210 and 211. The regulations were extended to manufactures of blood and blood components, in part 606. The regulations provide a detailed infrastructure to be used for manufacturing these types of products. This includes the design and operation of the facility , training and testing of staff, installation , cleaning and calibration of equipment , standard operating procedures for all aspects of operations, labeling, quality assurance and control programs, records, release testing, controls, and complaint files. It is not completely clear at the time of writing how cGMP will be applied to cellular therapy products. The FDA has indicated that it will use a sliding scale of implementation; such that products prepared for phase I trials will not require implementation of full cGMP or full validation of procedures. However, by phase III studies full validation specified in the pharmaceutical regulations will be required.

Product considerations for cardiac cellular therapies:

Whether the mechanisms of the cells involved in repair of cardiac damage is cardiomyocyte generation/regeneration, angiogenesis/revascularization, product of cytokines or other secreted factors, or a combination of these actions, is still being explored. Until these mechanisms are fully understood, many types of cells, alone or in combination, and prepared by a variety of methods will be candidates for clinical studies and investigational therapies, in the US and worldwide.

From the initiation of clinical investigation, product safety is the primary concern. Investigators must demonstrate that all devices and materials used for processing or administration of cellular products are compatible with the cell suspension components. In addition to safety, parameters of product characterization such as the source, phenotype, purity, number and proliferative potential of the cells should be considered early in product development to anticipate issues that may become important in the transition and scale-up from investigational to a licensed product.

Cell processing facility (CPF)

To ensure the safety of the cell donor and recipient requires the involvement of the cell processing facility (CFP) in all stages of development from basic research to the bedside. This information must be generated under good laboratory practice conditions (GLP). Although these regulations are described in the Code of Federal Regulations (Title 21 CFR, Part 58), many researchers are unaware of or are poorly informed about GLP. Sense many components of GLP resemble those of cGMP, review chart supra, a close interaction between the basic research laboratory and the CPF can facilitate the smooth transition of research into clinical studies. The CPF staff can also provide useful advice on the selection of cGMP-friendly reagents and methods, as well as expertise on the scale-up of cell preparation to a clinically applicable level.

Standard Operating Procedures that describe the production and testing methods used in manufacturing will be required and used in the manufacturing process. A manufacturing flow path and what testing will be used at each stage for monitoring product quality will be submitted and reviewed. Various criteria will be specified as to what tests results must be achieved for product release. Usually a Certificate of Analysis (C of A), which provides a list of all tests to be performed and the requisite level of acceptance, will be issued. Basic HLA typing of the original cell donor and confirmatory typing of the product will be required as an identity check. The panel that is routinely chosen contains assays that reflect product safety and include bacterial and fungal sterility, mycoplasma (all negative); and endotoxin (usually less than 5 EU/ml); product potency (a functional assay for product activity like secretion levels of a product or cytotoxic activity); viability (usually 70%), and purity (usually by flow cytometric analysis).

GMP operation of a CPF:

Regardless of the particulars of the procedures, the CPF must have in place SOP's that cover the infrastructure and daily operation of the cGMP facility. These include facility management, cleaning procedures, staff training, competency, and proficiency testing, quality assurance and control programs, process and equipment validation, materials management, and equipment maintenance and calibration

Operational SOP's:

These cover the daily operations and maintenance of the facility. There must be training files on all the staff. These include their job descriptions, curriculum vitae, documentation of training, mandatory training such as safety; blood borne pathogens, universal precautions, cGMP operations, continuing education, and evaluations. There should be a detailed plan of the facility indicating product, waste, personnel flow, air handling systems, and evacuation routes. The procedure for cleaning the facility must be described and cleaning agents should be validated for their efficacy against potential contaminating organisms. Efficacy of the cleaning and air handling systems must be documented, usually by means of an environmental monitoring program. This specifies the cleaning schedule and agents, monitoring of cleaning and contaminations, and when remedial action is required. The also must be cleaning procedures to describe cleaning procedures between different cellular products, during change over.

Specialized air handling systems must be calibrated, maintained, and shown to be within specifications by particle and viable counts. SOP's must be developed for ordering, quarantine testing, and release of supplies; reagents and management of inventory. Selection and audit of vendors, and specs for the product acceptance. Systems to track each product prepared using a particular piece of equipment, and all equipment used for the preparation of a particular product.

Each CPL should have procedures on file to deal with emergencies, system failures, evacuation, and actions to be taken in case of equipment alarms. Draft Guideline for the Validation of Blood Establishment Computer System, CBER, deals with electronic data entry management systems, and the agency has published a Guidance Document on the General Principles of Software Validation (CDER/CBER, 2002)

Cellular Manufacturing SOP's:

Manufacturing procedures require that procedures cover all aspects of management procedures (infra) and documentation that staff has been trained on specific procedures. Sense few cell therapy products are highly characterized when introduced into phase I studies, it is important to set realistic expectations in the SOP that provides sufficient flexibility in the procedure, that address biological variables. As the basic structure of all SOP's are the same; there should be standardized formats and numbering that allow the documents and revisions to be tracked. The format should include title, purpose, materials, reagents, and equipment, procedure, expected results, attachments, references, and sign-off section that show that the SOP has undergone review and acceptance. Effective SOP's are written in a style that provides sufficient information for an appropriately experienced individual to perform the procedure and achieve expected results. Overly detailed procedures may certainly be counter-productive, sense they tend to be lengthy, difficult to follow, and can result in the creation of multiple documents describing minor and unimportant aspects. The expected results section is important, which indicates when the procedure was performed. In addition, expected results may be written in a manor that allow for normal biological outcomes and variability. Establishment of expected results for cellular manufacturing procedures is achieved by validation and alert limits must be set that trigger remedial actions.

Validation:

Validation is an important component of a new procedure and provides evidence that the procedure is routinely capable of achieving the required and expected results In the case of manufacturing of cellular products; the validation process can be more complex, due to variability's of biological materials and processes. Those specified in the Certificate of Analysis can simplify selection of the criteria for acceptability. These studies should be designed in collaboration with quality/ assurance control personnel (QA.QC), who will ultimately be responsible for signing off on the validation. CBER has recently published a Guidance document titled "Validation of Procedures for Processing Human Tissues for Transplantation", which discusses validation measures intended to prevent contamination during processing (CBER, 2002). In some cases, procedures have been in use for a long time without formal validation. In these cases a retrospective validation should be performed. This can be accomplished by collecting historical results and comparing them to the published literature, and/or by the manufacturer of the equipment used.

Documentation;

Efficient documentation is at the core of the cGMP and provides evidence that the facility is in routine compliance with the regulations. A user-friendly system is necessary for recording the required data during manufacturing, and direct linkage to other associated data, and manufacturing data are usually assembled in the form of a batch record.

Good Tissue Practices:

The FDA published a proposed rule "Current Good Tissue Practice for Manufacturers of Human Cellular and Tissue Based Products; Inspection and Enforcement" The cGTP would provide the requisite applicable to all human cellular and tissue based products, regardless of their regulation category. Facilities preparing products that require an IND or IDE application would, in addition, be subject to the provisions of cGTP, which are considered a supplement and do not supersede existing cGMP regs.

Gene Therapy:

The controversies surrounding cellular therapies pale in comparison to those swirling around gene therapy in the United States, with more stringent regulations, oversight and implementations. Vector products' facilities will be expected to comply with cGMP and the expectation is likely to be maintained and held to a pharmaceutical manufacturing level.

Testing of Cellular Products for Cardiac Repair:

Regardless of the type of product and the manufacturing process, a variety of parameters must be evaluated by adequate and appropriate testing to ensure administration of a safe product.

This moves cell processing facilities clearly into the classification of product manufacturers, and in the case of products covered under IND's, the expectation is that manufacturing will resemble that of pharmaceuticals.

There is, however, a major difference between current types of cell therapy products and pharmaceuticals. In complete contrast to drugs, the vast majority of cellular therapies are currently prepared for a single recipient, where administration is under informed consent and the potential risks and benefits have been explained. Most of these therapies are in phase I or II clinical trials, and although the FDA has held that full compliance and product characterization will not be required until phase III; the problem is the degree of compliance required at earlier stages has not been fully elaborated.

Final legal considerations

A top-down approach is taken to introduce broad business and legal concepts to emerging biomedical companies, and relating them specifically to design, development, and commercialization of medical devices; cellular therapies and tissue engineered biopharmaceutical products. Topics include: corporate structure, corporate formation; and early-stage financing, contracts, licensing, intellectual property, patent portfolio, due diligence, securities regulations, mergers, spin-outs and exit strategies

1. Eschenhagen T, Zimmerman WH. Engineering myocardial tissue. Cir Res 2005; 97:1220-1231.
2. Christman KL, et al. Injectable fibrin scaffold improves cell transplant survival, reduces infarct expansion, and induces neovasculature formation in ischemic myocardium. J Am Coll Cardiol 2004; 44; 654-660.
3. Ryu JH, et al. Implantation of bone marrow mononuclear cells using injectable fibrin matrix enhances neovasculazition in infarcted myocardium. Biomaterials 2005; 26; 319-326.
4. Narmoneva DA, et al. Self assembling shortoligiopeptides and the promotion of angiogenesis. Biomaterials 2005; 26; 4873-4846.
5. Davis ME, et al. Injectable self-assembling peptide nanofibers create intramyocardial microenvironments for endothelial cells. Circulation 2005; 111; 442-450.
6. Hsieh PC, et al. Controlled delivery of PDGF-BB for myocardial protection using injectable self-assembling peptide nano-fibers. J Clin Invest 2006; 116; 237-248.
7. Brutsaert DL. Cardiac endothelial-myocardial signaling: its role in cardiac growth, contractile performance, and rhythmicity. Physiol Rev 2003; 83; 59-115.
8. Kuramochi Y, et al. Cardiac endothelial cells regulate reactive oxygen species-induced cardiomyocyte apoptosis through neuregulin-1beta/erbB4 signaling. J Biol Chem 2004; 279; 51141-51147.
9. Kofidis T, et al. 2005. Novel injectable bioartificial tissue facilitates targeted, less invasive, large-scale tissue restoration on the beating heart after myocardial surgery. Circulation 112 ;(9 supp), 1173-1177.

10. Kofidis T, et al. 2002. In vitro engineering of heart muscle: artificial myocardial tissue. J Thorac Cardiovasc Surg 2004; 128; 571-578.

11. Zhang S. Designer self-assembling peptide nanofiber scaffolds for 3-D tissue cell cultures. Simin Cancer Biol 2005; 15; 413-420.

12. Cannizzaro, C, et al. Practical Aspects of Cardiac Tissue Engineering with Electrical Stimulation. 2007 Tissue Engineering 2nd Edition; 291-307.

13. Cannizzaro SM, et al. A novel biotinylated degradable polymer for cell interaction applications. Biotechnol Bioeng 1998; 58; 529-535.

14. Giovangrandi, L, et al. 2006. Low-cost microelectrode array with integrated heater for extracellular recording of cardiomyocyte cultures using commercial flexible printed circuit technology. Sens. Actuat. B Chem.113; 545-554.

15. Lee KY, et al. Nanoscale adhesion ligand organization regulates osteoblast proliferation and differentiation. Nano Lett 2004; 4; 1501-1506.

16. Mwale F, et al. The effect of glow discharge plasma surface modifications of polymers on the osteogenic differentiation of committed human mesenchymal stem cells. Biomaterials 2006; 27; 2258-2264.

17. Karande TS. Diffusion in musculoskeletal tissue engineering scaffolds: design issues related to porosity, permeability, architecture, and nutrient mixing. Ann Biomed Eng 2004; 32; 1728-1743.

18. Askari AT, et al. Effect of stromal cell-derived factor 1 on stem cell homing and tissue regeneration in ischemic cardiomyopathy .Lancet 2003; 362; 697-703.

19. Baar K, Birla R, Heart muscle by design: Self-organization of rat cardiac cells into contractile 3-D cardiac tissue. FASEB Journal.4 A.D.

20. Dennis RG et al. Mesenchymal cell culture: Instrumentation and methods of evaluating engineered muscle; Methods of Tissue Engineering, Anthony Atala RPL, ed2002. Academic Press.

21. Kosnik PE, et al. Mesenchymal cell culture: Functional mammalian skeletal muscle constructs. Methods of tissue engineering, Anthony Atala RPL. Ed 2002. Academic Press.

22. 2002 Heart and Stroke Statistical Update, American heart Association. 2002,2004.

23. Eschenhagen T, Three-dimensional reconstruction of embryonic cardiomyocytes in a collagen matrix: a new heart muscle model system. FASEB Journal .1997.11; 683-694.

24. Zimmerman WH. Cardiac tissue engineering for replacement therapy. Review, 79 references, Heart Failure Review.2003; 15; 277-286.

25. Fedak PW, et al. Restoration and regeneration of failing myocardium with cell transplant and tissue engineering. (Review 78 references) Seminars in Thoracic & Cardiovascular Surgery; 2003; 15; 277-286.

26. R.K. Birla was supported by a grant from DARPA : Defense Advanced Research Projects ; contract #N66001-02-C-8034

27. Fields, RC, Niklason, LE, et al. Gene therapy of tissue engineered blood vessels. Tissue Eng.9 (6); 1281-1287.

28. L'Heureux, N, et al. 1993; In vitro construction of a human blood vessel from cultured vascular cells: a morphological study. J Vasc. Surg.17; 499-509.

29. L'Heureux, N et al.1998. A completely biological tissue-engineered human blood vessel. FASEB J.12; 47-56.

30. McKee, JA, et al. 2003; Human arteries engineered in vitro. EMBO Rep. 4(6); 633-638.

31. Mitchell, R. Niklason, LE. 2002; Requirements for growing tissue-engineered vascular grafts. Cardiovasc Pathol 12; 59-64.

32. Niklason LA. 1999. Replacement arteries made to order... Science 286; 1493-1494.

33. Remppis A, et al. 2004; S100A1 gene transfer: A strategy to strengthen engineered cardiac grafts. J. Gene Med. 6(4); 387-394.

34. Zimmermann WH, et al. 2003; Gewebeersatztherapie nach transmuralem myokardinfackt.Z. Kardiol.92; I/243 (abstract).

35. Buckberg GD.2002. Basic science review: the helix and the heart. J Thorac Cardiovasc Surg 124; 863-883.

36. Leor J, & Cohen, S. 2004; Myocardial tissue engineering: creating a muscle patch for a wounded heart. Ann. N.Y. Acad. Sci 1015; 312-319.

37. Barron V, et al. 2003; bioreactors for cardiovascular cell tissue growth: a review. Ann Biomed Eng 31(9) 1017-1030 (review).

38. Shachar M, Cohen, S.2003. Cardiac tissue engineering, ex-vivo: design principals in biomaterials and bioreactors. Heart Fail. Review 8; 271-276.

39. Bursac N et al. 2003. Cultivation in rotating bioreactors promotes maintenance of cardiac myocyte electrophysiology and molecular properties. Tissue Eng. 9; 1243-1253.

40. Narmoneva DA, et al. 2004. Endothelial cells promote cardiac myocyte survival and special reorganization: implications for cardiac regeneration. Circulation 110; 962-968.

41. Shimizu K, et al.2005; Enhanced cell seeding into 3-D porous scaffolds by use of magnetite nanoparticles. J Biomed Mater Res.B Appl Biomater. Oct.21 (Epub ahead of print).

42. Ozawa T, et al 2002. Optimal biomaterial for creation of autologous cardiac grafts. Circulation 106 ;(12 supp 1), 1176-1182.

43. Michalet, X et al. 2005; Quantum dots for live cells. In vivo imaging and diagnostics. Science 307; 538-544. (Review).

44. Radistic, M, Freed LE and Vunjak-Novakovic G 2004. Functional assembly of engineered myocardium by electrical stimulation of cardiac myocytes cultured on scaffolds. Proc Natl Acad Sci U.S. A. 101; 18129-18134.

45. Norlin A.2004. Investigation of Pt, Ti, Tin, and nanoporous carbon electrodes for implantable cardioverter-defibrillator applications. Electrochim Acta; 49; 4011-4020.

46. Lichtenberg, A, et al. 2006. Preclinical; testing of tissue engineered heart valves re-endothelialized under simulated physiological conditions. Circulation 114; 1559-65.

47. Sutherland F, et al. 2005. From stem cells to viable autologous semilunar heart valves. Circulation 111; 2783-2791.

48. Hoerstrup S, et al. 2002; Tissue engineering of functional trileafet heart valves from human marrow stromal cells. Circulation 106; 1143-1150.

49. Shinoka t, et al. 2005. Midterm clinical results of tissue engineered vascular autografts seeded with autologous bone marrow cells. J. Thorac Cardiovasc Surg 129; 1330-1338.

50. Mol, A, et al. 2005. Tissue engineering of human heart valve leaflets: a novel bioreactor for a strain-based conditioning approach. Ann Biomed Eng.33; 1778-1788.

51. Schmidt, D, et al. 2004. Umbilical cord blood derived endothelial progenitor cells for tissue engineering of vascular grafts. Ann Thorac Surg.78; 2094-2098.

52. Schmidt, D, et al. 2005. Living patches engineered from human umbilical cord derived fibroblasts and endothelial cells, Eur.J. Cardio-thorac. Surg.27, 795-800.

53. Masters KS, et al.2004; Designing scaffolds for vascular interstitial cell: cell adhesion and function on naturally derived materials. J. Biomed. Mater Res. A. 71,172-180.

54. Staub ME, et al.1998. Aortic valve homograft's in adults: a clinical perspective. Mayo Clin.Proc.73; 231-238.

55. Eagle, K, et al. 1999. Guidelines for coronary artery bypass graft surgery. J. Am. Coll. Cardiol. 34; 1262-1347.

56. Kelly, DE, et al. 1984; Baileys Textbook of Microscopic Anatomy. Baltimore, Williams and Wilkins.

57. Nerum, LE, Seliktar, D.2001, Vascular tissue engineering. Annu. Rev. Biomed. Emg.3:225-243.

58. Segers, V, Lee, R.2007; Bioengincered scaffolds: myocytes, endothelial cells and cardiac repair.

59. Atala, A, and L.RP.P.I.A.A.L.R.e. A. 2001. Methods of tissue engineering. Academy press, San Diego.

60. Atala, A, and M.D.P.I.A.A.ed.2005. Tissue engineering. Birkhauser Press, Boston.

61. Atala, A, et al.2006. Tissue engineered autologous bladders for patients needing cystoplasty. Lancet 367, 1241-1246.

62. De Filippo, RE 2003. Engineering of vagina tissue in vivo. Tissue Eng.9, 301-306.

63. Yoo, JJ 1999. Autologous engineered cartilage rods for penile reconstruction. J. Urol...162, 1119-1121.

64. Fukuda, K 2001. Development of regenerative cardiomyocytes from mesenchymal stem cells for cardiovascular tissue engineering. Artif. Organs 25,187-193.

65. Strauer, BE.2001. Intracoronary, human autologous stem cell transplantation for myocardial regeneration following myocardial infraction. Dtsch. Med. Wochenschr. 126,932-938.

66. Strem, B. et al. 2005. Multipotential differentiation of adipose tissue-derived stem cells. Keio J. Med.54, 132-141.

67. Xiao, J et al. 2005. Transplantation of a novel cell line population of umbilical cord blood stem cells ameliorates neurological defects associated with ischemic brain injury. Stem Cells Dev.14, 722-733.

68. Zhao, P.et al.2002. Human bone marrow stem cells exhibit neural phenotypes and ameliorate neurological deficits after grafting into the ischemic brain of rats. Exp.Neurol.174, 11-20.

69. Lavik, E., and Langer, R. 2004. Tissue engineering: Current state and perspectives. Appl Microbiol. Biotechnol.65,1-8.

70. Guo, XM, et al. 2006. Creation of engineered cardiac tissue in vitro from mouse embryonic stem cells. Circulation 113, 2229-2237.

71. Miyahara, Y., et al. 2006. Monolayered mesenchymal stem cells repair scarred myocardium after myocardial infarction. Nat. Med. 12,459-465.

72. Mao, JJ. 2005. Stem cell-driven regeneration of synovial joints. Biol.Cell97, 289-301.

73. Mao, JJ, et al., 2006. Craniofacial tissue engineering. J. Deny.Res.In press.

74. Marion, NW, et al. 2005. Borate glass supports the in vitro osteogenic differentiation of human mesenchymal stem cells. Mech.Adv.Mater.Struct. 3,239-246.

75. Friedenstein, AJ.1995. Marrow stromal fibroblasts. Calcif. Tissue Int.56,(-supp. 1) ,S17.

76. Spees, JL., et al. 2004. Internalized antigens must be removed to prepare hypo immunogenic mesenchymal stem cells for cell and gene therapy. Mol. Ther. 9,747-756.

77. Banfi, A.et al. 2000. Proliferation kinetics and differentiation potential of ex vivo expanded human bone marrow stromal cells: Implications for their use in cell therapy. Exp.Hematol. 28,707-715.

78. Bruder, SP., et al. 1997. Growth kinetics, self-renewal, and the osteogenic potential of purified human mesenchymal cells during extensive sub cultivation and following cryopreservation .J.Orthop. Res.64, 278-294.

79. Tsutsumi, S., et al. 2001. Retention of multi lineage differentiation potential of mesenchymal cells during proliferation in response to FGF. Biochem. Biophys. Res. Commun.288.413-419.

80. Caplan, AI, and Dennis, JE.2006. Mesenchymal stem cells as tropic mediators. J.Cell Biochem.

81. Scott, CT.2006. The Future of Medicine. Pearson LTD

82. 82. Christopher Reeve's interview with Jerone Groopman, http://www.jeronegroopman.com/reeve.html

83. American Heart Association's Heart Disease and Stroke Statistics-2004 update.

84. Atala,A.,and Koh,C.,2004 Tissue engineering applications of therapeutic cloning. Annual Review of Biomedical Engineering, 2, 27-40.

85. International Society for Heart and Lung Transplantation; current statistics; http://www.ishlt.org

86. Appelbaum, F.2001.Hematopoietic cell transplantationas immunotherapy. Nature, 411; 385-389.

87. Lennon, et al., 1996. Human and animal mesenchymal progenitors from bone marrow: identification of serum for optimal selection and proliferation. InVivo Cell Dev. Biol.Anim. 32; 602-611.

88. Bruder, SP., 1997. Growth kinetics, self renewal, and the osteogenic potential of purified human mesenchymal stem cells during extensive subcultivation and following cryopreservation.J. Cell.Biochem.64; 278-294.

89. Novakovic, GV, and Freshney, RI. 2006. Culture of cells for tissue engineering. John Wiley & Sons, Inc.

90. Anversa, P., et al. 2006. Life and death of cardiac stem cells: a paradigm shift in cardiac biology. Circulation; 113; 1451-1463.

To Seek the Holy Grail of Cardiac Progenitor Cells:

Neocardiogenesis

- Definition and Scope
- The term neocardiogenesis comes from cardiogenesis, which refers to the development of the heart in the embryo; neocardiogenesis, in turn, means the development of the heart in adults. The heart has mechanisms already in place that are responsible for small scale repair. However, these repair mechanisms are not sufficient for large scale repair, made necessary by events such as myocardial infarctions. Neocardiogenesis replaces dead

cardiac muscle cells with living cells so that both the structure and function of the heart are maintained. This improves myocardial pumping of fluid around the body. [2]

- Background The human heart has been thought of as a postmitotic organ. Cardiomyocytes (muscle cells of the heart) were thought to be terminally differentiated cells that were irreplaceable and thus required to maintain cardiac function throughout life. However, it is now known that the heart is able to regenerate new small vessels needed to repair an ischemic (lacking blood) myocardium. The belief that humans are born with a fixed number of cardiomyocytes, and that the growth of these cells was directly responsible for the growth of the heart, has also been disproven.[3] Reports of the heart's ability to repair itself have started to appear in peer reviewed journals [4] and papers have been published that have shown the potential of bone marrow cells to regenerate myocardium (myogenesis).[5] Other studies into the regeneration of myocardium have highlighted evidence of angiogenesis.[6] It has been reported that improvement in heart contractility has occurred as a result of the induction of angiogenesis.[7] The results of these studies suggest that there is a possibility that, during neocardiogenesis, angiogenesis and myogenesis are interlinked and operate simultaneously in the process of cardiac regeneration.
- Ischemic heart disease accounts for approximately 50% of all cardiovascular deaths and is the leading cause of congestive heart failure. Myocardial necrosis is due to myocardial infarction and is, by nature, an irreversible injury. After 15 to 20 minutes of coronary artery occlusion the cardiomyocytes are destroyed irreversibly. Many of the therapies, available to clinicians today, can significantly improve the prognosis of patients with acute myocardial infraction. However, the post infarcted heart remains a major challenge, resulting from ventricular remodeling processes, characterized by progressive expansion of the infract area and dilatation of the left ventricular (LV) cavity. The major goal to reverse LV remodeling would be the enhancement of regeneration of cardiac myocytes as well as the stimulation of neovascularization

within the infarcted area, by repopulation of the injured myocardium with healthy autologous cells, or by the induced proliferation of endogenous resident cardiac stem cells.

- Cardiac stem cells: A new view of cardiac biology.
- The heart has been found to be a self-renewing organ characterized by resident cardiac stem cells (CSC's) and early committed cells (ECC's) stored in niches. This novel view of the heart raises the possibility that defects in myocardial homeostasis and ventricular dysfunction occur because of a progressive increase in the number of CSC's-(minus) ECC's permanently withdrawn from the cell cycle. The heart is composed of myocytes that constitute a population of highly specialized cells. In self-renewing organs, cell number depends on the stem cell pool. Although stem cell antigens have been unequivocally detected in CSC's. There is no one marker capable of providing an absolute identification of stem cells in vivo. This is why the search for the "true" stem cell removed from its microenvironment has been elusive.
- Bone Marrow-Derived Stem Cells for Myocardial Regeneration:
- A rare subset of the homogenous bone marrow cellular mix, the mesenchymal stem/progenitor has been under intense investigation as a possible immuno – compatible, allogenic, universally usable biologic therapeutic.
- There is now considerable experimental evidence that transplantation of bone marrow cells into the heart induces angiogenesis and improves contractility. The use of the patient's own cells for the regeneration of cardiac muscle has the advantages that it is ethically acceptable and immunosuppression is unnecessary. The studies reviewed herein suggest that transplantation of unmanipulated autologous bone marrow may provide a novel and promising means of reversing post-infarction left ventricular dysfunction caused by scarred tissue, and may have important clinical implications for improving the long-term prognosis of these patients and possibly the prevention of the occurrence of heart failure.

- Different routes of stem cell delivery have been used to repair infracted myocardium after acute myocardial infraction. Of these, intracoronary administration of hematopoietic progenitors represents the best tried method for stem cell therapy in patients with acute myocardial infraction. The procedures described herein, are based upon experience, which have been empirically designed. It is clear that that the procedures proposed will partially or fully change in the future as new experimental and clinical evidence emerges. Stem cells can be obtained from bone marrow. In that case bone marrow is aspirated from the iliac crest under local anesthesia with an aspiration needle. At this time, the cells can be injected, or cultivated overnight before being infused into the coronary artery. It is not known yet whether all mononuclear cells or a specific sub-population of cells previously described should be given. Therefore, not only hematopoietic and mesenchymal stem cells, but also other mononuclear cells are infused to the necrotic area. Circulating progenitor cells can also serve as a source for stem cells. In that case, peripheral venous blood (250ml) is collected, mononuclear cells are purified and ex-vivo cultured for 3 days and then reinfused. For intracoronary delivery of cells, an over-the-wire angioplasty balloon is used. Then the guide wire is withdrawn and the central lumen of the balloon is used to infuse the cells. Intracoronary infusion of the cell suspension is carried out, manually or with a pump, alternating periods of occlusion –infusion and reperfusion until the entire dose is given.
- Epicardial local delivery has shown to be an easy and reliable method for gene and cell therapy. Although epicardial transplantation has been the most common route of delivery for cell transplant, an endoventricular approach has several advantages, including that the procedure can be used in high-risk patients and repeated with minimal risk to the patient. In addition, it is associated with lower morbidity rate than surgery, and is effectively used to treat areas normally inaccessible by surgery, such as the septum. At present, several endoventricular devices are under evaluation. They may be divided into two categories: the three -dimensional (3-D) guidance catheter delivery

system and the two-dimensional (2- D) fluoroscopy guidance systems. Endoventricular delivery is a more safe, accurate and reproducible delivery of cells, which ideally incorporates the visually, dynamic internal architecture of the ventricle, in real time. The catheter maneuverability and orientation of the catheter tip in three dimensional spaces, has the exacting ability to penetrate and inject into the thin, scarred myocardium. Endoventricular injection catheters have an exemplary safety record, with few reports of myocardial rupture leading to cardiac tamponade from overly aggressive catheter manipulation or injection.

- While catheter injection of cells is a relatively new innovation, the ability to access the heart without having to perform a medium sternotomy, is quietly revolutionizing the future of interventional cardiology. The procedure is likely to have application in a majority of patients with previous myocardial infarctions and congestive heart failure. The use of real time, 3-D guidance appears to be key in targeting areas that need to be treated. Cardiologists can pre-map, the heart for study and identify the afflicted parts of the heart; marking 25, to 75, target/injection points, pre-programmed into the imaging computer. Each one of these 77 target points actually express specific electrical output measurements, which immediately show if the scarred myocardium is completely dead or there is some evidence of viability. Before and after color photo images allows physicians to compare and contrast the efficacy over time. The complete procedure routinely takes 45 minutes.
- Whole Bone Marrow Transplantation
- Emerson C. Perin, MD, PhD, and Guilherme V. Silva, MD;Texas Heart Institute.
- Treating ischemic heart failure remains one of the most challenging tasks in current cardiology practice. Despite recent technological advances, many heart failure patients are not ideal candidates for percutaneous or surgical revasculation. This so-called "no-option" patient group usually comprises those individuals who have undergone multiple revascularization procedures and have significant residual myocardial ischemia. The hallmark of the so-called

"no-option" group of patients is that the current treatment approach yields unsatisfactory results and they continue to have unmanageable symptoms of refractory angina or heart failure. New insights into the mechanisms of cardiac repair have provided evidence that the heart can undergo a repair process in adulthood. Currently, several types of stem cells are under investigation for the use in cardiac stem cell therapy. Bone marrow-derived stem cells were among the first to be studied in clinical trials, and are the most widely used cell source for cardiac cell therapy.

Bone Marrow Cells and Vascular Growth

Takayuki Asahara, MD, PhD.

- Tissue regeneration by somatic stem/progenitor cells has been recognized as a system for maintenance of homeostasis in many organs. The isolation and investigation of these somatic stem/progenitor cells describes how these cells contribute to post-natal organogenesis. On the basis of their regenerative potency, these somatic stem/progenitor cells are considered a key therapeutic strategy for damaged organs. Recently, endothelial progenitor cells (EPC's) have been isolated from peripheral blood. EPC's share common stem/progenitor cells with hematopoietic stem cells (HSC's), both being derived from bone marrow (BM) and able to incorporate into foci of physiological or pathological neovascularization. The findings that EPC's home to sites of neovascularization and differentiate into endothelial cells (EC's) in situ is consistent with vasculogenesis- a critical paradigm... This discovery has drastically changed our understanding of adult blood vessel formation.

Conclusions –future directions

- Piero Anaversa MD, Edmund H. Sonnenblick, MD, & William H. Frishman. MD.
- In April 2001, the recognition that hematopoietic stem cells (HSC's) can acquire the cardiac cell lineages and regenerate the infarcted heart in mice started a scientific revolution that has dominated and continues to dominate the cardiovascular field biologically and clinically. This possibility, however, has generated profound enthusiasm and strong skepticism in the scientific and clinical community. The basis for this controversy is multifactorial and involves not only scientific reasons but also emotional beliefs. Under the ingrained conviction that HSC's cannot disobey lineage specification, the detractors of HSC plasticity immediately claimed that they were unable to reproduce published results, and reaffirmed their negative view regarding the therapeutic efficacy of bone marrow cells for human disease. In spite of the fact that the experimental design and methodological analysis of the myocardium

used in these negative studies were strikingly different from those employed in the original report;

- this data fomented the debate and repurposed the use of skeletal myoblasts as the only safe and promising cells to be implemented in patients with chronic heart failure. It is rather instructive that the disbelievers of HSC transdifferentiation are similarly against the possibility of cardiomyocyte regeneration by activation of endogenous stem cells. Their conviction is that we are born with a determined number of cardiomyocytes that can live for 100 years or more. Sense the majority of the cardiomyocytes are present at the death of the organ and organisms, according to this paradigm, these cells should be essentially immortal. (Editor's note; here the authors cite studies and counter-studies that refute this historical view of the heart)
- So far, experimental studies and clinical trials have employed rather heterogeneous bone marrow cell preparations, and this treatment has resulted in a consistent improvement in function of the infarcted heart. However, the search for the most effective HSC for cardio repair continues. An unusual, unexpected behavior has emerged with the explosion of stem cell biology. The scientific community is divided in several sectors, which tend to promote one cell type versus another. Embryonic stem cells (ESC's) are totipotent cells... problems related to rejection and tumor formations exist with this cell population... (Editor's note: the FDA has recently approved the first human clinical study)
- Mesenchymal stem cells have been defined as the nonhematopoietic progenitor cell compartment of the bone marrow. Marrow stromal cells are highly proliferative and clonogenic ...Cells beat spontaneously and synchronously; Importantly, MSC's lead to myocardium regeneration in vivo. Circulating bone-marrow-derived cells include a subset of the endothelial progenitor cells (EPC's), which promotes neovasculation in vivo. Evidence suggests that EPC's generate new vessels. Additionally, the ability of EPC's to acquire myocyte lineage has been documented in vitro and in vivo. The clinical importance of these findings is enormous.

- 1. Anaversa P. Nadal-Ginard B. Myocyte renewal and ventricular remodeling. Nature. 2002; 415; 240-3.
- 2. Scorsin M. Hagege A. Vilquin JT, Fiszman M. Marotte F, Samuel JL.,Rappaport L., Schwartz K. Menasche P. Comparison of the effects of fetal cardiomyocytes and skeletal myoblast transplantation on postinfarction left ventricular function. J. Thorac Cardiovasc. Surg. 2000; 119; 1169-75.
- 3. Kao RL, Chiu RC. Cellular Cardiomyoplasty: Myocardial Repair with Cell Implantation. Austin Texas: Landes Bioscience; 1997.
- 4. Murray CE, Wiseman RW, Schwartz SM, Hauschka SD. Skeletal myoblast transplantation for repair of myocardial necrosis. J. Clin Invest. 1996; 98:2512-23.
- 5. Taylor DA et al; Regenerating functional myocardium; improved performance after skeletal myoblast transplantation. Nat Med. 1998; 4:929-33.
- 6. Orlic et al; Mobilized bone marrow cells repair the infarcted heart, improving function and survival. Proc Natl Acad Sci USA 2001; 98; 10344-9.
- 7. Toma C. Pittenger MF, et al; Human Mesenchymal stem cells differentiate to a cardiomyocyte phenotype in the adult murine heart. Circulation. 2002; 105; 93-8.
- 8. Tomita S. et al; Autologous transplantation of bone marrow cells improves damaged heart function. Circulation. 1999; 100; 11247-56.
- 9. Fukuda K. Development of regenerative cardiomyocytes from mesenchymal stem cells cardiovascular tissue engineering. Artif Organs, 2001; 25; 187-93.
- 10. Ferarrari G. et al. Muscle regeneration by bone marrow-derived myogenic progenitors. Science. 1998; 279; 1528-30.
- 11. Perin EC, et al. Transendocardial, autologous bone marrow transplantation for severe, chronic ischemic heart failure. Circulation. 2003; 107:2294-302.
- 12. Strauer BE, et al. Repair of infracted myocardium by autologous intracoronary mononuclear bone marrow cell transplantation in humans. Circulation. 2002; 106; 1913-8.

- 13. Mosca JD et al. Mesenchymal stem cells as vehicles for gene delivery. Clin Orthop: 2000: S71-90.
- 14. Pittenger MF, et al. Multilineage potential of adult human mesenchymal stem cells. Science, 1999; 284; 143-7.
- 15. Menasche P. et al. Autologous skeletal myoblast transplantation for severe post infarction left ventricular dysfunction. J.Am Coll Cardiol. 2003; 41;; 1078-83.
- 16. Gronthos et al. Mononuclear and cellular characterization of highly purified stromal stem cells derived from bone marrow. J Cell Sci.2003; 116; 1827-35.
- 17. Mc Intosh et al. Stromal cell modulation of the immune system: A potential role for mesenchymal stem cells. Graft. 2000; 3; 324-328.
- 18. Tse et al. T-cell proliferation by human marrow stromal cells; Implications in transplantation. Transplantation. 2003; 389-97.
- 19. Di Nicola et al. Human bone marrow stromal cells suppress T-lymphocyte proliferation induced by cellular or nonspecific mitogenic stimuli. Blood 2002; 99; 3838-43.
- 20. Saito T. et al. Xenotransplant cardiac chimera: immune tolerance of adult stem cells. Ann Thorac Surg. 2002; 74; 19-24.
- 21.Mangi AA et al. Mesenchymal stem cells modified with Akt prevent remodeling and restore performance of infracted hearts. Nat Med. 2003; 10; 10.
- 22. Orlic D. et al. Bone marrow cells regenerate infarcted myocardium. Nature. 2001; 410; 701-5.
- 23. Stamm C. et al. Autologous bone-marrow stem cell transplantation for
- myocardial regeneration. Lancet. 2003; 361; 45-6.
- 24. Barbash IM et al. Systemic delivery of bone-marrow derived mesenchymal stem cells to infarcted myocardium; feasibility, cell migration, and body distribution. Circulation. 2003; 108; 863-8.

- 25. Kraithman DL et al. In vivo magnetic resonance imaging of mesenchymal stem cells in myocardial infraction. Circulation. 2003; 107; 2290-3.
- 26. Hill JM et al. Serial Cardiac Magnetic Resonance Imaging of injected Mesenchymal Stem Cells. Circulation. 2003; 11; 11.
- 27. Asahara T et al. Bone marrow origin of endothelial progenitor cells responsible for postnatal vasculogenesis in physiological and pathological neovascularization. Circ Res. 1999; 85; 221-8.
- 28. Kalka C. et al. Transplantation of ex-vivo expanded endothelial progenitor cells for therapeutic neovascularization. Proc Natl Acad Sci USA. 2000; 97; 3422-7.
- 29. Kawamoto A. et al. Therapuetic potential of ex-vivo expanded endothelial progenitor cells for myocardial ischemia. Circulation. 2001; 103; 634-7.
- 30. Kocher AA. Et al. Neovascularization of ischemic myocardium by human bone marrow derived angioblasts prevents cardiomyocyte apoptosis, reduces remodeling and improves cardiac function. Nat Med. 2001; 7; 430-6.
- 31. Al-Khaldi A et al. Therapeutic angiogenesis using autologous bone marrow stromal cells: Improved blood flow in chronic limb ischemia model. Ann Thorac Surg. 2003; 75; 204-9.
- 32. Jackson KA et al. Regeneration of ischemic cardiac muscle and vascular
- endothelium by adult stem cells. J Clin Invest. 2001; 107; 1395-401.
- 33. Price MJ et al. Intravenous allogenic mesenchymal stem cells home to myocardial injury and reduce left ventricular remodeling in a porcine balloon occlusion-reperfusion model of myocardial infraction. J. Am. Coll. Card. 2003; 41; 269A.
- 34. Silva GV, et al. Mesenchymal stem cells differentiate into an endothelial phenotype, enhance vascular density and improve heart function in a chronic myocardial ischemic model. Circulation 2005. 111 ;(2); 150-156.

- 35. Duan HF, et al. Treatment of myocardial ischemia with bone marrow derived mesenchymal stem cells over expressing hepatocyte growth factor. Mol Ther2003; 3; 467-474.
- 36. Li RK. Et al. Autologous porcine heart cell transplantation improved heart function after myocardial infraction. J. Thorac Cardiovasc Surg.119; 62-68; 2000.
- 37. Kamihata H. et al. Implantation of bone marrow mononuclear cells into ischemic myocardium enhances perfusion and regional function via side supply of angioblasts, angiogenic legands, cytokines. Circulation. 104; 1046-1052; 2001.
- 38. Tomita, S. et al. Improved heart function with myogenesis and angiogenesis after autologous porcine bone marrow stromal cell transplantation. J Thorac Cardiovasc Surg. 123; 1132-1140; 2002.
- 39. Balsam, LB. et al. Haematopoietic stem cells adopt mature hematopoietic fates in ischaemic myocardium. Nature. 429; 668-673; 2004.
- 40. Galinanes, M. et al. Autotransplantation of unmanipulated bone marrow into scarred myocardium is safe and enhances cardiac function in humans. Cell Transpl.13-7-13; 2004.
- 41. Krause, DS. et al. Multi-organ, multi-linage engraftment by single bone marrow –derived stem cell. Cell.105; 369-337; 2001.
- 42. Fuchs, S. et al. Catheter based autologous bone marrow myocardial injection in no-option patients with advanced coronary artery disease. J Am Coll Cardiol. 41; 1721-1724; 2003.
- 43. Beltrami, AP.et al. Adult cardiac stem cells are multipotent and support myocardial regeneration. Cell.114; 763-776; 2003.
- 44. Oh.H. et al. Cardiac progenitor cells from adult myocardium; homing, differentiation, and fusion after infarction. PNAS. 100; 12313-12318; 2003.
- 45. Kinnaird, T. et al. Marrow-derived stromal cells express genes encoding a broad spectrum of arteriogenic cytokines and promote in vitro and in

vivoarteriogenesis through paracrine mechanisms. Circ. Res. 94; 678-685; 2004.

- 46. Mathur, A. et al. Stem cells and the repair of the heart. Lancet. 364; 183-192; 2004.
- 47. Kinnaird T, et al. Local delivery of marrow-derived stromal cells augments collateral perfusion through paracrine mechanisms. Circulation 2004; 109; 1543-1549.
- 48.Anversa P, et al. Molecular genetic advances in cardiovascular medicine focus on the myocyte. Circulation 2004; 109; 2832-2838.
- 49. Urbanek K, et al. Intense myocyte formation from cardiac stem cells in human cardiac hypertrophy. Proc Natl Acad Sci USA 2003; 100; 10; 440-445.
- 50. Ryan TJ. Et al. ACC/AHA guidelines for the management of patients with acute myocardial infraction. A report of the American College of Cardiology/ American Heart Association Task Force on Practice Guidelines. J Am Coll Cardiol 1999; 34; 890-911.
- 52. Graf T. et al. Differentiation plasticity of hematopoietic cells. Blood 2002; 99; 3089-3101.
- 53. Reyes M. et al. Purification and ex-vivo expansion of postnatal human mesodermal progenitor cells. Blood. 2001; 98; 2615-2625.
- 54. Grounds MD, et al. The role of stem cells in skeletal and cardiac muscle repair. J Histochem Cytochem 2002; 50; 589-610.
- 55. Beltrami AP, et al. Evidence that human cardio myocytes divide after myocardial infraction. N Engl J Med 2001; 344; 1750-1757.
- 56. Laflamme MA. Et al. Evidence for cardiomyocyte repopulation by extra cardiac progenitors in transplanted human hearts. Circ Res. 2002; 90; 634-640.
- 57. Strauer BE, et al. Intracoronary, human autologous stem cell transplantation for myocardial regeneration following myocardial infraction. Dtsch Med Wochenschr 2001; 126; 932-938.

- 58. Tse HF, et al. Angiogenesis in ischaemic myocardium by intramyocardial autologous bone marrow mononuclear cell implantation. Lancet 2003; 361; 47-49.
- 59. Menasche P. et al. Myoblast transplantation for heart failure. Lancet 2001; 357; 279-280.
- 60. Hamano K. et al. Local implantation of autologous bone marrow cells for therapeutic angiogenesis in patients with ischemic heart disease: Clinical trial and preliminary results. Jpn Circ J2001; 65; 845-847.
- 61.Garot JJ. Et al. Magnetic resonance imaging of targeted catheter-based implantation of myogenic precursor cells into infarcted left ventricular myocardium. J Am Coll Cardiol 2003; 41; 1841-1846.
- 62. Lederman RJ.et al. Catheter based endomyocardial injection with real time magnetic resonance imaging. Circulation 2002; 105; 1282-1284.
- 63. Hagege AA, et al. Viability and differentiation of autologous skeletal myoblast grafts in ischaemic cardiomyopathy. Lancet 2003; 361; 491-492.
- 64. Muller P, et al. Cardiomyocytes of noncardiac origin in myocardial biopsies of human transplanted hearts. Circulation 2002. 106; 31-35.
- 65. Lee M, et al. Stem cell transplantation in myocardial infraction. Rev Cardiovasc Med. 2004; 5(2); 82-98.
- 66. Pittenger MF et al. Mesenchymal stem cells and their potential as cardiac therapeutics. Circulation Res. 2004; 95:9-20.
- 67. Tosh D. et al. How cells change their phenotype. Nat Rev Mol Cell Biol 2002; 3; 187-194.
- 68. Beltrami AP, et al. Adult cardiac stem cells are multipotent and support myocardial regeneration. Cell 2003; 114; 763-776.
- 69. Beltrani AP et al. Evidence that human cardiac myocytes divide after myocardial infraction. N Engl J Med 2001; 334; 1750-1757.
- 70. Thiele J, et al. Regeneration of heart muscle tissue: quantification of chimeric cardiomyocytes and endothelial cells following transplantation. Histol Histopatathol 2004; 19; 201-209.

- 71. Deb A, ET al. Bone marrow derived cardiomyocytes are present in adult human heart: A study of gender- mismatched bone marrow transplantation patients. Circulation 2003. 107; 1247-9.
- 72. Kang HJ. Et al. Effects of intracoronary infusion of peripheral blood stem cells with granulocyte-colony stimulating factor on left ventricular systolic function and restenosis after coronary stenting in myocardial infarction: the MAGIC cell randomized clinical trial. Lancet 2004; 363; 751-756.
- 73. Menasche P, et al. Autologous skeletal myoblast transplantation for severe postinfarction left ventricular dysfunction. J Am Coll Cardiol. 2003; 41;1078-83.
- 74. Herreros J, et al. Autologous intramyocardial injection of cultured skeletal muscle-derived stem cells in patients with non-acute myocardial infarction. Eur Heart J 2003; 24; 2012-2020.
- 75. Pagani FD, et al. Autologous skeletal myoblasts transplanted to ischemic-damaged myocardium in humans. Histological analysis of cell survival and differentiation. J Am Coll Cardiol 2003; 41; 879-888.
- 76. Galinanes M, et al. Autotransplantation of unmanipulated bone marrow is safe and enhances cardiac function in humans. Cell Transplant 2004; 13; 7-13.
- 77. Smits PC, et al. Catheter-based intramyocardial injection of autologous skeletal myoblasts as a primary treatment of ischemic heart failure: clinical experience with six-month follow up. J Am Coll Cardiol 2003; 42; 2063-2069.
- 78. Assmus B, et al. Transplantation of progenitor cells and regeneration enhancement in acute myocardial infarction. (TOPCARE-AMI). Circulation 2002; 106; 3009-3017.
- 79.Fernandez-Aviles F, et al. Experimental and clinical regenerative capability of human bone marrow cells after myocardial infraction. Cir Res. 2004; 95; 742-748.
- 80. Wollert KC, et al. Intracoronary bone –marrow cell transfer after myocardial infraction: the BOOST randomized controlled clinical trial. Lancet 2004; 364; 141-148.

- 81. Chen SL, et al. Effect on left ventricular function of intracoronary transplantation of autologous bone-marrow mesenchymal stem cell in patients with acute myocardial infraction. Am J Cardiol 2004; 94; 92-5.
- 82.Perin EC, et al. Transendocardial, autologous bone marrow transplantation for severe, chronic ischemic heart failure. Circulation. 2003; 107:2294-302.
- 83. Pagani FD, et al. Autologous skeletal myoblasts transplanted to ischemic-damaged myocardium in humans. Histological analysis of cell survival and differentiation. J Am Coll Cardiol 2003; 41; 879-888.
- 84. Smits PC, et al. Catheter-based intramyocardial injection of autologous skeletal myoblasts as a primary treatment of ischemic heart failure: clinical experience with six-month follow up. J Am Coll Cardiol 2003; 42; 2063-2069.
- 85. Fuchs, S. et al. Catheter based autologous bone marrow myocardial injection in no-option patients with advanced coronary artery disease. J Am Coll Cardiol. 41; 1721-1724; 2003.
- 86. Menasche P, et al. Autologous skeletal myoblast transplantation for severe post infarction left ventricular dysfunction. J Am Coll Cardiol. 2003; 41; 1078-83.
- 87. Fortuin FD, Losordo DW, et al. One-year follow up of direct myocardial gene transfer of vascular endothelial growth factor-2 using naked plasmid deoxyribonucleic acid by way of thoracotmy in no-option patients. J.Am. Coll. Cardiol.92, 436-9.
- 88. Dib N, et al. Safety and feasibility of autologous myoblast transplantation in patients with ischemic cardiomyopathy: Interim results from the United States experience. Circulation. 106,II-463. 2002
- 89. Vale PR, Losordo DW, et al. Randomized, single-blind, placebo-controlled pilot study of catheter-based myocardial gene transfer for therapeutic angiogenesis using left ventricular electromechanical mapping in patients with chronic myocardial ischemia. Circulation. 103, 2138-43, 2001.

- 90. Dib N, et al. Feasibility and safety of autologous myoblast transplantation in patients with ischemic cardiomyopathy. Cell Transplantation. 14. 2003.
- 91.Fuchs S, et al. A randomized double-blind placebo controlled multi-center pilot study of the safety and feasibility of AdGVVEGF121.10 via an intramyocardial injection catheter in patients with advanced coronary artery disease. J Am Coll Cardiol. 41, 21A, 2003.
- 92. Ince H, et al. Transcatheter transplantation of autologous skeletal myoblasts in post infarction patients with severe left ventricular dysfunction. J.Endovas.Ther.6; 695-704. 2004.
- 93. Dib N, et al. Endoventricular transplantation of allogenic skeletal myoblasts in a porcine model of myocardial infraction. J. Endovas. Ther. 9, 313-9. 2002.
- 94.Yoon PD, et al. Myocardial regeneration. Transplanting satellite cells into damaged myocardium. Texas Heart Inst. J. 1995; 22; 119-125.
- 95.Kornowski R, et al. Preliminary animal and clinical experiences using an electromechanical mapping procedure to distinguish infarcted from healthy myocardium. Circulation. 1998; 98; 1116-1124.
- 96.Deutsch E, et al. Autologous skeletal muscle transplantation in the swine heart: feasibility and viability endocardial delivery. Circulation. 1999; 100; 1-164.
- 97. Hennebry TA, et al. No-Option Patients: a nightmare today, a future with hope. J Inv Cardiol 2004; 17; 93-4.
- 98. Perin E, Willerson JT, et al. Adult stem cell therapy in perspective. Circulation. 2003; 107; 935-938.
- 99. Kornowski R, et al. Evaluation of the acute and chronic safety of the biosense injection catheter system in porcine hearts. Cathet Cardiovas Intervent 1999; 48; 447-453.
- 100. Sarmento-Leite R, Silva GV, et al. Comparison of left ventricular electromechanical mapping and left ventricular angiography: Defining practical standards for analysis of NOGA maps. Texas Heart Inst J. 2003; 30; 9-6.

- 101.Forrester JS, et al. Stem cell repair of infarcted myocardium: An overview for clinicians. Circulation 2003. 108; 1139-1145.
- 102.Perin EC, et al. Assessing myocardial viability and infract transmurality with left ventricular electromechanical mapping inpatients with stable coronary artery disease: Validation by delayed-enhancements magnetic resonance imaging. Circulation.2002;106;957-961.
- 103. Perin EC, Dohmann HF, et al. Improved exercise capacity and ischemia 6 and 12 months after transendocardial injection of autologous bone marrow mononuclear cells for ischemic cardiomyopathy. Circulation 2004; 110(supp II); 213-218.
- 104. Dohmann HF, et al. Transendocardial autologous bone marrow mononuclear cell injection in ischemic heart failure: Postmortem anautomicopathologic and immunohistochemical findings. Circulation 2005. 112; 521-526.
- 105. Assmus B. et al. Transcoronary transplantation of progenitor cells and recovery of left ventricular function in patients with chronic heart disease: Results of randomized, controlled, clinical trial. Circulation 2004; 110(supp III) ;238.
- 106. Shintani S, et al. Mobilization of endothelial progenitor cells in patients with acute myocardial infraction. Circulation 2001; 103; 2776-2779.
- 107. Asahara, T, et al. Isolation of putative progenitor endothelial cells for angiogenesis. Science 1997; 275; 964-967.
- 108. Shi Q, et al. Evidence for circulating bone marrow –derived endothelial cells. Blood 1998; 92; 362-367.
- 109. Asahara T, et al. Bone marrow origin of endothelial progenitor cells responsible for postnatal vasculogenesis in physiological and pathological neovascularization. Circ Res 1999; 85; 221-228.
- 110. Tamaki T, et al. Identification of myogenic-endothelial progenitor cells in the interstitial spaces of skeletal muscle. J Cell Biol 2002; 157; 571-577.

- 111. Gill M, et al. Vascular trauma induces rapid but transient mobilization of VEGFR2 (+) AC133 (+) endothelial precursor cells. Circ Res 2001; 88; 167-174.
- 112. Choi K, et al. A common precursor for hematopoietic and endothelial cells. Development 1998; 125; 725-732.
- 113. Yin AH, et al. AC133, a novel marker for human hematopoietic stem and progenitor cells. Blood 1997; 90; 5002-5012.
- 114. Piechev M, et al. Expression of VEGFR-2 and AC133 by circulating human CD34+ cells indentifies a population of functional endothelial precursors. Blood 2000; 95; 952-958.
- 115. Nieda M, et al. Endothelial cell precursors are normal components of human umbilical cord blood. Br J Haematol 1997; 98; 775-777.
- 116. Murohara T. et al. Transplanted cord-blood derived endothelial precursors cells augment post natal neovasculazition. J Clin Invest 2000; 105; 1527-1536.
- 117. Crosby JR, et al. Endothelial cells of hematopoietic origin make a significant contribution to adult blood vessel formation. Circ Res 2000; 87; 728-730.
- 118. Murayama T, et al. Determination of bone marrow-derived endothelial progenitor cell significance in angiogenic growth factor-induced neovascularization in vivo. Exp Hermatol 2002; 30; 967-972.
- 119. Reyes M, et al. Origin of endothelial progenitors in human postnatal bone marrow. J Clin Invest 2002; 109; 337-346.
- 120. Boyer M, et al. Isolation of endothelial cells and their progenitor cells from human peripheral blood. J Vasc Surg 2000; 31; 181-189.
- 121. Kalka C, et al. Transplantation of ex vivo expanded endothelial progenitor cells for therapeutic neovascularization. Proc Natl Acad Sci USA 2000; 97; 3422-3427.
- 122. Quirici N, et al. Differentiation and expansion of endothelial cells from human bone marrow CD34 (+) cells. Br J Haematol 2001; 115; 186-194.

- 123. Takahashi T, et al. Ischemia and cytokine-induced mobilization of bone marrow-derived endothelial progenitor cells for neovascularization. Nat Med 1999; 5; 434-438.
- 124. Asahara T, et al. VEGF contributes to postnatal neovascularization by mobilizing bone marrow-derived endothelial progenitor cells. EMBO J 1999; 18; 3964-3972.
- 125. Dimmeler S, et al. HMG-CoA reductase inhibitors (statins) increase endothelial progenitor cells via the PI3-kinase/Akt pathway. J Clin invest 2001; 108; 391-397.
- 126. Vasa M. et al. Increase in circulating endothelial progenitor cells by statin therapy in patients with stable coronary artery disease. Circulation 2001; 103; 2885-2890.
- 127. Urbich C, et al. Double- edged role of statins in angiogenesis signaling. Circ Res 2002; 90; 737-744.
- 128. Murayama T, et al. Aging impairs therapeutic contributions of human endothelial progenitor cells postnatal neovascularization. (Abstract) Circulation 2001; 104; 11-68.
- 129. Vasa M, et al Number and migratory activity activity of circulating endothelial progenitor cells inversely correlate with risk factors for coronary artery disease. Circ Res 2001; 89; E1-E7.
- 130.Hill JM, et al. Circulating endothelial progenitor cells, vascular function, and cardiovascular risk. N Engl J Med 2003; 348; 593-600.
- 131. Werner N, et al. Circulating endothelial progenitor cells and cardiovascular outcomes. N Engl J Med 2005; 353; 999-1007.
- 132. Kawamoto A, et al. Therapeutic potential of ex-vivo expanded endothelial progenitor cells for myocardial ischemia. Circulation 2001; 103; 634-637.
- 133. Kocher AA, et al. Neovascularization of ischemic myocardium by human bone marrow-derived angioblasts prevents cardiomyocyte apoptosis, reduces remodeling and improves cardiac function. Nat Med 2001; 7; 430-436.

- 134. Iwasaki H, et al. Dose dependent contribution of CD34 positive cell transplantation to concurrent vasculogenesis and cardiomyogenesis for functional regenerative recovery post myocardial infarction. Circulation 2006; 113; 1311-1325.
- 135. Iwaguro H, et al. Endothelial progenitor cell vascular endothelial growth factor gene transfer for vascular regeneration. Circulation 2002; 105; 732-738.
- 136. Shintani S., et al. Augmentation of postnatal neovascularization with autologous bone marrow transplant. Circulation 2001; 103; 897-903.
- 137. Hamano K et al. The induction of angiogenesisby the implantation of bone marrow cells a novel and simple therapeutic method. Surgery 2001; 130;44-54.
- 138. Kamihata H, et al. Implantation of bone marrow mononuclear cells into ischemic myocardium enhances collateral perfusion and regional function via side supply of angioblasts, angiogenic ligands, and cytokines. Circulation 2001; 104; 1046-1052.
- 139. Bhattacharya V, et al. Enhanced endothelialization and microvessel formation in polyester grafts seeded with CD34+ bone marrow cells. Blood 2000; 95; 581-585.
- 140. Shimizu T, et al. Fabrication of pulsatile cardiac tissue grafts using 3- dimensional cell sheet manipulation technique and temperature-responsive cell culture surfaces. Circ Res 2002; 90; e40.
- 141. Shimizu T, et al. Electrically communicating three-dimensional cardiac tissue mimic fabricated by layered cultured cardiomyocyte sheets. J Biomed Mater Res 2002; 60; 110-117. Cardiac stem cells: A new view of cardiac biology.
- 142. Anversa P, et al. Life and death of cardiac stem cells: a paradigm shift in cardiac biology. Circulation 2006; 113; 1451-1463.
- 143. Leri A, et al. Cardiac stem cells and mechanisms of myocardial regeneration. Physiol Rev 2005; 85; 1373-1416.

- 144. Chien KR, et al. Stem cells: Lost in translation. Nature 2004; 428; 607-608.
- 145. Urbanek K, et al. Intense myocyte formation from cardiac stem cells in human cardiac hypertrophy. Proc Natl Acad Sci USA 2003; 100; 10440-10445.
- 146. Chimenti C, et al. Senescence and death of primitive cells and myocytes lead to premature cardiac aging and heart failure. Circ Res 2003; 93; 604-613.
- 147. Anversa P, et al. Primitive cells and tissue regeneration. Circ Res 2003; 92; 579-582.
- 148. Palmer TD, et al. Vascular niche for adult hippocampal neurogenesis. J Comp Neurol 2000; 425; 479-494.
- 149. Leri A, et al. Symmetric and asymmetric division of cardiac stem cells in the mouse heart. Circulation 2003; 108; iv-33.
- 150. Oh H, et al. Cardiac progenitor cells from adult myocardium: homing, differentiation, and fusion after infraction. Proc Natl Acad Sci USA 2003; 100; 12313-12318.
- 151. Matsuura K, et al. Adult cardiac Sca-1-positive cells differentiate into beating cardiomyocytes. J Biol Chem 2004; 279; 11384-11391.
- 152. Rosenblatt-Velin N, et al. FGF-2 controls the differentiation of resident cardiac precursors into functional cardiomyocytes. J Chin Invest 2005; 115; 1724-1733.
- 153. Urbanek K, et al . Myocardial regeneration by activation of multipotent cardiac stem cell in the ischemic heart failure. Proc Natl Acad Sci USA 2005; 102; 8692-8697.
- 154. Leri A, MD, Piero Anversa MD & William FrishmanMD. Cardiovascular Regeneration and stem cell therapy. Professor's medicine/chairman; vice-chairman; Cardiovascular Research Institute; New York Medical College.
- 155. Yoon YS, et al. Clonally expanded novel multipotent stem cells from human bone marrow regenerate myocardium after myocardial infraction. J Clin Invest 2005; 115 ;(2):326-338.

- 156. Iwasaki H, et al. Dose dependent contribution of CD34 positive cell transplantation to concurrent vasculogenesis and cardiomyogenesis for functional regenerative recovery post myocardiodial infarction. Circulation 2006; 113; 1311-1325.
- 157. Losordo DW, et al. Therapeutic angiogenesis and vasculogenesis for ischemic disease: part II: cell-based therapies. Circulation 2004; 109(22):2692-2697.
- 158. Orlic D, et al. Bone marrow cells regenerate infarcted myocardium. Nature 2001; 401; 701-705.
- 159. Orlic D, et al. Mobilized bone marrow cells repair the infarcted heart, improving function and survival. Proc Natl Acad Sci USA 2001; 98(18) :10344-10349.
- 160. Badorff C, et al. Transdifferentiation of blood-derived human adult endothelial progenitor cells into functionally active cardiomyocytes. Circulation 2003; 107 ;(7):1024-1032.
- 161. Dimmeler S, et al. Unchain my heart: the scientific foundation of cardiac repair. J Clin Invest 2005; 115(3):572-583.
- 162. Ma N, et al. Human cord blood cells induce angiogenesis following myocardial infraction in NOD/SCID-mice. Cardiovas Res 2005; 66(1):45-54.
- 163. Zhang S, et al. Both cell fusion and transdifferentiation account for the transformation of human peripheral blood CD34-positive cells into cardiomyocytes in vivo. Circulation 2004; 110(25):3803-3807.
- 164. Yeh ET, et al. Transdifferentiation of human peripheral blood CD34+ enriched cell population into cardiomyocytes, endothelial cells, and smooth muscle cells in vivo. Circulation 2003; 108(17): 2070-2073.
- 165. Gibson CM, et al. Relationship of TIMI myocardial perfusion grades, flow grades, frame count, and percutaneous coronary intervention to long term outcomes after thrombolytic administration in acute myocardial infraction. Circulation 2002; 105(16): 1909-1913.

- 166. Balsam LB, et al. Haematopoietic stem cells adopt mature haematopoietic fates in the ischaemic myocardium. Nature 2004; 428(6983):668-673.
- 167. Askari AT, et al. Effect of stromal-cell-derived factor I on stem-cell homing and tissue regeneration in ischaemic cardiomyopathy. Lancet 2003: 362(9385): 697-703.
- 168. Terada N, et al. Bone marrow cells adopt the phenotype of other cells by spontaneous cell fusion. Nature 2002; 416(6880): 542-545.
- 169.Ying GL, et al. Changing potency by spontaneous fusion. Nature 2002; 416(6880); 545-548.
- 170. Losordo DW. Et al. Phase ½ placebo –controlled, double blind, dose escalating trial of myocardial vascular growth 2 gene transfer by catheter delivery in patients with chronic myocardial ischemia. Circulation 2002; 105; 2012-2018.
- 171. Britten MB, et al. Infract remodeling after intracoronary progenitor cell treatment in patients with acute myocardial infraction (TOPCARE-AMI): mechanistic insights from serial contrast-enhanced magnetic resonance imaging. Circulation 2003; 109(18): 2212-2218.
- 172. Meyer GP, et al. Intracoronary bone marrow cell transfer after myocardial infraction: eighteen months' follow-up data from the randomized controlled BOOST (bone marrow transfer to enhance ST-elevation infract regeneration) trial. Circulation 2006; 113 ;(10) 1287-1294.
- 173. Welt FG, Losordo DW. Cell therapy for acute myocardial infraction: curb your enthusiasm? Circulation 2006; 113(10): 1272-1274.
- 174. Assmus B, et al. Transcoronary transplantation of progenitor cells after myocardial infraction. N Engl J Med 2006; 355: 1222-1232.
- 175. Schachinger V, et al. Intracoronary bone marrow-derived progenitor cells in acute myocardial infraction. N Engl J Med 2006; 355: 1210-1231.
- 176. Lunde K, et al. Intracoronary injection of mononuclear bone marrow cells in acute myocardial infraction. N Engl J Med 2006; 355:1199-1209

CardioMatrex ™: A Cardio Combination Biologic Tissue-engineering, Self-assembling Molecular Injection Matrex: patent pending

References

1. Metallo CM, Azarin SM, Ji L, de Pablo JJ, Palecek SP. Engineering tissue from human embryonic stem cells. Nat Inst Health. 2009;12(3):709–29.
2. Atala A. Regenerative medicine strategies. J Pediatr Surg. 2012;47(1):17–28.
3. Valarmathi MT, Goodwin RL, Fuseler JW, Davis JM, Yost MJ, Potts JD. A 3-D cardiac muscle construct for exploring adult marrow stem cell based myocardial regeneration. Biomaterials. 2010;31(12):3185–200.
4. Naderi H, Matin MM, Bahrami AR. Review paper: critical issues in tissue engineering: biomaterials, cell sources, angiogenesis, and drug delivery systems. J Biomater Appl. 2011;26(4):383–417.
5. Huang C, Wei H, Yeh Y, Wang J, Lin W, Lee T, Hwang S, Choi S, Xia Y, Chang Y, Sung H. Injectable PLGA porous beads cellularized by hAFSCs for cellular cardiomyoplasty. Biomaterials. 2012;33(16):4069–77.
6. Chen Q-Z, Harding SE, Ali NN, Lyon AR, Boccaccini AR. Biomaterials in cardiac tissue engineering: ten years of research survey. Mater Sci Eng. 2008;59:1–37.
7. Venugopal JR, Prabhakaran MP, Mukherjee S, Ravichandran R, Dan K, Ramakrishna S. Biomaterial strategies for alleviation of myocardial infarction. J Royal Soc Interface. 2012;9(66):1–19.
8. Demirbag B, Huri PY, Kose GT, Buyuksungur A, Hasirci V. Advanced cell therapies with and without scaffolds. Biotechnol J. 2011;6(12):1437–53.
9. Langer R, Vancanti JP. Tissue engineering. Science. 1993;260:920–6.
10. Campbell CD, Goldfarb D, Roe R. A small arterial substitute: expanded microporous polytetrafluoroethylene: patency versus porosity. Ann Surg. 1975;182:138–43.

11. DeBakey ME, Jordan GL, Abbott JP, O'Neal RM. The fate of dacron vascular grafts. Arch Surg. 1964;89:757–82.
12. Molina JE, Carr M, Yarnoz MD. Coronary bypass with Gore-Tex graft. J Thorac Cardiovasc Surg. 1978;75:769–71.
13. Roh JR, Sawh-Martinez R, Brennan MP, Jay SM, Devine L, Rao DA, Yi T, Mirensky TL, Nalbandian A, Udelsman B. Tissue-engineered vascular grafts transform into mature blood vessels via an inflammation-mediated process of vascular remodeling. Proc Natl Acad Sci. 2010; 107:4669–74.
14. Nelson DM, Ma Z, Fujimoto KL, Hashizume R, Wagner WR. Intramyocardial biomaterial injection therapy in the treatment of heart failure: materials, outcomes and challenges. Nat Inst Health. 2012;7(1):1–15.
15. Dib N, Menasche P, Bartunek JJ, Zeiher AM, Terzic A, Chronos NA, Henry TD, Peters NS, Fernández-Avilés F, Yacoub M, Sanborn TA, Demaria A, Schatz RA, Taylor DA, Fuchs S, Itescu S, Miller LW, Dinsmore JH, Dangas GD, Popma JJ, Hall JL, Holmes DR. Recommendations for successful training on methods of delivery of biologics for cardiac regeneration: a report of the International Society for Cardiovascular Translational Research. JACC Cardio Int. 2010;3(3):265–75.
16. Giraud M-N, Guex AG, Tevaearai HT. Cell therapies for heart function recovery: focus on myocardial tissue engineering and nanotechnologies. Cardiol Res Pract. 2012; 2012:971614.
17. Ptaszek LM, Mansour M, Ruskin JN, Chien KR. Towards regenerative therapy for cardiac disease. Series Stem Cells. 2012; 379:933–42.
18. Karam J-P, Muscari C, Montero-Menei CN. Combining adult stem cells and polymeric devices for tissue engineering in infarcted myocardium. Biomaterials. 2012;33(23):5683–95.
19. Nelson DM, Ma Z, Fujimoto KL, Hashizume R, Wagner WR. Intra-myocardial biomaterial injection therapy in the treatment of heart failure: materials, outcomes and challenges. Acta Biomaterialia. 2011;7(1):1–15.

20. Chiu LLY, Radisic M, Vunjak-novakovic G. Bioactive scaffolds for engineering vascularized cardiac tissues. Macromol Biosci. 2010; 10:1286–301.

21. Hwang NS, Elisseeff J. Controlled differentiation of stem cells. Nat Inst Health. 2009;60(2):199–214.

22. Reis LA, Chiu LLY, Liang Y, Hyunh K, Momen A, Radisic M. A peptide-modified chitosan-collagen hydrogel for cardiac cell culture and delivery. Acta Biomaterialia. 2012;8(3):1022–36.

23. Xiang Z, Liao R, Kelly MS, Spector M. Collagen–GAG scaffolds grafted onto myocardial infarcts in a rat model: a delivery vehicle for mesenchymal stem cells. Tissue Eng. 2006;12(9):2467–78.

24. Chiu LLY, Radisic M. Controlled release of thymosin β4 using collagen–chitosan composite hydrogels promotes epicardial cell migration and angiogenesis. J Cont Rel. 2011; 155:376–85.

25. Chimenti I, Rizzitelli G, Gaetani R, Angelini F, Ionta V, Forte E, Frati G, Schussler O, Barbetta A, Messina E, Dentini M, Giacomello A. Human cardiosphere-seeded gelatin and collagen scaffolds as cardiogenic engineered bioconstructs. Biomaterials. 2011; 32:9271–81.

26. Gao J, Liu J, Gao Y, Wang C, Zhao Y, Chen B, Xiao Z, Miao Q, Dai J. A myocardial patch made of collagen membranes loaded with collagen-binding human vascular endothelial growth factor accelerates healing of the injured rabbit heart. Tissue Eng. 2011;17(21–22):2739–47.

27. Shi C, Li Q, Zhao Y, Chen W, Chen B, Xiao Z, Lin H, Nie L, Wang D, Dai J. Stem-cell-capturing collagen scaffold promotes cardiac tissue regeneration. Biomaterials. 2011;32(10):2508–15.

28. Cheng K, Blusztajn A, Shen D, Li T-S, Sun B, Galang G, Zarembinski TI, Prestwich GD, Marbán E, Smith RR, Marbán L. Functional performance of human cardiosphere-derived cells delivered in an in situ polymerizable hyaluronan-gelatin hydrogel. Biomaterials. 2012;33(21):5317–24.

29. Shachar M, Tsur-gang O, Dvir T, Leor J, Cohen S. The effect of immobilized RGD peptide in alginate scaffolds on cardiac tissue engineering. Acta Biomaterialia. 2011;7(1):152–62.

30. Sapir Y, Kryukov O, Cohen S. Integration of multiple cell-matrix interactions into alginate scaffolds for promoting cardiac tissue regeneration. Biomaterials. 2011; 32:1838–47.

31. Binsalamah ZM, Paul A, Khan AA, Prakash S, Shum-Tim D. Intramyocardial sustained delivery of placental growth factor using nanoparticles as a vehicle for delivery in the rat infarct model. Int J Nanomed. 2011; 6:2667–78.

32. Ruvinov E, Leor J, Cohen S. The promotion of myocardial repair by the sequential delivery of IGF-1 and HGF from an injectable alginate biomaterial in a model of acute myocardial infarction. Biomaterials. 2011;32(2):565–78.

33. Liu Z, Wang H, Wang Y, Lin Q, Yao A, Cao F, Li D, Zhou J, Duan C, Du Z, Wang Y, Wang C. The influence of chitosan hydrogel on stem cell engraftment, survival and homing in the ischemic myocardial microenvironment. Biomaterials. 2012;33(11):3093–106.

34. Li Z, Guo X, Guan J. A thermosensitive hydrogel capable of releasing bFGF for enhanced differentiation of mesenchymal stem cell into cardiomyocyte-like cells under ischemic conditions. Biomacromolecules. 2012;13(6):1956–64.

35. Baumann L, Prokoph S, Gabriel C, Freudenberg U, Werner C, Beck-Sickinger AG. A novel, biased-like SDF-1 derivative acts synergistically with starPEG-based heparin hydrogels and improves eEPC migration in vitro. J Cont Rel. 2012;162(1):68–75.

36. Zhang S. Fabrication of novel biomaterials through molecular self-assembly. Nat Biotechnol. 2003;21(10):1171–8.

37. Zhang S, Gelain F, Zhao X. Designer self-assembling peptide nanofiber scaffolds for 3D tissue cell cultures. Sem Cancer Bio. 2005; 15:413–20.

38. Quintana L, Fernandez Muinos T, Genove E, Olmos MDM, Borros S, Semino CE. Early tissue patterning recreated by mouse embryonic fibroblasts in a three-dimensional environment. Tissue Eng. 2009;15(1):45–54.

39. Kyle S, Aggeli A, Ingham E, McPherson MJ. Production of self-assembling biomaterials for tissue engineering. Trends Biotechnol. 2009;27(7):423–33.

40. Gelain F, Bottai D, Vescovi A, Zhang S. Designer self-assembling peptide nanofiber scaffolds for adult mouse neural stem cell 3-dimensional cultures. PloS one. 2006;1(1):119.

41. Genové E, Shen C, Zhang S, Semino CE. The effect of functionalized self-assembling peptide scaffolds on human aortic endothelial cell function. Biomaterials. 2005; 26:3341–51.

42. Branco MC, Pochan DJ, Wagner NJ, Schneider JP. Macromolecular diffusion and release from self-assembled b-hairpin peptide hydrogels. Nat Inst Health. 2010;30(7):1339–47.

43. Genové E, Schmitmeier S, Sala A, Borrós S, Bader A, Griffith LG, Semino CE. Functionalized self-assembling peptide hydrogel enhance maintenance of hepatocyte activity in vitro. J Cell Mol Med. 2009; XX:1–12.

44. Branco MC, Schneider JP. Self-assembling materials for therapeutic delivery. Nat Inst Health. 2009;5(3):817–31.

45. Standley SM, Toft DJ, Cheng H, Soukasene S, Chen J, Raja SM, Band V, Band H, Cryns VL, Stupp SI. Induction of cancer cell death by self-assembling nanostructures incorporating a cytotoxic peptide. Nat Inst Health. 2011;70(8):3020–6.

46. Jung JP, Nagaraj AK, Fox EK, Rudra JS, Devgun JM, Collier JH. Co-assembling peptides as defined matrices for endothelial cells. Nat Inst Health. 2010;30(12):2400–10.

47. Sieminski AL, Semino CE, Gong H, Kamm RD. Primary sequence of ionic self-assembling peptide gels affects endothelial cell adhesion and capillary morphogenesis. J Biomed Mater Res. 2008;87(2):494–504.

48. Bergmann O, Bhardwaj RD, Bernard S, Zdunek S, Barnabé-Heider F, Walsh S, Zupicich J, Alkass K, Buchholz BA, Druid H, Jovinge S, Frisén J. Evidence for cardiomyocyte renewal in humans. Nat Inst Health. 2010;324(5923):98–102.

49. Davis ME, Motion JPM, Narmoneva DA, Takahashi T, Hakuno D, Kamm RD, Zhang S, Lee RT. Injectable self-assembling peptide nanofibers create intramyocardial microenvironments for endothelial cells. Nat Inst Health. 2009;111(4):442–50.

50. Guo H, Cui G, Wang H, Tan Y. Transplantation of marrow-derived cardiac stem cells carried in designer self-assembling peptide nanofibers improves cardiac function after myocardial infarction. Biochem Biophys Res Commun. 2010;399(1):42–8.

51. Chan SS-K, Li H-J, Hsueh Y-C, Lee DS, Chen J-H, Hwang S-M, Chen C-Y, Shih E, Hsieh PCH. Fibroblast growth factor-10 promotes cardiomyocyte differentiation from embryonic and induced pluripotent stem cells. PLoS One. 2010;5(12):14414.

52. Guo H, Cui G, Yang J, Wang C, Zhu J, Zhang L, Jiang J, Shao S. Sustained delivery of VEGF from designer self-assembling peptides improves cardiac function after myocardial infarction. Biochem Biophys Res Commun. 2012;424:105–11.

53. Altunbas A, Lee SJ, Rajasekaran SA, Schneider JP, Pochan DJ. Encapsulation of curcumin in self-assembling peptide hydrogels as injectable drug delivery vehicles. Nat Inst Health. 2011;32(25):5906–14.

54. Hsieh PCH, MacGillivray C, Gannon J, Cruz FU, Lee RT. Local controlled intramyocardial delivery of platelet-derived growth factor improves post-infarction ventricular function without pulmonary toxicity. Circulation. 2006;114(7):637–44.

55. Narmoneva DA, Vukmirovic R, Davis ME, Kamm RD, Lee RT. Endothelial cells promote cardiac myocyte survival and spatial reorganization. Nat Inst Health. 2009;110(8):962–8.

56. Padin-Iruegas ME, Misao Y, Davis ME, Segers VFM, Esposito G, Tokunou T, Urbanek K, Hosoda T, Rota M, Anversa P, Leri A, Lee RT, Kajstura J. Cardiac progenitor cells and biotinylated IGF-1 nanofibers improve endogenous and exogenous myocardial regeneration after infarction. Nat Inst Health. 2010;30(7):1339–47.

57. Davis ME, Hsieh PCH, Takahashi T, Song Q, Zhang S, Kamm RD, Grodzinsky AJ, Anversa P, Lee RT. Local myocardial insulin-like growth factor 1 (IGF-1) delivery with biotinylated peptide nanofibers improves cell therapy for myocardial infarction. PNAS. 2006;103(21):8155–60.

58. Kim JH, Jung Y, Kim S-H, Sun K, Choi J, Kim HC, Park Y, Kim SH. The enhancement of mature vessel formation and cardiac function in infarcted hearts using dual growth factor delivery with self-assembling peptides. Biomaterials. 2011;32(26):6080–8.

59. Dubois G, Segers VFM, Bellamy V, Sabbah L, Peyrard S, Bruneval P, Hagège AA, Lee RT, Menasché P. Self-assembling peptide nanofibers and skeletal myoblast transplantation in infarcted myocardium. J Biomed Mater Res. 2008;87(1):222–8.

60. Segers VFM, Tokunou T, Higgins LJ, MacGillivray C, Gannon J, Lee RT. Local delivery of protease-resistant stromal cell derived factor-1 for stem cell recruitment after myocardial infarction. Circulation. 2007;116(15):1683–92.

61. Kopesky PW, Vanderploeg EJ, Kisiday JD, Frisbie DD, Sandy JD, Grodzinsky AJ. Controlled delivery of transforming growth factor b1 by self-assembling peptide hydrogels induces chondrogenesis of bone marrow stromal cells and modulates Smad2/3 signaling. Tissue Eng. 2011;17(1–2):83–9

62. Miller RE, Kopesky PW, Grodzinsky AJ. Growth factor delivery through self-assembling peptide scaffolds. Clin Orthop Relat Res. 2011;469(10):2716–24.

63. Gelain F, Unsworth LD, Zhang S. Slow and sustained release of active cytokines from self-assembling peptide scaffolds. J Cont Rel. 2010;145(3):231–9.

64. Davis ME, Hsieh PCH, Grodzinsky AJ, Lee RT. Custom design of the cardiac microenvironment with biomaterials. Nat Inst Health. 2009;97(1):8–15.

65. Kraehenbuehl TP, Zammaretti P, Van der Vlies A, Schoenmakers RG, Lutolf MP, Jaconi ME, Hubbell JA. Three-dimensional extracellular matrix-directed cardioprogenitor differentiation: systematic modulation of a synthetic cell-responsive PEG-hydrogel. Biomaterials. 2008; 29:2757–66.

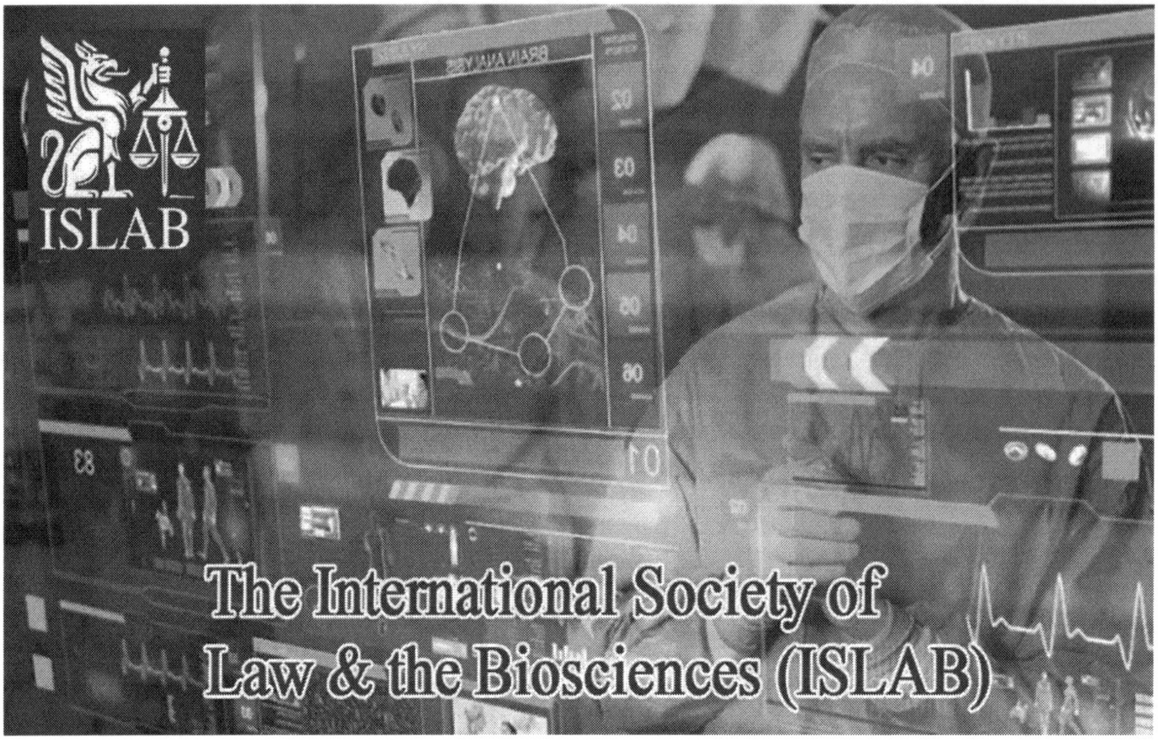

Biotechnology Law and Practice

Fundamentals of the Biosciences

Legal, Regulatory, Corporate Strategy

Case Law and Best Practices

The International Society of Law and the Biosciences (ISLAB): a non-profit educational and public benefits corporation exists primarily to educate students, lawyers, physician researchers, and management professionals regarding the extraordinarily complex set of laws that govern the creation, development, and marketing of new drugs, biologics, medical devices, and other advanced technologies.

Furthermore, ISLAB research fellows produce scholarly white papers, and recommendations for policy on the varied and complex issues posed by the explosion of new biomedical discoveries and other emerging technologies, creating a need for awareness and diligence at the crossroads of biotechnology and the law.

LEGAL AND PRIVACY POLICY

The Health Insurance Portability & Accountability Act of 1996 (HIPAA) requires all health care records and other individually identifiable health information used or disclosed to us in any form, whether electronically, on paper, or orally, be kept confidential.

This federal law gives you, the patient, significant new rights to understand and control how your health information is used. HIPAA provides penalties for covered entitles that misuse personal health information.

Nothing in the Terms of Use shall be construed as a solicitation for or promotion of, any product or the use of any product that is not authorized by the laws and regulations of the state where you reside or access the Sites. Patents. All patents issued to and patent applications filed or assigned conditionally to ISLAB are the property of company and are protected by United States and foreign patent laws. Any use of these patented or patentable assets is prohibited without the specific prior written consent of ISLAB. Forward-Looking Statements: Our public communications and SEC filings may contain "forward looking statements" – that is, statements related to future, not past, events. In this context, forward-looking statements often address our expected future business and financial performance and financial condition, and often contain words such as "expect," "anticipate," "intend," "plan," "believe," "seek," "see," "will," "would," or "target." Forward-looking statements by their nature address matters that are, to different degrees, uncertain, such as statements about our announced plan filing a Reg A+ securities offering affecting the products and services businesses, (Verticals); expected income; earnings per share; revenues; organic growth; growth of our Digital business; margins; cost structure; restructuring charges; cash flows; return on capital; capital expenditures, capital allocation or capital structure; dividends; and the split between earnings. For us, particular uncertainties that could cause our actual results to be materially different than those expressed in our forward-looking statements include: obtaining (or the timing of obtaining) any required regulatory reviews or approvals or any other consents or our ability to reduce costs as we execute that plan; changes in law, economic and financial conditions, including interest and exchange rate volatility, commodity and equity prices and the value of financial assets, including the impact of these conditions on our ability to sell or the value of incremental assets to be sold as part of our announced plan. Fair Use Notice: This message may contain copyrighted material the use of which has not always been specifically authorized by the copyright owner. We are making such material available in our efforts to advance the understanding of environmental, political, human rights, economic, democracy, scientific, healthcare, social justice issues, etc. We believe this constitutes a 'fair use' of any copyrighted material as provided for in Section 17 U.S.C. Section 107.

Index

D

I

J

O

P

Q

R

S

Made in the USA
Monee, IL
05 November 2026

67849404R00185